CONTE

CHAPTER ONE

MAXIMIZING YOUR ABILITIES AND EXPANDING YOUR HORIZONS

It's not what the disability is but, rather, what the ability is. What do you have to offer a potential employer? With a development of self-knowledge along with careful planning, you can make a potential employer an offer he can't refuse.

The Americans with Disabilities Act (ADA) has underscored the belief that anyone who is willing to work and who has mastered a set of skills or a particular skill that is marketable should be allowed to work, whether or not that person has a disability.

Do Your Homework

Before you can present yourself as a viable candidate for a job, you must have done your homework. You must have developed job skills, a good set of ethics, a positive attitude, and the willingness to learn. Just as the world is rapidly changing so are the demands for certain skills. New jobs are being developed each year. Emerging fields such as robotics continue to generate jobs. The ADA does not guarantee that you will find a job because you have a disability. What it does provide is a legal framework for assuring that you will not be discriminated against because you happen to have a disability. So, the good news is that you will have a chance at bat. But you will have to put in some practice before you come to bat in the big leagues.

The Employment Picture

The present trend of downsizing means more work for less staff, according to the Chicago Private Industry Council. Because of this, job candidates with a variety of skills are in demand. Restructuring and re-engineering have taken their toll. Human resource people have greater workloads and must wear many hats. They don't have time to linger over a résumé that is "iffy" or incomplete or does not offer up-to-date marketable skills.

You are not alone in your quest for work. There are 49 million people with disabilities in America or 19.4 percent of the entire U.S. population. Seventy-nine percent of nonworking Americans with disabilities say they are both capable and willing to work, according to a report recently issued by the President's Committee on Employment of People with Disabilities; one of the reasons for their unemployment cited by 32 percent of those surveyed is that they lack the necessary training. Sixteen percent said they need special equipment for work. Forty percent said that employers won't recognize their capabilities. Although employer attitude remains one of the greatest barriers toward employment, this book is dedicated to the proposition that you can find employment if you really want to work and if you take the time to prepare for the work you seek. This book will show you how to discover and to pursue a career that is right for you, an individual with unique interests, personality, and abilities.

Nationwide Survey Results

Almost three quarters of the top industries across the United States are currently hiring people with disabilities, according to a survey conducted by Global Strategy Group for the President's Committee on Employment of People with Disabilities. The survey was concluded in October of 1995. Results were presented to the executive board of the President's committee on December 15 of that year. The survey was a nationwide random sampling of 300 chief executive officers and human resource managers of Fortune 500 companies. A sizable majority of people who make the hiring decisions in their companies claim that the ADA has had a positive impact on corporations.

The results of this survey can be broken down by type of industry. Two thirds of the executives in the field of technology believe that the ADA has had a positive impact as do a majority of executives in the communications industry. Slightly less than one half of all manufacturing human resource managers think the ADA has made a positive impact on companies across the United States.

Comparing regions of the country led to some interesting differences among executives. Fifty-nine percent of those in the East as well as 51 percent of those in the South find the ADA to have made a positive impact. A slightly lower number, 47 percent, in the Midwest and West say the same.

Technology-based industries are not only the most likely to extol the virtues of the ADA, but also demonstrate the most impressive record of hiring people with disabilities. Although technology-based industries post a hiring record of 76 percent, the manufacturing industry is not far behind with a record of 74 percent. This is very encouraging because technology-based industries offer a bright employment picture for the future. While communications industry personnel are less likely to hire people with disabilities, their record is still impressive at 69 percent.

Another interesting fact is that the hiring of people with disabilities appears to correlate more with the size of companies than the type of companies. An inspiring 87 percent of companies with more than 200 employees are hiring people with disabilities as are 75 percent of companies that employ 51 to 200 people. More than one half of companies with less than 50 employees are hiring people with disabilities. Furthermore, a majority of these companies are looking for qualified applicants so they can hire more individuals with disabilities.

Examine Your Interests and Attitude

Don't be afraid to test the water. Dr. David Helfand, a career counselor and author of *Career Change*, (published by VGM Career Horizons, 1994), says that it's never too early to begin career planning. Whether you are in high school or college, or are just beginning to enter the job market, start planning. David Schnell, a vocational counselor who is blind, says those with disabilities must develop self-esteem. He says that the ability to imagine yourself successfully accomplishing your goals is a powerful tool. Making major decisions about what to do with your life can be very challenging, even overwhelming: "Decision making can be even more challenging for people with disabilities, many of whom have been receiving the message for all of their lives that they are not equal to or as capable as the average person." Yet, Schnell offers these words of consolation:

"You do have control over how you feel about yourself, and you should take control over the major decisions that influence your life." Don't let others make the decisions you yourself should make. One vital area of decision making is your career. With good planning, your career can last a lifetime.

A person should begin career planning with a survey of his or her interests. Most people will not become rich by working for others so to plan a career simply on the basis of what jobs are currently the highest-paying is not worth it in the long run, economically or psychologically. With few exceptions, the entry-level salary of jobs across a broad spectrum are roughly equivalent, especially when you consider that the highest-level entry salaries belong to careers in which entry-level preparation has required long years of study and financial outlay, such as careers in engineering or in science.

Being happy in a career motivates a person to learn as much as possible about the career. Enjoyment translates into enthusiasm. The person who likes his job will feel that time on the job passes quickly. Such a person will most likely strive to do his or her best, and outstanding performance will get a person noticed the next time candidates are needed for further training or when a promotion is possible. When performance time rolls around, the supervisor won't have difficulty in justifying why that person should receive a raise.

Interest leads advancement in a chosen career. Attitude is like fuel in the engine—it makes us go fast and true toward our goal. And who has a better attitude than a person who has triumphed over numerous obstacles in the quest to become as self-sufficient and independent as possible? If you weren't eager to succeed, you wouldn't be reading this book. Tom Thomson, director of the Learning Assistance Program at Harper College in Palatine, Illinois, states that anyone who has persevered in his or her career path despite the challenge of being physically disabled is someone who deserves to be admired and recognized as an achiever.

Every step you take toward independence leads you closer to your career goal. You have had to make an effort whereas some young people today have had it too easy. Whether due to parents wanting to ensure that the lives of their offspring would be easier than their own or whether modern-day conveniences have made this an instant-gratification society, young people in general seem to have become desensitized to the value of hard work. Instead, a sense of entitlement has developed throughout all levels of society. Yet, working truly has its own rewards, not the least of which are:

Dignity and self-esteem for those who do a good job;

Possibly making a contribution and improving the world in some way;

Helping others;

Learning something new;

Testing one's limits;

Making new friends; and,

Receiving a regular paycheck, a testimony to the value of the contribution.

Not only is the paycheck a symbol of achievement, it is a necessity if you are to establish some measure of economic self-sufficiency.

Whether we intend to work part-time or full-time, our job is central to our identity. And, increasingly, the person with physical disabilities has the chance to make it in the world of work. Speaking in 1995, Alan Reich, president of the National Organization on Disability located in Washington, D.C., said that in the previous 2 years, "We have seen America lead the world as it became a more open society for people with disabilities." Thomas Warren of Merrill Lynch says, "We are seeing more people with disabilities coming into our office for jobs than we have in our entire history."

Not only are people coming in for entry-level jobs, people with disabilities are applying for jobs on the professional and managerial levels. People with disabilities are indeed moving up the corporate ladder. Barbara Bode, vice president and executive director of the Council for Better Business Bureau in Arlington, Virginia, claims to have witnessed changes in the attitudes of businesses during the past 10 years. "As more people with disabilities have come into the work force and employers see what they can do, employers' attitudes will change for the better." Our society is large, and we cannot expect progress overnight. Thomson notes that employer attitudes have improved in the field of government and in those industries that depend on government contracts as well as big business in general. But he feels more progress must be made in educating medium-sized companies and small businesses.

Because small business is the current engine driving job creation in this country, a person with a disability cannot exclude smaller-size businesses from his or her job-search plan. Many small businesses have hired those with disabilities and will continue to do so as long as those with disabilities match their abilities with those listed in job descriptions.

Because a small business usually cannot afford a training staff, it is even more important that the skills of a job candidate closely match those of a posted opening; the candidate will most likely be expected to be up to par with a minimum of training.

Scan the employment ads in a journal such as *Careers & the disABLED*. Many companies advertise in publications especially designed to reach those with disabilities. When reading advertisements in general periodicals and newspapers, note any advertisements that specifically mention that the potential employer is an equal opportunity employer. You will be pleased to see that many so advertise themselves.

In the article "Ten Years of Change," published in *Careers & the disABLED*, author John M. Williams describes the past decade in relation to the disability movement. He cites advances in technology, ADA awareness, and increased visibility as having led the disability movement. A survey of 25 people with disabilities conducted by the magazine reveals that within the last 10 years, there have been significant changes in the rights and opportunities of people with disabilities. Respondents to the survey note that the roughest barrier confronting people with disabilities is an attitudinal one. The report indicates that the ADA and the appearance of people with disabilities in the media are changing attitudes. Wilson Hayes, a plant manager for Boeing Corporation, observes, "We have more people with disabilities working for us than ever before. Workers who have disabilities have proven that they are capable and determined. I see more of these professionals with disabilities in our factories and our offices." So no longer is a blind student necessarily destined to become a teacher of the blind or a Braille typesetter. The student cannot be a pilot, but he or she can do almost anything else in the world of work.

Technology Can Help

Recent advances in assistive technology devices have pried the door of employment opportunity open a bit wider. Warren tells of ten people with hearing problems who work for Merrill Lynch. The company has set up teletypewriter devices for the deaf (TDDs) to provide information to customers who are hearing impaired who call into the company to inquire about investment opportunities. Hundreds of customers have benefitted from this equipment.

Ken Loloski, a person with a disability, is a bookkeeper for Boeing who has been aided in his work by advancements in technology that have taken place in the past decade. He worked for Sears for 3 years before he came to Boeing. "I use large-print software and next-to-speech keyboards to do my work. When I started working 10 years ago, no one could believe I could do the work. Now everyone is a believer. All I asked is to be judged on my ability to do the job."

Most people who work in the field of rehabilitation say that the opportunity for placing people with disabilities into competitive employment is greater than ever before. All 50 states have been participating in supported employment and have shown dramatic increases in numbers of people successfully working. Whereas in 1986 the numbers were less than 10,000 placements per year, as of 1991 the numbers have exceeded 90,000.

If meaningful work can be found for those with the most profound disabilities, surely you can find work for yourself. It will not be easy, but it can be done. Thomson says that in order to be successful in the marketplace of today, every job seeker must take a proactive stance. This applies doubly to those seeking to enter the job market who happen to have a physical disability. Developing a positive and confident attitude together with a touch of humor can see you through to a successful career, according to Thomson.

You may have to be a pioneer. John St. Leger is a window clerk at the Barrington (Illinois) Post Office. His premature birth resulted in a hearing impairment detected at age five. After holding a few jobs that he felt were not rewarding and did not hold much promise for advancement, St. Leger visited the Illinois State Vocational and Rehabilitation Office to get some counseling. He spoke with a job specialist, took an interest test, and then decided to try for the post office. He liked the fact that the postal service has a union; to him that means job security and many benefits, including insurance. After successfully passing a test for post office employment, he waited for a position to open. He turned down the first location offered, but accepted the second opening—in Barrington, a northwest suburb of Chicago. After he had some years of experience as a postal worker, St. Leger decided to put a bid for the position of window clerk. Within the post office system, bids are considered in order of seniority on the job. At the time of his application, St. Leger was the candidate with the most years of employment at the post office. After successfully bidding, he then received training for the window-clerk position and had to submit to tests. During the last 5 years, his hearing problem has worsened, so he began to post a sign at his window informing customers that he is hearing-impaired. He has had no difficulty in relating with customers and in carrying out his multiple tasks. In fact, I frequented his window on a weekly basis for more than 2 years before I became aware of his impairment. He states proudly that his brother-in-law was the first deaf person to be hired for the post office within the State of Illinois. His brother-in-law works in another suburb. He has developed a system of signs communicating the various postal services and encourages his customers to point to what they need. So far he has had no complaints concerning this job accommodation.

Others have succeeded in careers of their own choosing so why can't you? Howard E. Figler in the 37th annual edition of *Planning Job Choices* dares you to "Give Yourself Permission to Pursue the Career You Really Want." He claims that career choice comes alive when you fire up an idea of your own and launch it into a world that says, "I'm not sure you can do that." He relates that older as well as younger students may resist giving themselves permission to pursue ambitious careers that reflect their deepest values and beliefs. Figler feels that caution is not related to age, but to the fear of making a mistake. He advises, "Accept it: sooner or later you are going to make a mistake somewhere along the line. The economic sands will shift. So you just don't know which way they will go and neither do the professional forecasters of economic trends." So what should you do about it, he asks. Shrink and fade away? Or look for safe careers? Very few careers are totally secure, and often those that are safe are so boring that you wouldn't want them anyway.

There are always those who are brave enough to test limits. Inis Cohen was not about to limit her son's capabilities merely because he was born with multiple sclerosis. While David Cohen was still a baby, doctors told his mother that he was very bright and should be stimulated as much as possible. His mother took this to heart, often reading aloud with her son and taking him to all sorts of museums, sports events, and other outings during his early years. When a special education teacher discouraged her son by failing to provide a chair that would enable David to reach the computer keyboard comfortably and by subtly sabotaging his career plans through her low level of daily performance expectations for David, Inis gave her son pep talks at night and provided him with continuous supplemental instruction and enrichment activities. Despite the teacher's low expectations for his achievement, David has gone right ahead to follow his dream of becoming a lawyer—a lawyer who will specialize in helping those with disabilities. He is in law school right now, earning top grades.

1986 Harris Survey

In a 1986 nationwide survey of 1,000 people with disabilities conducted by Louis Harris and Associates for the International Center for the Disabled in cooperation with the National Council on the Handicapped in Washington, D.C., not working was seen to be the truest definition of what it means to be disabled in this country. Two-thirds of all disabled Americans between the ages of 16 and 64 were found to be not working. Only one in four worked full-time, and another 10 percent were working part-time. No other demographic group less than 65 years of age of any size has a similar proportion of people who are not working. People with disabilities are excluded from the mainstream of American life mainly in the area of work, even more than social or leisure activities. For the average American, the striving to reach one's abilities amounts to working to achieve career and financial goals. Our society expects people to work, and the preeminent criterion by which most people are judged and measured is the job that they hold. Americans below the age of retirement who are not working live somewhat apart from the mainstream of life in this country. Unemployment excludes people from many of the common experiences known by most Americans.

In this Harris survey, nonworking disabled Americans less than 65 were asked if they would like to be working. A substantial portion—66 percent—responded that they would like to have a job. The challenge now becomes how a society can effect policies and programs to bring these people into the working mainstream. To prove how much a job means and how much those with disabilities look forward to working, 52 percent of those polled who worked replied that they were very satisfied with the kind of work they were doing. Thirty-one percent admitted to being somewhat satisfied. Some 5 percent were neither satisfied nor dissatisfied, while only 9 percent were somewhat dissatisfied. An equally small percentage were either not sure or refused to answer. Compare that with the attitudes toward work expressed by most or many people without disabilities.

Interestingly enough and in line with the idea that work provides a place of socialization, the great majority of disabled persons, both those working and those not working, would prefer to work in an office or other workplace and not at home. Seventy percent said they would prefer to work in an office, while only 26 percent would prefer to work at home. Or, in other words, seven out of ten prefer to work outside of their home, just as most Americans do. The two factors leading the list of reasons why people with disabilities limited their mobility or social activities were self-consciousness about their disability and their lack of education and marketable skills. Again, self-esteem and the development of specific job-related skills must form the basis of career planning.

After Carol Waskiewicz suffered a brain aneurism, she was subject to collapsing. To her the worst part of collapsing was not the possibility of physical injury, but the embarrassment of walking along a sidewalk and suddenly falling down in front of people. What would they think? She became increasingly hesitant to go out in public, although she had always been an affable person. Fortunately she had formed a friendship with one of the women she had met during her rehabilitation in the hospital. Carol wondered how her friend had been making the adjustment to side effects of having had an aneurism. On impulse, Carol phoned her friend. While exchanging bits of news, they began to laugh at each other's stories. They kidded each other about being clumsy. The laughter took hold, and they were able to put their problems into perspective. They were having such a good time commiserating with one another that they soon asked a few friends to join. Now, they have a support group that meets regularly, if informally. Carol claims it was her ticket to survival.

Bringing a disability out into the open is a step toward healing. Many years ago when it was the fashion to hide certain disabilities, I taught a regular classroom of seventh-grade students. As one of the students stood to recite, another student fell out of his chair and began to writhe on the floor. Several of the girls pointed at him and laughed because Jim had always been the class clown. Suddenly, one of the girls grew quiet. She looked at me, imploringly. "We've got to do something. He's not kidding. He's really in trouble." That's when I realized that he might be having an epileptic seizure. I never ran so fast in my life as I did down the school corridor to the nurse's office. Fortunately, the nurse was in and came to Jim's rescue. After that episode, which ended happily, I decided to learn all I could about epileptic seizures. Today, the teacher would be informed that Jim was subject to epileptic seizures and would be given information as to how such seizures could be simply and effectively dealt with should they happen in the classroom.

It has been my experience as a teacher, career counselor, and human relations professional that when people without disabilities are introduced to those with disabilities, they soon begin to accept those with disabilities as individuals. It just takes a bit of time. Encouraging signs taking place in the elementary school of today, such as mainstreaming of students with disabilities, awareness seminars, workshops, and even puppet plays that feature puppets with disabilities as just kids on the block, point to better acceptance of people with disabilities in the workplace when these students reach working age. The more those without disabilities meet those with disabilities, the less distance is felt between them. Those without disabilities tend to grow more tolerant.

With most job fields increasingly open to people with abilities who happen to have a disability or two, there is no longer any excuse for a person with disabilities not to pursue the occupation of his or her own choosing. There may be some loose bricks along the yellow brick road, but with determination, the road can be traveled.

Though he boasts of a never-quit attitude, Luis Estrella, who was born with cerebral palsy, admits that career prospects for a person with his severe disability were dim in 1986. To achieve his goals, he is quoted by author Eric Minton as saying that the environment and attitudes had to change. In 1987, Estrella got a Touchtalker—a laptop computer with speaking capabilities—to replace his communications board. Unfortunately, training did not come with the board. Then, he got the Liberator—a synthesized speech output communications device produced by the Prentke Romich Company—in 1994, which came with extensive training and support. Upon his college graduation, Estrella began to substitute teach in Tucson, Arizona, schools. When he came to substitute for a friend's class in economics, the assistant principal resisted his appointment, complaining that he was disabled. "I had to bite my tongue, since I wanted the job, but what I was thinking was, 'What was your first clue—the wheelchair?'" Even after relenting, the assistant principal frequently checked in on the class. But, Estrella must have been doing something right because 6 months later, he was employed full-time as an augmentative communication assistant at two elementary, one middle, and one high school—a job that led to his winning of the United Cerebral Palsy Association fellowship in 1995. Eric Minton concludes from Estrella's experience that many people with disabilities today face the same obstacles faced by Estrella in 1986. However, most people with disabilities in 1986 could not achieve positions of the type that Estrella holds now. "It is fair to say that opportunities for people with severe disabilities are much greater today than they were 10 years ago." Indeed as Estrella is proving, people with disabilities are playing on a considerably more level field than existed in 1986.

Ten Developments

In celebration of *Careers & the disABLED*'s tenth anniversary and the progress of people with disabilities during the past 10 years, the Winter 1995 issue listed the ten most significant developments for the workplace since 1986. The developments are to be seen as a continuum of progress. Together they have expanded the opportunities available to persons with disabilities.

1. The first is education. Before the ADA there was IDEA, the Individuals with Disabilities Education Act. The first version was enacted into law in 1975. Under IDEA schools were required to mainstream students with disabilities to the greatest degree possible. By the mid-1980s, the first generation of IDEA students were graduating from high school. Joseph P. Shapiro, senior editor of *U.S. News and World Report* and author of *No Pity*, says this first generation of mainstreamed students entered the workforce with a mindset of inclusion. "They have grown up expecting to be treated as equals."

2. The second concerns wheelchairs. Sunrise Medical purchased the independent wheelchair manufacturer Quickie in 1986, leading to the widespread marketing of the lightweight, stylish, manual wheelchair. Imitators quickly followed. Wheelchair technology has made significant progress in power chairs, too. Scooters have become a major market force. Serving originally as a long-distance transportation mode for people with walking disorders, they have become lighter, sturdier, and more maneuverable than many power chairs.

3. Then, along came the personal computer revolution of the early 1980s. Once the sole domain of publishing, financial, and scientific institutions, computers now occupy a place of honor in most workstations in virtually every industry. Computer technology has created personal notetakers and environmental controls, and has opened many jobs traditionally denied people with disabilities.

4. With the rise of the computer came the rise in repetitive motion syndrome. Suddenly ergonomics surfaced as a serious subject of study in the workplace. "Ergonomically correct" became a rallying

cry for sophisticated advertisers and marketers. Emphasis was placed on designing with people and their individualities in mind. This interest in accommodation of individuality has in turn created more job opportunities for people with disabilities because it has made job accommodation easier to accomplish.

5. The ADA became both the culmination of and a catalyst to a growing self-advocacy among those with disabilities. People began expecting and demanding suitable accommodations at stores, restaurants, and other public places.

6. In the mid-1980s Prentke Romich began to manufacture communication devices using Semantic Compaction Systems' Minspeak, a linguistic program that employs icons to supplement the standard English alphabet. The user can press a combination of two or three icons to speak a whole sentence, thus speeding up communications. Minspeak revolutionized the effectiveness of augmentative communication devices, which Prentke Romich and others have further developed to integrate with wheelchairs, climate controls, and computers. In fact, computers themselves entered the age of augmentative communication with the proliferation of laptops.

7. Although many municipal and national transportation systems have yet to abide by the 1973 Rehabilitation Act's standards, full accessibility at least appears to be within grasp. Much headway has been made through passage of the Air Carriers Act of 1986 and the ADA. The Air Carriers Act made the skies friendly to people with disabilities, allowing them to freely engage in business travel. On other fronts, the ADA has made it difficult for regional transportation authorities to continue to ignore their obligations. Many cities now have widespread accessibility to public transit, and most others are converting buses and trains or have plans in the works to do so.

8. The growing market represented by drivers with disabilities has inspired automakers. Automobile manufacturers have begun providing rebate programs for modifications of cars, vans, and trucks to accommodate disabilities. Parking spaces designated for people with disabilities has now become the norm—not the exception.

9. Voice Recognition Technology (VRT) has revolutionized access to personal computers. Today, all computer functions are available for everyone. Access ranges from an on/off button to sip-and-puff access. Refinement in VRT is continuing at a rapid pace. Voice recognition programs can be adapted to career fields or trained to understand even the most garbled speech. Also, the application of VRT is expanding. It is now being utilized to operate sewing machines, looms, and other machinery. At the opposite end is voice output, which has made computers accessible to people with visual impairments. Once limited to Braille readers and screen magnifiers, computer programs now talk people through applications, in addition to text documents.

10. The Internet has expanded communication to international networks. People are awakening to the potential of the World Wide Web. From in-office e-mail to the Internet, computers have created a whole new form of communication, one especially conducive to people with disabilities, who, because of various impairments, have limited interaction with others. But when you're communicating on the Internet, the message is you, totally and completely.

Finally, people with disabilities are no longer regarded as an aftermarket for product manufacturers. Now, people with disabilities have come to represent consumers and skilled labor. Whereas a few years ago you could order a voice synthesizer to put in your computer, now all televisions come with captioning chips.

Paul G. Hearne, president of the Dole Foundation, has observed that technology that adheres to principles of universal design will include the disabled population globally, thereby eliminating all barriers while proving the point that if any article is accessible to and usable by people with disabilities, they will buy it. "Technology is the key reason that people with disabilities will work together in the next decade so that it becomes a great equalizer for access to information for everybody."

CHAPTER TWO

WHAT DO YOU WANT TO DO? DEFINING AND FOLLOWING YOUR DREAMS

"Select a career because you have a passion for it. The idea that all persons with disabilities should be in particular careers is itself wrong and, certainly, a limiting factor in your choice." David Schnell maintains that by choosing a career based on your interests, you will be able to sustain motivation for many years, or even a lifetime. Merging your career with your interests will enable you to carry on successfully through the hurdles and setbacks that are inevitable along any career path. The world is so full of a number of things, you'd think we'd all be as happy as kings. So spoke Lewis Carroll. Yes, the career choices are so many. Unless we begin to sort through them in advance of applying for a job, we might settle for any job we can get. The secret to discovering the best jobs for you is much more than an external search for "where the jobs are."

Begin with Yourself

While searching out job announcements and writing résumés are essential tasks in a job search, they are not part of the first stage. They are not even the second or third things you need to do, according to Ronald L. Krannich and Caryl Rae Krannich, Ph.Ds, authors of *Discover the Best Jobs for You*, published by Impact Publications, 1991. Finding the best jobs for you begins with you—knowing your interests, values, skills, abilities, motivations, and dreams. You must analyze, synthesize, and reformulate this self-assessment information into a powerful objective. This objective, in turn, will build the foundation for a well-organized and fruitful job search because your strengths and goals will direct you to the employers who are looking for someone with your interests and talents. It is fairly well-established in psychology that where there is an interest there is usually a talent.

When author Robert Boles asked, "What Color Is Your Parachute?" he threw out a challenge to people to find their own particular work niche based on interests rather than on consideration of salary or prestige or even on ease of entry into the field. I can relate very well to his message. In my own life, although I have changed jobs frequently, my main interests have always served me well. I love to hear the sounds of people speaking. I enjoy helping people. I love music and laughter. I like to solve problems, and I enjoy learning and communicating. That combination of interests has led me into teaching, coaching, editing, proofreading, selling books, and, finally, into writing technical material, general feature articles, and how-to books. And I intend to keep going as long as I can because I love what I am doing.

I'm always amazed when people tell me how much they hate their jobs or how much they're looking forward to the weekend or how they intend to retire early. "Retire to what?" I ask myself because I have the luxury of doing what I enjoy doing and getting paid for it. But that luxury did not come easily. I spent many years in formal education, many years as an apprentice in the communications field, and I have written a number of articles that never made it into print. But, all the time, I was pursuing my dream. In the early days, it often felt like ten rejections before one sale. Logic might have insisted that I quit because there seemed to be little or no return for my efforts, but my heart told me to go on. The deep passion I have for writing impelled me to continue despite the long odds, irregular hours, and the necessity of keeping a full-time job while I pursued the elusive muse. Interestingly enough, the experiences from my full-time jobs, including teaching, gave me a rich variety of material to feed my creative imagination, and the experiences were eventually transformed into articles and books.

With most job fields wide open to people with ability who happen to have a physical disability, there is no longer any excuse not to select a career based on what you truly wish to do for the rest of your life. This is not to say the path is easy. But, the path is there, if you choose to follow your dream.

Consider this story reported in the Chicago Tribune on March 4, 1996:

On February 19, 1995, Stephanie Bostos was in a serious automobile accident. Her upper right leg was smashed, requiring the implantation of a steel rod and screws in her hip and knee. More catastrophic, her right foot had to be amputated. Yet, she recently danced on one of America's premier venues: the Kennedy Center for the Performing Arts.

How could this be? According to Michael Kilian, staff writer for the Chicago Tribune, Stephanie is quoted as saying, "Dancing—it's me. It's like eating food. You can't go without eating food, or breathing. Dancing is like breathing to me."

Stephanie's perseverance began within a few days of the accident. She began dancing again even before she'd been fitted with a prosthesis. Once she was fitted with and had mastered a prosthesis, she made great progress, but in her first official performance, she did the duet without it. She put it on when she went into the wings, but then came out and walked across the stage to make a statement.

If you are aware of your true interests, you will find a way to incorporate the interest within your career pattern. For instance, my friend Bob Bove was a very good accordion player in his youth. As an adult, he developed into a gifted teacher and coach. Although he made his lifetime career as a teacher and coach, he held onto his interest in accordion playing. During the Korean War, he met a professional accordion player named Dick Contino who was entertaining for the troops behind the lines. They became fast friends due to their mutual interest in the accordion. After Bove retired, he wrote the first biography of Dick Contino. Bove is now touring the country with the book and his hoping to have it made into a movie. A person with a true passion is hard to stop.

Another friend who was always interested in art and in painting but had made a living as an office worker was hit by a car while in her early twenties. The accident paralyzed her, and she no longer had the use of her arms. After she had time to adjust to her new situation, her thoughts turned to her love of art. She knew she could not go back to her old career. Painstakingly, she taught herself to paint by holding a paintbrush between her toes. After some time, she is finally at the stage where she has decided her efforts are good enough to present to the public, and her paintings are selling.

Find Your Pattern of Interests

The Mix-and-Match Game

Carole Hyatt, a nationally known lecturer and author of *Lifetime Employ-ability*, often has her lecture audience do an exercise designed to ferret out their interests. She asks each person to jot down his or her interests. Then, she shows the person how to sort through his or her list to put a new spin on the career goals. First, she asks the audience to form teams of two people each. One person is designated an "A," while the other is a "B." Each writes a list of skills used in previous and current jobs (List 1). Next, a list is made of skills or interests that have never been used for financial gain (List 2). Finally, each compiles a list of current and past hobbies (List 3). Then, "A" and "B" are asked to exchange lists. What item can "A" take from B's List 1 (occupational skills) and combine it with an item on B's List 2 (skills not used in a previous occupation)? Finally, a third item is selected from B's List 3 (hobbies and activities). Voila! The combinations can be startling. For example, "A" took "the skill of organizing and planning," combined it with "workshops in animal breeding and animal showing," and added "the keeping of a variety of exotic pets." She suggested "B" open a pet store with the unique angle of breeding and offering exotic pets and providing workshops for the public on the proper feeding and care of exotic animals.

Try this mix-and-match game with a friend or family member:

- What career would you suggest for someone who has run a lawn-maintenance business during summer vacations, has spent years assembling small kits, is skilled in rope tricks, and has a hobby of making designs with strings?

- What career could you suggest for someone who has worked part-time teaching crafts in a summer camp for children, fixes small appliances, and likes to read about new machines and inventions?

- Make a list of your skills, hobbies, and interests and then come up with creative suggestions for what you might do for a living.

Other Informal Methods

Another way to find your pattern of interests is to keep a diary. See what types of activities you engage in and which hold the greatest interest for you. Write an essay or short autobiography about yourself and what makes you tick. Another exercise is for you and a friend or two to buy a copy of the same issue of a newspaper. Then, supply each person with a pair of scissors. Each person should cut out as many articles as interest them personally. After you're done clipping, compare and contrast the subject matter of the articles to see what your interests tell about you. The game can be modified so that stories selected are not cut out but read aloud by the person who selected the story. Or, one person can be the cutter while a friend can be the reader and the third can be the listener.

The Career Exploration Inventory

There are many formal methods of determining interests. One straight-forward and easy to administer interest inventory is called the Career Exploration Inventory (CEI) developed by John J. Liptak, Ed.D. This is used by many career counselors as a guide for exploring work, leisure, and learning. According to the introduction to the inventory, the CEI is more than a career interest "test." It is an instrument designed to help you explore and plan three major areas of your life—your work, leisure activities, and education or learning. You are asked to respond to 120 items, and your responses are scored relative to 15 major clusters or groupings of interest. In addition, the test aids in locating additional sources of information on occupations, leisure activities, and related educational programs. To find out more, call the toll-free number (800) 648-JIST.

Here are some examples from the inventory:

- If your interest cluster is mechanical, which includes operating machines for mass production and using tools to build and repair things, the corresponding occupations would include engineer, drafter, cable splicer, mechanic, and TV repairperson. Typical jobs and leisure applications are mentioned, such as fixing appliances, model boat building, and dollhouse construction.

- Should the interest cluster be plants, which refers to the cultivating and gathering of crops and the growing and tending of plants, related occupations include landscape gardener, cemetery worker, forest ecologist, and soil conservationist, and typical leisure activities are 4-H activities, conservation clubs, growing house plants, and cactus gardening.

- Another cluster is physical sciences, which encompasses conducting research and collecting data about the natural world. Physical sciences would take in such occupations as astronomer, geologist, meteorologist, chemist, and environmental analyst. Related hobbies and activities are collecting rocks, solving mathematical puzzles, and gazing at stars.

You can make a list of your interests on separate cards or have them cut out from a sheet of paper in small strips. Now deal them out singly as you would deal out a deck of cards. Begin to sort through the individual interests and form clusters. Try to prioritize in order of preference. For example, helping your little sister with homework and explaining how to solve a math problem to a friend could be a cluster of helping others. Taking apart old clocks to see what makes them tick is part of a mechanical cluster. When you begin to narrow down your interest clusters to one or a few, try to seek out people in your chosen field of interest. Ask each person what interests he or she had as a young person. What interests do they now have? Another idea is to read biographies of famous people in fields you hope to explore. What activities and interests do famous inventors have in common? This is one way to see if you fit into a field as a whole. You may never be able to be an inventor, but you might be a repairperson. You may never be a famous explorer, but you might go on to teach geography. At first, be more concerned with the field of interest rather than rushing to narrow it down to a specific position or job within the general field. If you narrow too soon, you might miss an opportunity or two within your chosen field.

Organizations and Clubs

After you have narrowed some of your interests, investigate organizations and clubs geared to those interests. Such organizations may be listed in your local phone book or, by calling the national office, you may be referred to a club in your local area.

Another way to find clubs connected with your interests is to visit the library and search the bulletin boards. Very often local clubs post a general description of what they do, who is eligible to join, and how a person may go about joining or contacting the organization for further information.

Teachers are often excellent sources of clubs, whether in-school clubs or clubs in the larger community. For example, Junior Achievement helps students to further their interest in business careers by providing actual hands-on experience. Under the direction of a successful businessperson who volunteers time to work with a small group of young people, the club members themselves organize a work group and even form their own little company. Then, they select a product or service to sell or practice for a fee and off they go, hopefully into the land of profit. But even a lack of profit is a good learning experience. Not only are communication skills and leadership skills taught, but the individuals within the group learn to work together as a team as they develop a bird's-eye view of the business world.

Boy Scouts and Girl Scouts help you explore different careers by working on specific badges, visiting local community groups, and having a number of people in the community present lectures on their hobbies, careers, and interests.

Form your own career club. Do not limit members to those with physical disabilities. Take in anyone who is interested in exploring careers. By establishing regular meetings, you will be able to spread out some of the fact-finding work about careers. One member can dig out information about becoming a medical technician. Another may search for information having to do with general office work. Members can be asked to come up with names of local people who can be contacted to speak to the group or invite the group to inspect their places of business. Members can be asked to clip items from newspapers, magazines, newsletters, and other sources with the object of tracking salary data on specific career fields, surveying entry-level requirements for the field, or finding out any number of things. Money may be pooled to invest in software that will aid in the job search or career exploration. Many hands do lighten the load. You yourself will be taken more seriously in your quest for information when you can see that you have taken the time and interest to form a career club.

Job Titles

When life was simpler, each community was sufficient unto itself. There was the silversmith, the blacksmith, the farmer, the storekeeper, and the barkeeper, among others. They were plainly visible within the small village, and children could observe how they made their daily rounds. Now, however, there are so many occupations that it would take years to observe just a fraction of the many jobs.

One helpful hint in narrowing things down is to consult the *Dictionary of Occupational Titles* found in most every library or school career center. The current edition lists more than 12,000 titles. You will find lots of titles you've never heard of. By reading the introduction to the book, you'll see how the occupations are arranged, and it will make it easier to browse through the book.

Love to fill out forms? A form analyst designs, examines, and evaluates formats of business forms. The analyst makes recommendations for improvement of form design. A form analyst may design, draft, and prepare finished forms along with writing copy that will appear on the form.

Interested in measurement? A freight clerk verifies and keeps records of incoming and outgoing shipments and prepares items for shipping. This type of clerk composes and compares information and counts, weighs, and measures items, including the counting of shipments to verify against the bills of lading, invoices, orders, and other records.

Good in math? Like to predict? An estimator prepares cost estimates of products manufactured or services requested to aid in bidding or in determining what the price of products or services should be.

Interested in foreign languages and interacting with foreign countries? An export clerk must be handy with computers. An export clerk computes the duties, tariffs, weight values, and price conversions of merchandise exported to or imported from foreign countries. He or she examines documents, such as invoices, bills of lading, and shipping status, to verify conversion of merchandise weights or values into the monetary system used by the other country.

Good at balancing your budget? A credit counselor provides financial counseling to individuals who are in debt. The counselor ascertains the monthly income available to meet credit obligations, establishes the method of payoff, and estimates time for debts and liquidation. He or she contacts creditors in order to set up payment adjustments so the creditor can pay his or her bills.

The *Dictionary of Occupational Titles* is produced by the U.S. Employment Service. In order to properly match jobs and workers, the public employment service system requires that a uniform occupational language be used in all of its local job service offices. Under each occupation, such as a cloth printer, there will be seven basic parts to the occupational definition—from giving it a code number to alternate titles and statements of task elements, such as turns screws to align register marks on printing rollers with register marks on machine, or uses allen wrench. What's interesting about the occupational code is that the middle three digits represent the worker functions ratings of the task performed in the occupation. Because every job requires a worker to function to some degree in relation to data, people, and things, the fourth digit ranks the job as it relates to data, while the fifth digit ranks according to relations with people during the performance of the job, and the sixth digit ranks the category of things with relation to performance of the job. Thus, if a person is interested in becoming a general physician because he likes to work with people, a scrutiny of specific medical specialties may introduce the fact that a physician must work with his hands as well as with his eyes and heart. Even though medicine is considered a helping profession, science and mechanical ability are involved in the medical professions, as is knowledge of mathematics.

It's fun to run down the alphabetical index of occupational titles, exploring those that seem very unusual or that contain a key word of your interest area such as *machine*. Selecting "machine," you will find machine setter, machine sneller, machine-tank operator, just for starters. No doubt you will be intrigued enough to continue on to *machinist*, which covers machinist helper, machinist, linotype machinist, marine engine machinist, and others.

Countless jobs were not common a decade ago. Many jobs were unheard of until quite recently. One way to keep up with new jobs is to consult *Restructured America: A Streamlined Encyclopedia of 1992 Job Descriptions*. This guide was inspired by the *Encyclopedia of Managerial Job Descriptions*. According to the introduction of *Restructured America*, the 1980s were a time of great expansion of American business. Now the challenge facing American business is not expansion but contraction. With the downturn of the business cycle, many companies have concluded that the 1980s led them into overexpansion. Thus, corporate restructuring and downsizing have become the order of the day. But the new business environment requires new tools to help in the reorganization process. *Restructured America* presents essential job descriptions for the 1990s. Within its covers are found valuable job descriptions for such growing disciplines as Information Resources Management and Office Automation together with complete but concise job descriptions for every corporate task from entry level to the boardroom.

Twelve Interest Areas

Another valuable source for checking out possible occupations is the *Enhanced Guide for Occupational Exploration*. This guide contains 2,800 occupational descriptions and covers more than 95 percent of all workers in the United States. Its cross-referencing system allows you to locate jobs by skills, interests, education required, industry, and other factors. The U.S. Department of Labor has segmented all jobs into 12 major areas or groupings based on interests. These are the same groupings that are used in other career information systems.

Area 1: Artistic. You have artistic interests when you creatively express feelings or ideas. Subcategories of artistic interests are: literary arts such as editing, creative writing, critiquing; visual arts such as instructing and appraising; studio art; commercial arts; performing arts such as drama, music, or dance; craft arts such as graphic arts and related crafts; arts and crafts; hand lettering, painting, and decorating; elemental arts such as announcing and entertaining, and, modeling, including personal appearance. You could make a checklist next to each of the subcategories, indicating those in which you have participated and those in which you hope to become involved. Several checks may indicate a career interest.

Area 2: Scientific. Subcategories are physical sciences; life sciences, which includes animal specialization, plant specialization, and food research; medical sciences, which covers medicine and surgery, dentistry, veterinary medicine and health specialties, and laboratory technology. If you're interested in these fields, enroll in a laboratory course in the area of your interest. It will help to tell you whether you will be able to sustain your interest.

Area 3: Plants and Animals. Under this heading is managerial work with plants and animals, as well as animal training and animal service and elemental work with plants and animals separated into farming, forestry and logging, hunting and fishing, nursery and groundskeeping, and general services.

Area 4: Protective. This includes safety and law enforcement and security services.

Area 5: Mechanical. This category along with the next category, Industrial, has the most subdivisions, ranging from engineering, craft technology and quality control, to material control.

Area 6: Industrial. There are dozens of specific subcategories such as machine work with metal and plastics; machine work with wood; machine work with paper; down to manual work involving stamping, labeling, wrapping, and packing.

Area 7: Business Detail. It is a good thing to check each subheading should your interests lie in general business. This is a large category. Business Detail includes administrative detail; mathematical detail, such as bookkeeping and auditing; financial detail, such as paying and receiving; oral communications, such as interviewing, receiving, and information giving; records processing; clerical machine operation, such as computer operation, which is in itself constantly expanding; clerical machine operation; and clerical handling, which includes filing, sorting, distribution, and general clerical work as subcategories.

Area 8: Selling. Selling runs the gamut of functions from sales technology and general sales to vending.

Area 9: Accommodating. Includes hospitality services, barber and beauty services, passenger services, customer services, such as food services and sales services; and attendant services.

Area 10: Humanitarian. Under Humanitarian is found social services, such as religious services, counseling, and social work; nursing; therapy; specialized teaching services, and child and adult care.

Area 11: Leading-Influencing. There are many subheadings, including mathematics and statistics with a further subcategory of data processing design, followed by data analysis, educational and library services, and communications and business.

Area 12: Physical Performing. Includes sports and physical feats.

As you check off your inventory interest list against these headings, you may find your interests clustering in accommodating, which will then lead you to narrow choices into the subcategories within that field. As you begin to read about hospitality services, you may become attracted more to food services than safety and comfort services. Narrowing down even further, you may be interested in hotel food services. From there, you can narrow down to specific jobs, such as nutritionist. After you have a definite interest in an industry such as the hotel industry, try to write to hotels in your area or call up to schedule a visit. Carefully read any literature the hotel might furnish. While you are there, don't forget to pick up an application form and start to practice even though you may be a year or more away from actually applying.

Associations

From the initial stages of career exploration to the final stages of searching for specific job openings, making friends with appropriate associations will be a big boost up the career ladder of your choice. The granddaddy of association guidebooks is the *Encyclopedia of Associations*, which currently comes in three volumes. Don't let its size intimidate you. Its indexes and appendixes are easy to follow. Each of the volumes explains in simple language how to use the book. Next, how to use the index is explained followed by a list of abbreviations and symbols and, finally, a keyword list. By means of the keyword list, you can zero right in on familiar territory, such as trade, business and commercial organizations, environmental and agricultural organizations, cultural organizations, and social welfare organizations. Let's say you are interested in electronics. There are approximately 25 listings of associations having to do with the keyword of *electronics*. It's always a good idea to write to a general association, which is usually pinpointed by having "America," "American," or "National" in its title. There is a listing for the American Electronics Association. Immediately following the name of this association is its address and phone and fax number. Other details may be given, such as the year of its founding and the number of members. It lists field offices, if any, and regional groups. Its purpose is clearly displayed. In this case, its purpose is to foster a healthy business climate and conduct networking programs for industry executives. Toward the end of the entry, there is information regarding publications of the association. In this case, the American

Electronics Association publishes the AEA *Directory*, which is an annual, and a membership directory. There is also a newsletter. In addition, the organization issues bulletins. You might write for career information along with a schedule of conventions or workshops in your area. Ask for a copy of the newsletter, too. In this way, you will keep current with issues in the field and who is who, the latter invaluable for networking, which will be discussed later in the book.

Other listings are specific to subcategories of electronics, such as the American Loudspeaker Manufacturers Association. There is also a manufacturers association for Asian-American Manufacturers. If you are of Asian origin, here's a unique chance to network and make your career interests known. While writing or calling an association, inquire as to what type of placement activities it sponsors and what types of training it offers. Going to a convention and meeting with a group of professionals in your intended field allows an in-depth look at who is successful in the field and what it takes to be successful in the field. It's worth the price of admission, and, as a student, you may receive a discount or may be admitted free, depending on how well you plead your case and depending on the interests of the association in recruiting young people into the profession.

You can gain a lot by reading listings in the career area of your choice. We will look further at one example. The Earth Island Institute is listed under Environmental and Agricultural Organizations. The listing mentions the type of projects in which it is interested. Perhaps there is a chance of an internship, an assistanceship, or a volunteer opportunity. Perhaps you can use one of the projects as a resource for a term paper in general science or geography. The entry further notes that the institute compiles statistics and maintains a reference library. It also publishes brochures and *Earth Island Journal: An International Environmental News Magazine*. At the very least, send for a back copy of the publication.

The HEATH Directory

The HEATH *National Resource Directory on Postsecondary Education and Disability* (1996) was prepared by the American Council on Education under cooperative agreement with the U.S. Department of Education. Published biennially, it offers a selection of resources in the major interest areas in the field of postsecondary education and disability.

The directory is full of information and easy to use. The index arranges all organizations in alphabetical order, from ABLEDATA to Worldwide Disability Solutions Group. Also listed in the index is the organization's 800 number. For example, the phone number for the National Center for Youth with Disabilities (NCYD) is (800) 333-6293. You will find the complete entry in alphabetical order within the listings of the individual organizations. Under NCYD's entry on page 24, additional phone numbers are supplied, including a fax number and teletypewriter (TT) number. You will learn that NCYD maintains the National Resource Library, a computerized database containing interdisciplinary information on current research, model programs, training and educational materials, and a technical assistance network of consultants with expertise in adolescence and disability issues. Also, the library may be accessed by calling an information specialist to request a database search. Its publications include *Connections*, a newsletter that highlights critical issues for youth with chronic illness or disability; annotated bibliographies; and a series of statistical data fact sheets.

Another helpful listing is for the American Foundation for the Blind (AFB). The AFB mission is to enable people who are blind or visually impaired to achieve equality of access and opportunity that will ensure freedom of choice in their lives. This mission is fulfilled through: development, collection, and dissemination of information; identification, analysis, and resolution of critical issues; education of the public and policymakers; and production and distribution of talking books and other audio materials. Why not write for career materials? Services provided include information and consultation in the areas of education, rehabilitation, employment, and special products. *AFB News*, which is published twice a year, is available at no cost, as is the catalog of publications. You may subscribe for a fee to the *Journal of Visual Impairment & Blindness*.

Under the heading of National Alliance of Blind Students (NABS) is listed a national newsletter called *The Student Advocate*. It is available to members. The alliance also sponsors a program to assist with employment. Dues are $10 per year.

Disabled American Veterans (DAV) has a listing that says it works to lower the rate of unemployment among veterans with disabilities and to prevent discrimination against them. The organization's voluntary services operates nationwide as does its transportation network. Its national service office advises members and nonmembers across the country.

Vocational Tests

The *Twelfth Mental Measurements Yearbook*, edited by Jane Close Conoley and James C. Impara, lists interest tests by title, by subject, and by publisher. Along with old favorites, such as the Kuder General Interest Survey, there are newer, intriguing tests, like the Employability Inventory, the Guilford-Zimmerman Interest Inventory for College Students and Adults, and tests geared to specific professions. The latter include the Nurse Aide Practice Test, the Candidate Profile Record (for applications for clerical positions) and a sales potential inventory for real estate called ASPIRE. If a test is available in a special edition, for instance in Braille, this information is noted.

Several interesting tests are noted below:

- The purpose of the Job Seeking Skills Assessment (Arkansas Research and Training Center in Vocational Rehabilitation, 1988) is to determine a person's ability to complete a job application form and to participate in the employment interview. The target population is vocational rehabilitation clients. It also serves as a guide for integrating the results into program planning. Its authors are Suki Hinman, Bob Means, Sandra Parerson, and Betty Odendahl.

- The Vocational Learning Styles (Piney Mountain Press) is another fairly recent test in the vocational area. It was developed by author Helena Hendrix-Frye to assess learning styles and preferred working conditions. The test is geared to Grades 7 through 12 and is also intended for adults. This test uncovers an area of concern that has gone largely unaddressed—what type of environment are you interested in working in or interested in avoiding? Five areas are covered:

    1. Physical domain explores the kinesthetic, visual, tactile, and auditory.

    2. Social domain addresses group versus individual.

    3. Environmental domain explores formal design, informal design, bright lights, dim lights, warm temperature, cool temperature, with sound and without sound.

    4. Mode of expression domain refers to whether you are orientated toward oral communication or written communication.

5. Work characteristics domain refers to working outdoors or indoors, sedentary work versus nonsedentary, lifting versus nonlifting, data, people, and things.

The score reports include a profile in story form as to how an employer or an instructor might structure a learning or working environment.

- The Voc-Tech Quick Screener (VTQS) identifies career interests. Its target population is non-college–bound high school students and adults. Its authors are Robert Kauk and Robert Tobinett; the test publisher is CFKR Career Materials, Inc. The test was reviewed by Del Eberhardt, program administrator of the Greenwich Public Schools in Greenwich, Connecticut. Eberhardt said that the Strong Interest Inventory and Holland's Self-Directed Search provide better techniques, but that the VTQS can help high school students gain new information about the technical occupations under the careful guidance of a teacher or guidance counselor. He did not recommend it for in-depth or serious career guidance. Still, it does supply a start with its 14 cluster groups of occupations, each of which contains more than a dozen disparate occupations. After the testee's interests are matched to occupational profiles, he or she is instructed to complete the final portion of the VTQS. The testtaker lists the three fields receiving the highest number of points and then rates his or her interests in gaining the skills and in completing the studies needed to enter the field, chances of success, and interest in jobs related to the fields. Information to aid in each task is provided. Points earned are again summed, and the high score indicates the field in which the testee has the greatest interest.

The three tests most often used with job candidates for the purpose of choosing a career are:

1. The Miller Analogy Test;

2. Minnesota Multiphasic Test; and

3. Strong-Campbell Interest Test.

Placement centers call this battery of tests "value clarification."

Career Clustering

Bill Houze, a personnel executive with high-technology experience in General Electric and Rockwell International, coined the term *Career Veer* to describe a process of gaining the essential tools for a lifelong career by becoming a cluster specialist. According to Houze's theory, a person can build and sustain an enjoyable, rewarding career in the new order of things, if he or she will take the time to become a cluster specialist. By the new order, Houze is referring to America's transformation from a nation of heavy industry to a world leader in the supplying of information, knowledge, and certain services and technologies. It does not matter whether you are aiming for a white-collar or a blue-collar career. Becoming a cluster specialist should be your goal in our rapidly changing society. By doing so you will reduce the hazards that accompany change. By clustering or being well-versed in a wide variety of subspecialties, such as office work, you will have a reasonable chance to continue to learn and to grow in your chosen field of work.

In addition, career clustering provides more satisfaction because cluster specialists rely more on broad aptitudes, attitudes, and skills than on detailed knowledge. This gives you flexibility and transferable skills as you come face-to-face with downsizing, outplacement, and the company push towards early retirement. A cluster specialist bridges the gap between the specialist who knows too much about too little and the generalist who knows too little about too much. The cluster specialist works at reasonable technical depth in several related areas and will be more successful than either the generalist or the specialist in the marketplace of the future.

Five Vocational Tests

Think about the relationship of work to interest patterns. Certain types of work attract people who share the same or similar interests. This theory of mutual interest became the basis for predicting a tendency to succeed or fail in any given job.

1. Edward K. Strong of Stanford University was one of the first to develop an interest test as a predictor of career success. The Strong Vocational Interest Bank was designed to uncover an individual's pattern of interests. Bankers often enjoy cultivating roses as a

hobby. Given a forced choice between growing roses and tending cattle, those with an interest in banking presumably would opt for the roses.

2. Frederic J. Kuder, a specialist in vocational guidance, set out to determine what interests were desirable for or were commonly associated with certain jobs. In his research, Kuder uncovered clear associations that he then used to develop the Kuder Preference Record, which is a pen-and-pencil survey in the form of forced choices. Each set of choices comes in a series of three: for example, would you rather dig ditches, plan a survey, or clean teeth.

3. The purpose of the Occupational Interests Surveyor (OIS) is to measure interest in five basic fields of work and to measure five sources of job satisfaction. It is usually administered to students and adults who have minimal educational qualifications. It can be given to a group in a period of 30 to 40 minutes. Its author is Tony Crowley and the test is published by Hobsons Publishing Company of England. The OIS is based on the rationale that people are more motivated and satisfied at occupations and tasks that interest them and that those who select occupations consistent with their interests remain with the position longer and report more work satisfaction. The surveyor also includes a checklist of 75 occupational activities that complement the five categories of job titles.

4. The Occupational Interests Explorer is designed to assess interest in several general fields of work and over a wide range of occupational activities. Its target population is ages 15 and older with above-average intelligence. The interest areas are: practical/active; enterprising/persuasive; scientific/investigative; clerical/administrative; artistic/creative; and social/supportive. Work satisfactions are classified both as intrinsic or within the work itself and extrinsic such as pay and prestige associated with the work. It can be administered to a group in about 20 minutes. Its author is Tony Crowley and its publisher is Hobsons Publishing Company.

5. Job-O, also known as Judgement of Occupational Behavior Orientation, aims to facilitate self-awareness, career awareness, and career exploration. It is designed to be administered in a group. Its authors are Arthur Cutler, Francis Ferry, Robert Kauk, and Robert Robinett. It is published by CFKR Career Materials. Targeted at

Grades 4 to 7, it rates interests among the categories of mechanical/ construction, scientific/technical, creative/artistic, social/legal/educational, managers/sales, and administrative support. Test booklets in Spanish and Vietnamese are available. It can be administered in about an hour. An advanced form is intended for Grades 10 through 12 and for the adult population. This version delineates occupational interest, training time, reasoning skills, mathematical skills, language skills, working with data, working with people, working with things, working conditions, physical demands, leadership, helping people, problem solving, initiative, teamwork, and public contact. It may be self-administered. It can run on IBM software. The authors of the test feel that it provides job matches that facilitate career exploration.

All of these tests as well as others are described in great detail in the *Twelfth Mental Measurements Yearbook* mentioned previously.

Question Yourself

There are many insightful questions you can ask yourself that will also help you to zone in on your interests. Do you enjoy working with your mind, your hands, your whole body? Do you like work that occasionally leads you outdoors or do you prefer to spend your working hours indoors? Do you like to work in a large building with its own cafeteria or in a small office setting? Do you enjoy the open pit arrangement of many offices or do you prefer an enclosed cubicle for an office? Are you content working alone or do you need a support staff? Do you need close supervision or can you easily work on your own with minimal directions? Do you work at a very fast pace or at a relatively slow pace? Do you crave regular work hours or enjoy a variety of schedules? Do you like sporadic work activity where you put in a lot of effort for relatively short periods of time or do you like to work at a steady pace throughout the day? Do you want to be paid weekly or biweekly or monthly? Do you demand a straight salary or would you consider straight commission or a combination of salary and commission?

How would you describe your value system? Are you money-oriented? Love to be praised? Like to feel responsible? Put your family first? Crave job security? Enjoy meeting new people? Love the thrill of power? Enjoy exercising authority over others? Like a prestige career? Be honest.

Keeping career clusters in mind, jot down clusters next to each appropriate value such as "business" next to "money-oriented" and "social work" next to "liking to feel responsible" and so on. What career clusters interest you and satisfy your value scheme?

Gary Shufelt in the Fall 1995 issue of *Careers & the disABLED* lists the top habits to cultivate while searching for the right career. Three of them summarize this chapter:

1. Take an honest look at career ambitions. By this, Shufelt means not only thinking about getting ahead or figuring out what you want to do, but staying interested. Are you where you want to be now? Are you headed where you believe you'll want to be? Consider your career options.

2. Appreciate your self-worth. It's easier for you to achieve more when you have a better sense of who you are. For people with disabilities, it is essential to maintain self-esteem.

3. Understand that career decisions usually aren't forever. If you're pressuring yourself to find a career path that will be the answer to your entire working life, you may be adding unnecessary anxiety. Just as one job leads to another, so can one career lead to another.

Thanks to the federal School to Work Opportunities Act passed in May of 1994, a growing number of states are receiving grants for programs that help young people make the transition from school to careers. "The money is intended to bring together what employers need and what students are learning," according to J.D. Hoye, director of the National School to Work office in Washington, D.C. All 50 states, plus the District of Columbia and Puerto Rico, have received initial funding, and 27 more now have advanced-stage implementation grants, money that will go not only to work-based learning programs but also to encourage schools and businesses to create curricula that help students understand the relationship between academics and work. For more information on school-to-work programs in your area, contact the National School to Work Learning and Information Center at (800) 251-7236 or visit the School to Work home page on the Internet at http://www.stw.ed.gov.

The *Directory of College Facilities and Services for People with Disabilities* is a very helpful reference. Written by Carol H. Thomas and James L. Thomas and published by Oryx Press in 1991, this directory lists colleges and universities serving those with physical disabilities in terms of type of university, technical school, or other designation. It includes categories of disabilities represented, accessibility of various facilities, including classrooms and labs, and provisions for living arrangements. The first index arranges colleges and universities alphabetically. The second index is a categorical listing of disabilities served and programs followed by institutions that offer specific services. The directory concludes with a resource list of associations, centers, organizations, and societies providing services, clearinghouses, and databases and print sources for information.

CHAPTER THREE

BUILDING A FOUNDATION OF CAREER SKILLS

An old saying goes, "If wishes were horses, beggars would ride." Even though interests should point the way and act as arrows to the career target, a successful career cannot be had unless a person develops skills necessary to enter the field of choice and to stay in the field. Skill development should begin at least in junior high and should proceed with active guidance and counseling from not only guidance counselors, but also teachers and other members of the school staff. Families should also play a part in career guidance and skill development.

Early Skill Development

Career development can begin as early as kindergarten. In Notus, Idaho, where Vera Kenyon is a guidance counselor for kindergarten through 12th grade, guidance starts in kindergarten. By 4th grade, the students are ready to be introduced to the Idaho Career Information System (CIS). From 4th through 6th grade, Kenyon talks to students about the kinds of courses from which they will choose in the future and how these choices relate to the work they want to do. Kenyon has students use a worksheet to select occupations that are of interest. Then she provides the students with printed descriptions for occupations in which they have expressed interest. She uses the Idaho CIS for these printouts.

According to the National Occupational Information Coordinating Committee, elementary schools were equipped with CIS at more than 1,200 sites in 1994.

The method by which students gain access to CIS differs in secondary and postsecondary schools. In many secondary schools, counselors are active in introducing the system to students, but college counselors more often put students on their own. Increasingly, according to *Occupational Outlook Quarterly*, high school students use the system on networked computers.

College students traditionally work on stand-alone computer terminals. Schools and colleges are integrating career development into their curricula by tieing in their subject matter to career development information and activities and by focusing specifically on career information.

Computer-assisted systems usually have one or more on-line assessments that help users to learn about themselves and the qualities they might prefer in a career. In the on-line assessment, students answer questions dealing with their values, interests, skills, aptitudes, or experiences as they relate to work. They also explore the importance of occupational characteristics such as anticipated demand for workers, physical requirements, salary, working conditions, and amount of education required.

In addition, most systems can accept results from additional standardized assessment surveys, such as Self-Directed Search, Strong Interest Inventory, Career Adjustment Inventory, Career Occupational Preference System, and Harrington-O'Shea CDM.

A student's career search can get a big boost from the search feature in CIS. The search takes one of three broad forms:

1. In the first, students have the system generate a list of occupations based on the results of their completed assessment survey.

2. In the second, they choose search variables from a list. When they enter the value for each variable, the computer tells them how many remaining occupations meet the criteria. Users can often specify job characteristics they wish to avoid as well as ones they desire.

3. In the third type of search, the user types in keywords from the name of an occupation or selects it from an index. Then the description relating to the occupation is projected on the screen.

Most systems contain descriptions of from 300 to 500 occupations. Many systems permit users to compare two occupations side by side on one display or printout according to working conditions, numbers employed, recommended school courses, earnings, physical demands, and sources for more information. Thus, the student can carry on much of his career search without continual supervision from his counselor.

Further information about the various career information systems is available from national groups, CIS developers, and the state CIS directors. NOICC, a federal interagency program, has fostered the development of career programs since 1979 in cooperation with State Occupational Information Coordinating Committees and state CIS programs. NOICC can be contacted at 2100 M Street, Suite 800, Washington, DC 20036-1193.

Starting with junior high, you should take at least one interest test. Deaf students are not usually given the Kuder Occupational Interest Survey because it is highly dependent upon verbal response. Braille answer sheets for the Kuder Preference are easily obtained. Due to the fact that those with disabilities often underestimate their ability and potential, the PRG Interest Inventory for the Blind has been developed. This inventory reflects hobbies and jobs commonly undertaken by people who are sight-impaired. The test can be administered orally or by using a tape recorder.

Special Needs and Skill Development

The new law for integrating children with special needs into the mainstream states that the child and the parents have something to say about if and when testing should occur, as well as how test results are to be used and the type of tests that may be given. Personality tests as well as vocational, aptitude, and interest tests are geared to approximately an 8th-grade reading level. Check with the guidance department as to possible modification of test materials and any change in the time limits, if necessary. Blind students should be given access to the use of a Braille or oral test. For further information regarding disability rights and testing, write for a copy of The Independent, a quarterly magazine by and about people with disabilities. The magazine is free to members of the Center for Independent Living, 2539 Telegraph Avenue, Berkeley, CA 94704.

Career training should include maximum use of hands and speech. Check with your physical and occupational therapists, the school nurse, and the school speech pathologist as to how your condition may improve and how you can extend your skills. Many jobs require or are greatly enhanced when a person has good perceptual ability. Have you had your ability to discriminate objects, pictures, form, and color measured?

Students with physical disabilities should not shy away from driver education. Quadriplegic and visually impaired students are capable of learning to drive and are eligible for licenses. Remember that independent living as well as occupational choices are linked to the ability to drive. Also, a new level of confidence comes with every skill mastered. You may take driving lessons individually. Cars can be equipped with adapted devices. Many state departments of education have special programs for disabled students within the state's driver education program.

You may send for *Tips on Car Care and Safety for Deaf Drivers*. This booklet discusses safety tips and other matters pertinent to learning to drive. Write to the U.S. Department of Transportation, National Highway Traffic Safety Administration, Washington, DC 20590.

High School Skill Development

Your teachers and vocational education teachers can help make certain your program provides career exploration and, possibly, a work-study component while you are still in school so you can continue to learn about different careers and be better prepared to make choices at a later time.

Talk with your school guidance counselor or vocational rehabilitation counselor about taking an interest inventory and the availability of a vocational assessment. In addition, you may visit your school library and public library for books and pamphlets that describe various postsecondary education programs, such as trade, vocational-technical, college, or university. Be sure to read as much as you can about the many jobs and career opportunities open to you.

Write for the *Transition Resource Guide*, a booklet on different types of programs, including a variety of vocational-technical programs and adult education. The booklet is available from the HEATH Resource Center, One Dupont Circle, N.W., Suite 800, Washington, DC 20036-1193.

While still in high school, take the time to study the best programs available for the subject matter you wish to master. According to HEATH, advisors of disabled students agree that selecting school and educational programs should begin with a list of the best programs in your chosen field of study. The list can then be narrowed by investigating which of these best and most appropriate to your needs. Do it in three steps:

- Step One is to gather information about schools that offer training in your field of choice.

- Step Two is to become aware of any accommodations and special services available in programs of interest.

- Step Three is to become aware of any accommodations you may need.

For additional information regarding this topic, write to HEATH for the fact sheet, "Strategies for Advising Students with Disabilities for Postsecondary Education."

Individualized Education Programs

Individualized Education Programs (IEPs) are federally-regulated. The federal regulations are contained in the Individuals with Disabilities Education Act (IDEA) and Appendix C to Part 300: Notice of Interpretation issued by the Department of Education, Office of Special Education and Rehabilitative Services. This law is one of several amendments to Public Law 94-142, The Education of the Handicapped Act (EHA). IDEA is used by school systems throughout the country to guide the way in which special education and related services are determined for a provided to eligible children and youth with disabilities.

Passed in 1975, EHA requires that an Individualized Education Program be developed by a multidisciplinary team for each child or youth with a disability who is eligible for special education and related services. The IEP was intended to set forth a plan for the services that would be provided to the child. In 1981, in response to queries from the public regarding the EHA's requirements for the Individualized Education Program, the U.S. Department of Education released Appendix C to Part 300 to provide additional explanation of EHA's regulations.

The major components of the IEP are: (1) the IEP meetings where parents and school personnel jointly make decisions about an educational program for a child with a disability, and (2) the IEP document itself, that is, a written record of the decisions reached at the meeting. The IEP meeting is meant to serve as a communications and planning vehicle between parents and school personnel and enables them, as equal participants, to jointly decide what the needs of the child are, what services should be provided to meet those needs, and what outcomes should be anticipated. The IEP process provides an opportunity for resolving any differences between parents and agency concerning the needs of a child with a disability. The IEP sets forth in writing a commitment of resources necessary to enable a child with a disability to receive needed special education and related services. Among other things, the IEP is a management tool and also serves as an evaluation device for use in determining the extent of the child's progress toward meeting the projected outcomes.

With the new trend toward mainstreaming those with physical disabilities, it is especially important for the parent to step forward in the planning process. If the parents will take a little extra time to study accommodation devices and emerging technology for people with the type of physical disability that matches the child's, the parents can encourage and suggest ways of helping to successfully mainstream a child. The parents can see to it that the child has access to needed programs.

A school must be concerned with the safety of a child participating in a program. With input from a parent or from a group of parents who have children with physical disabilities, sports equipment may be modified or special sports equipment purchased so that the child with physical disabilities can participate in sports programs. The same is true with regard to shop classes. Whereas a particular child may not be able to adequately handle a certain tool or machine, with a bit of ingenuity and modification, that same child may be successful. This is the same principle as modification of the workplace, which has caught on with increasing success in business and in industry. In fact, technologies for those with physical disabilities has led to career opportunities in manufacturing for those with disabilities. More on this in Chapter 9.

Each public agency shall take steps to ensure that one or both of the parents are present at each meeting or are afforded the opportunity to participate. Parents are to be notified of the meeting early enough to ensure that they will have an opportunity to attend. The meeting is to be scheduled at a mutually agreed-upon time and place. If a purpose of the meeting is the consideration of transition services for a student, the notice must also indicate this purpose; indicate that the agency will invite the student and identify any other agency that will be invited to send a representative. If neither parent can attend, the public agency shall use other methods to ensure parent participation, including individual or conference telephone calls. The public agency shall give the parent, on request, a copy of the IEP.

Questions and Answers about IEPs

Does the IEP include ways for parents to check the progress of their children? In general, yes. The IEP document is a written record of decisions jointly made by parents and school personnel at the IEP meeting. That record includes agreed-upon items, such as goals and objectives and the specific special education and related services to be provided to the child. The goals and objectives should be helpful as a general guide. However, the IEP is not intended to include specifics about the total educational program planned for a child such as might be found in a daily or weekly instructional plan. Parents will need to obtain more specific ongoing information about the child's progress and should arrange for teacher conferences, review report cards carefully, and pay attention to reporting procedures.

Must IEPs include specific checkpoint intervals for parents to confer with teachers and to revise or update their children's IEPs? No, the IEP of a child with a disability is not required to include specific checkpoint intervals for review of progress. However, in individual situations, specific meeting dates could be designated in the IEP, if the parents and school personnel believe that it would be helpful to do so.

Are transition services included in the IEP? The IEP for each student, beginning no later than when the student turns 16 (and even at a younger age, if determined to be appropriate) must include a statement of the needed transition services, including, if appropriate, a statement of each public agency's and each participating agency's responsibilities or linkages or both before the student leaves the school setting. This is why parents should keep in close contact with agencies and organizations set up to specifically help those people having physical disabilities that match their child's, such as United Cerebral Palsy, Spina Bifida Association, or Arthritis Foundation. These associations can suggest ways of helping the child get the training he or she deserves and can put the parents in touch with manufacturers or distributors of specialized equipment. These organizations often have support groups that enable parents to network with other parents.

The more knowledge and support parents have about how a child can reach full potential, the greater the chances that the child's high school and elementary school program will provide full resources. Each public agency must provide free appropriate public education (FAPE) to all children with disabilities under its jurisdiction. The IEP for a child with a disability must include all of the specific special education and related services needed by the child as determined by the child's current evaluation. This means that the services must be listed in the IEP even if they are not directly available from the local agency and must be provided by the agency through contract or other arrangements. If the parent is an informed consumer of special education services, he or she will be able to determine whether the IEP has been broad enough to include needed services, some of which may not be known by the local school district; or a service might not be brought up because it cannot be provided by the local agency.

If modifications are necessary for a child with a disability to participate in a regular education program, must they be included in the IEP? Yes, if modifications (supplementary aids and services) to the regular education program are necessary to ensure the child's participation in that program, those modifications must be described in the child's IEP. For example, for a child with a hearing impairment, this may be special seating arrangements or the provision of assignments in writing. This applies to any regular education program in which the student may participate, including physical education, art, music, and vocational education.

When must physical education (PE) be described or referred to in the IEP? Section 300.307 (a) provides that physical education services, specially designed if necessary, must be made available to every child with a disability receiving FAPE. If a student with a disability can participate fully in the regular PE program without any special modifications to compensate for the disability, it would not be necessary to describe or refer to PE in the IEP. On the other hand, were some modifications necessary, those modifications must be described in the IEP.

If a student with a disability needs a specially designed PE program, that program must be addressed in all applicable areas of the IEP; for example, present levels of educational performance, goals, and objectives and services to be provided. However, these statements would not have to be presented in any more detail than other special education services mentioned in the IEP.

If a student with a disability is educated in a separate facility, the PE program for that student must be described or referred to in the IEP. However, the kind and amount of information to be included in the IEP would depend on the physical-motor needs of the student and the type of PE program that is to be provided. Thus, if a student is in a separate facility that has a standard PE program; for example, a residential school for students with deafness, and if it is determined based on the student's most recent evaluation that the student is able to participate in that program without any modifications, then the IEP need only note such participation. On the other hand, if special modifications to the PE program are needed for the student to participate, those modifications must be described in the IEP. Moreover, if the student needs an individually designed PE program, that program must be addressed under all applicable parts of the IEP.

If a student with a disability is to receive vocational education, must it be described or referred to in the student's IEP? The answer depends on the kind of vocational education program to be provided. If a student with a disability is able to participate in the regular vocational education program without any modifications to compensate for the student's disability, it would not be necessary to include vocational education in the student's IEP. On the other hand, if modifications to the regular vocational education program are necessary in order for that student to participate in that program, those modifications must be included in the IEP. Moreover, if the student needs a specially designed vocational education program, then vocational education must be described in all applicable areas of the IEP. However, these statements would not have to be presented in any more detail than the other special education services included in the IEP.

Must the IEP specify the amount of services or may it simply list the services provided? The amount of services to be provided must be stated in the IEP so that the level of the agency's commitment of resources will be clear to parents and other IEP team members. The amount of time to be committed to each of the various services to be provided must be appropriate to that specific service and must be stated in the IEP in a manner that is clear to all who are involved in both the development and implementation of the IEP.

Changes in the amount of services listed in the IEP cannot be made without the holding of another IEP meeting.

Must the IEP of a child with a disability indicate the extent to which that child will be educated in the regular educational program? Yes. Section 300.346 (a) (3) provides that the IEP for each child with a disability must include a statement of the extent that the child will be able to participate in regular educational programs. One method of meeting this requirement is to indicate the percent of time the child will be spending in the regular education program with nondisabled students. Another way is to list the specific regular education classes the child will be attending. If a child with a severe disability, for example, is expected to be in a special classroom setting most of the time, it is recommended that, in meeting the above requirement, the IEP include any noncurriculum activities in which the child will be participating with nondisabled students, such as lunch, assembly periods, club activities, and other special events.

What about private school placement by public agencies? Before a public agency places a child with a disability in, or refers a child to, a private school or facility, the agency shall initiate and conduct a meeting to develop an IEP for the child in accordance with Section 300.343. The agency shall ensure that a representative of the private school or facility attends the meeting. If the representative cannot attend, the agency shall use other methods to ensure participation by the private school or facility. After a child with a disability enters a private school or facility, any meetings to review or revise a child's IEP may be initiated and conducted by the private school or facility at the discretion of the public agency. If the private school or facility initiates and conducts these meetings, the public agency shall ensure that the parents and an agency representative are involved in any decision about the child's IEP and agree to any proposed changes in the program before those changes are implemented. Even if a private school or facility implements a child's IEP, responsibility for compliance with this part remains with the public agency and the State Education Authority (SEA).

If a child with a disability is enrolled in a parochial or other private school and receives special education or related services from a public agency, the public agency shall initiate and conduct meetings to develop, review, and revise an IEP for the child in accordance with Section 300.343 and ensure that a representative of the parochial or private school attends each meeting. If the representative cannot attend, the agency shall use other methods to ensure participation by the private school, including individual or conference telephone calls.

Reading will give you a head start on dealing with IEP issues. *Special Education and Related Services: Communicating Through Letter Writing: A Parent's Guide*, II (1) by S. Ferguson and S. Ripley is available from NICHCY, P.O. Box 1492, Washington, DC, 20013. This book was published in 1991.

Another helpful guide is *Choosing Options and Accommodations for Children: A Guide to Planning Inclusive Education* by M.F. Giangreco, C.J. Cloninger, and V.S. Iverson available from Paul H. Brookes Publishing, P.O. Box 10624, Baltimore, MD 21285-0624. It was published in 1993. "Parents can be the key . . . to an appropriate education for their child with disabilities," by the Parent Advocacy Coalition for Education Rights is available from PACER Center, 4826 Chicago Avenue South, Minneapolis, MN 55417. It was published in 1992. *Optimizing Special Education: How Parents Can Make a Difference* by N.O. Wilson is available from Insight Books, Division of Plenum Press, 233 Spring Street, New York, NY 10013. It was published in 1992.

Transition Programs

The national movement toward improving transition outcomes has been gaining momentum. Professionals are increasing their assistance to young people trying to make a transition to adult life. Better approaches are being adopted in planning, modifying, and redesigning curricula.

Students have wider choices. According to Daniel E. Steere in *The Advance* of September 1994, those in counseling and teaching are beginning to remember what it feels like to be an adolescent. For young people the transition from school to adulthood is difficult. Steere feels that the heart of successful transition is the realization that students with disabilities are simply young people facing a challenging time of life.

Steere makes several suggestions for improving transition programs:

1. Young people need a base of experience upon which to make informed choices about jobs, places to live, and a host of other decisions. "A measure of our effectiveness in designing curricula, then, is the degree to which these experiences are afforded."

2. Families, not just students, experience transition. Professionals must consider the pressure on families and provide needed supports to them.

3. The dreams of students and their parents may not always be the same. Transition is a time in life in which young people struggle for independence and self-definition.

4. Many young people struggle to develop a sense of themselves. Although much of our formal transition-planning efforts focus on employment and independent living, a broader goal for most young people is to figure out who they are and why they are valued.

5. Many students and their families prefer to conduct planning away from the pressures of a traditional school-based planning meeting. Transition planning should be built upon the dreams and aspirations of students and families. Transition goals should reflect these visions of postschool success. The increased use of maps and other approaches to lifestyle planning are positive steps in this direction.

6. Young people are often heavily influenced by their peers. It is logical that the involvement of peers in the transition-planning process should be the rule and not the exception.

7. Transition does not end when one leaves schools. Few attain optimal outcomes immediately upon graduation or the end of education services. Many struggle for some time.

8. One's greatest allies stand by during transition periods. Those people who are willing to go the distance in providing support are often most important to a student. Professionals may not be in a

position to provide longitudinal support, but they can certainly assist young people in strengthening their connections to their allies and in developing new ones.

9. Young people of today face pressures that many of us never experienced.

Beyond the Classroom: Transition Strategies for Young People with Disabilities by Paul Wehman, published in 1992 by Paul H. Brookes Publishing Company, goes into depth on these topics.

Career Days

Encourage your school to organize a career day. Help in planning it. Roosevelt Junior High School in Bellwood, Illinois, has had a steady success with its career day. Usually held in the spring, the event begins to get organized early in the fall. Students are surveyed on what fields of work interest them. Then, teachers, parents, and students give suggestions as to community members who might be called upon to talk about their work.

Although sessions are planned as formal talks, time is set aside for questions and some one-to-one discussion. Students make out the invitations to the event and print a brochure describing the purpose and organization of career day along with a list of topics and speakers. A few weeks before the actual event, student volunteers are enlisted to serve as room captains and as guides for the speakers. Then, the school's outdoor bulletin board announces the event. Shortly before career day, teachers prepare their students. What questions are not allowed: for example, How much money do you make? However, the emphasis is to encourage the students to participate freely and in a businesslike manner.

Following the event, teachers usually are satisfied with the general deportment of the students. Some students who never speak up actually engaged a speaker or two. Some students who always speak up found an opportunity to listen creatively. Students seem to mature before the eyes of the teachers. Afterwards, most students report getting new ideas concerning which career paths they might follow. Students feel satisfied that the speakers had given them ways to follow up their quest for information in a particular field. Some students begin to show interest in their school work as if their eyes were opened to a definite connection between school and the world of work.

Parents can expose their children to the world of work by setting aside time to have children visit them at work or, if the work of a parent is not of interest to a child, the parent may schedule a visit to the work site of a friend, a member of the local chamber of commerce, a public institution, or a hospital. If careful ground rules are laid down prior to the visit, including length of stay and what equipment or machinery might be demonstrated, the experience will be gratifying for both student and businessperson.

Volunteering

Young people, especially those with physical disabilities, are used to being catered to. Volunteering turns the tables, giving a young person the chance to wait on others. Volunteers gain in self-confidence and in self-esteem. And there is no shortage of volunteer opportunities. They can be found in the school itself—volunteering for school committees, in student organizations, or simply helping a fellow student catch up on his or her work. There are countless volunteer opportunities in churches and synagogues—from general office work to babysitting during services to janitorial work. Parks, hospitals, retirement centers, art councils, garden clubs, and conservation groups all have special projects that are crying for volunteers.

Survey the opportunities and then from those that will give you exposure to the type of work you might like in the future or the type of people with whom you might like to work. Being a candy striper can appeal to someone interested in a career in medicine or social work. Volunteering in the hospital gift shop can spark the beginning of a career in retail. Volunteering to work with senior citizens sets the stage for many careers, such as being a therapist, an activities director, a geriatric nurse, a rehabilitation specialist, or a religious minister. The local library is always open to volunteers—from book shelvers to assistants with special programs, to display creators. A student interested in history can volunteer at a local historical society or museum. Call your local United Way to discover the various social service organizations in your area that need help.

A successful newsletter writer I know got her start writing newsletters for various organizations for which she had been a volunteer. Volunteering can provide a meaningful work experience. Sometimes, volunteering does an indirect service by turning you away from a career you mistakenly thought you would like. It happened to me. I had a longstanding interest in teaching. I often volunteered to teach arts and crafts during the summer and to entertain small groups of children. What I discovered on my first encounter with preschoolers is that I couldn't control them. While I chased one to the left, another ran off to the right. They had a jolly good time, but I was exhausted. The experience taught me well. Even though I subsequently have taught at every grade level from third on up, I never ventured into a kindergarten or primary classroom.

Volunteering will develop your skill base. You will learn to appear to your assignment on time and on a regular basis. You will be expected to call in, if you cannot make it. Often volunteers become floaters and learn to work in various departments at a variety of tasks.

I remember the young girl with a physical disability who volunteered to work in my elementary school library. She was shy, and the first task I assigned her was to dust the shelves. This was easy for her. I, then, asked her to shelve books. She said she enjoyed putting things in order. I noticed that she always seemed to enjoy working alone. Because this was not developing her social skills, I asked her eventually to tutor a third-grader who had just come from Germany and was having difficulty learning English. At first, my volunteer balked. Why should she take on a new task when she was doing so well at shelving books? I didn't argue with her, but the next afternoon I introduced her to the third-grader. Something clicked. She began to tutor. When she did well with that assignment, I asked if she would read to a small group of children who needed extra reading time. She was not too happy but, again, when she saw the children, she agreed to try. Up the ladder of social communication she climbed until now she has attained success in a career in elementary teaching.

John Dewey said, "We learn by doing" and I believe that hands-on learning is vital to our education. Volunteering is the one way of achieving hands-on learning.

Name Your Dreams

Dare to Dream is a guide to planning your future prepared by the Florida Department of Education. What is your dream? What kind of job would you like to have? What kinds of things do you like to do for fun? How will you get around your community? Imagine you are having a meeting to plan ways to make your dream come true. The reason for the meeting is to share your desired postschool outcome with the people who are important to you and can help make your dreams come true—teachers, parents, counselors, employers, and friends.

As you meet with these people in real life, ask each what he or she does for a living. What is their title and what are their duties? Write down those of interest to you. Read articles in the paper about what people do and save those that appeal to you. After a while, make a list of jobs you might like to do and those you would not like to do. Also, mention the kinds of things you do well and those you don't do well.

As you begin to narrow your choices, ask how you can prepare for each job. What education will you need? On-the-job training usually is given to a janitor or clerk. University training is needed to become a lawyer or teacher. Vocational or technical school can be a step on the way to being an electronics technician or draftsman. Community college is the training ground for practical nurses or police officers.

Plan for free time. What things do you like to do? What things don't you like to do? Make a list of things you already do and things you would like to try. High school is a time to explore new activities and meet new friends. Choose friends whether they are disabled or not.

A program at the University of Washington increases the involvement of high school students with disabilities in the fields of science, technology, and engineering. Called "Disability, Opportunities, Internetworking and Technology in Science, Engineering and Mathematics," the program hopes to stimulate and inspire bright young scientists with disabilities from Washington and Oregon states.

In the 1993 summer sessions at the University of Washington in Seattle, participants studied engineering, mathematics, and sciences through lectures, labs, and the use of additional electronic applications. In addition to operating on sheep hearts, the group attended a lecture by an astronaut on space travel; utilized computer technology to experiment with the various forces affecting the global climate; conducted a lab on techniques in forensic analysis; and explored the possibilities presented by virtual reality at the university's Human Interface Technology Laboratory.

Students with various disabilities were represented. Some had visual, hearing, mobility, or speech impairments. Program Director Sheryl Burgstahler said, "Students learned how to work in teams, how to build on their strengths, and how to compensate for their weaknesses."

When the session ended, another important element of the program began. Participants were supplied any needed adaptive technology such as computers, modems, a connection to the Internet network, sip-and-puff, and talking screen readers so that they could communicate with one another and their mentors.

The mentors are practicing professionals, professors, and college students, many of whom have disabilities themselves.

Parents should provide their children with extracurriculum activities that expose them to a larger world and that introduce and reinforce skills that will be useful in later careers. My daughter's training in piano did not result in a musical career, but it did give her strength in her hands to allow her to successfully pursue a career as a hair stylist. A weight-lifting hobby later enabled a young man with atrophied leg muscles to walk quickly and powerfully with crutches. A young man paralyzed from the waist down due to a car accident took up singing. He began to join local chorus groups. His singing gave him self-confidence along with developing a pleasing voice. He has used these skills in his present sales occupation.

Having a physical disability has no relationship to mental ability. There is no good reason for a person with a physical disability to neglect the development of his or her mental potential. Students with physical disabilities should challenge themselves mentally and expect to undertake rigorous courses in math, science, and computers so that they will be ready to compete for future jobs. Those jobs will increasingly require mental alertness and knowledge rather than brute, physical strength. Remember, you were not the cause of your physical disability, and you should be proud that you are managing quite well in spite of it. Now, it is up to you not to create a mental disability by aiming too low in terms of subject matter studied and grades to be awarded. Don't create a mental block by refusing to discover the uniqueness of your personality, intelligence, interest, and skill base. Expect great things of yourself. Don't make your own attitude your barrier to achieving your personal best. People with physical disabilities have proven that they can intern with NASA; they can engage in sports; they can climb mountains; they can handle virtually every career. Why put a stop to your success? Visualize yourself in the occupation of your choice and you will be there!

There are new directions in the vocational curriculum in the public school system. Decreasing deviance is an intervention aimed at decreasing differences between nondisabled and the disabled. Deviations in behavior are first identified, and then the training of the individual is channeled toward reducing or even eliminating these differences. As deviance is decreased, programmatic goals increase competence. A more positive view is taken as to the potential for achievement. Providing individuals with disabilities the chance to expand their opportunities for training will encourage such individuals to choose whether or not to become paid workers. It gives people with profound disabilities a chance to decide if they wish to compete and shows them a plan for competing.

In their study, *Vocational Assessment and Curriculum Guide*, published by Exceptional Education in Seattle, Washington, F. Rusch and R. Schutz pinpoint the survival skills necessary for entry-level competitive employment. According to the supervisors Rush and Schutz surveyed:

- Employees should be capable of demonstrating basic arithmetic skills.

- They should be able to tell and follow time in increments of hours and minutes.

- Employees should have the capability of coming to work an average of five times per week.

- Employees must recognize the importance of attendance and punctuality.

- They must complete repetitive tasks that they have learned for at least 30- to 60-minute intervals.

- They must be able to move with safety about the work setting.

- They must understand what work routine requires and not exhibit disruptive behavior.

- They should have the desire to work for money.

- They should be able to read at least one- or two-word sentences.

- They should learn, at least at a level of minimum proficiency, new job tasks whenever they are given a maximum of 6 to 12 hours of instruction.

- They must be able to participate in a work environment for a sustained period of at least 3 to 4 hours.

For those with severe disabilities, efforts must begin at a young age. Public schools should identify home-related vocational skills. Service occupations that are similar to home duties include housekeeping/janitorial, food service, and laundry. Parents who help their children to learn such skills go a long way toward persuading their children's high school teachers that the children deserve a chance at vocational education. Regardless of level of disability, a school's program should include development of independence, persistence, productivity, and stick-to-it-tiveness.

If you are in high school it is time to give serious thought to your academic and career goals. The HEATH Resource Center newsletter advises students with disabilities to plan and discuss with parents, friends, and other people their career goals and how to reach them. It also urges students to discuss academic programs with teachers. Not only special education teachers, but regular education teachers and vocational education teachers to make certain the program contains career exploration and, possibly, a work-study component so you can learn about different careers and be better prepared to make choices later on.

Talk with your school guidance counselor and/or vocational rehabilitation counselor about interest inventories and the availability of a vocational assessment. Visit your school library as well as your public library for books and pamphlets describing the various types of postsecondary programs, such as trade, vocational-technical, and college or university. Be sure to read information on the variety of jobs and career opportunities available to you. Finally, write to HEATH for its *Transition Resource Guide*, a booklet that describes different kinds of programs, including a variety of vocational-technical programs and adult education. The address of the HEATH Resource Center is One Dupont Circle, NW, Suite 800, Washington, DC, 20036-1193.

CHAPTER FOUR

Selecting a College and Optimizing Your College Experiences

One obvious occupational split is the one between low-paid subsistence jobs and skilled and professional careers that pay well and offer good benefits. To the educated belong the spoils. Aspiring to a high-level career requires education beyond high school. Nancy J. Gorman of the Chicago Private Industry Council explains that many large corporations are looking to fill, not entry-level positions, but positions that demand more sophisticated skill sets. Candidates are expected to know Windows and Microsoft Word. "Although candidates could once expect to get hands-on training and a period of orientation, those days are past. Now, employees expect a high level of ability on the part of the new employee and an ability to get right down to work from the first day forward."

The purpose of any type of postsecondary education, whether at a two- or four-year college or vocational-technical school, is to prepare students to be active and productive members of society. While some students choose to continue their formal schooling upon graduating from college, most enter the workforce. The challenges of identifying career interests and developing job search and job maintenance skills are formidable for many students—whether or not they have disabilities. Students must narrow and articulate career interests, create a résumé, learn how to set up interviews and how to interview effectively. In addition, students with disabilities must be knowledgeable about disability-related issues, including the pros and cons of disclosing one's disability to a potential employer. Disability service providers and career development staff may assist students with disabilities by making opportunities for structured job development activities available as well as providing general guidance and support.

Choosing a College

How to Choose a College: Guide for the Student with a Disability is a joint project of the Association on Handicapped Student Service Programs in Postsecondary Education and the HEATH Resource Center. The booklet encourages the student to ask himself/herself questions:

- What size school is most comfortable for me? How big was my high school? A larger college means more opportunity, but it also may mean less individual assistance.

- Am I assertive enough to get what I need in a larger, more impersonal system?

- What are my financial limitations?

After you have narrowed your choices by size and cost within a given geographic area, you are ready to look at the academic requirements and offerings of the schools that fit your general guidelines.

Most campuses will give you a chance to identify yourself as a student with a disability at some point during the admissions process. There may be a place to check on the application blank, or with the information sent to you after your acceptance concerning housing, athletic events, and the like. If the college invites you to identify yourself as a student with a disability and in need of accommodation, it is to your advantage to do so as quickly and completely as possible. By law, your disability cannot be used to discriminate against you in the admissions process.

In high school, the school district was responsible for providing any and all support services you needed to encourage your full participation in the educational process. The college or university does not have the same legal obligation. It is required, however, by law, to provide any reasonable accommodation that may be necessary for you to have equal access to educational opportunities and services available to your nondisabled peers, if you request them. The college is under no obligation to seek you out to see if there is something you need. This is your chance to make contact with the people on campus who can and will provide the support services you need.

After you have identified the Disabled Students Services Office, or the Learning Assistance office, or a similar-sounding office, you should ask very specific questions. Colleges will vary in how much support they provide, according to the HEATH Resource Center, but seldom will the level of support equal the level you received in high school. You are free to ask about the accommodations that you must have and the things it would be nice to have. Later, you will put together this information regarding extras and necessities. A student who uses a wheelchair might ask if there is an adapted transportation system on campus or if there are any buildings on campus that are not accessible. Students with a hearing impairment might ask how to make arrangements for notetakers or who makes arrangements for interpreters or what kind of accommodations are available for taking tests because the disability may interfere understanding oral instructions. When you visit the campus, make arrangements to meet another hearing impaired student to find out how that student manages.

Many students with disabilities are eligible for some financial support through their state's Vocational Rehabilitation Services Agency. If you have not made contact with someone from this agency to determine the possibility of financial support, you should investigate this source immediately. Money may be available to you for support of your education through the Social Security Administration. You can locate those offices in the telephone directory under the listing for State Agencies.

Narrowing Your Choices

Ask yourself the following questions in relation to each college on your list: How good is my academic background compared to that of the other students? What academic support services are available to me on this campus? What will the living situation be for me, if I go to this school? What kinds of nonclassroom experiences are available to me on this campus? What are the possibilities for financial assistance, if I attend this school?

According to HEATH Center, often the availability of good academic support is the prime consideration in making a decision regarding schooling. If you cannot compete with your peers academically, you will not be around long enough to worry about extracurricular activities. For individuals who have severe restrictions on their physical capabilities, the availability of a suitable living situation must outweigh the consideration of extras available for classroom support. Those with very limited funding may find it necessary to consider financial support even before considering academic offerings and quality of the institution.

Remember, you are not alone on the college campus. The American Council on Education reports that since 1995, the percentage of first-year college students with disabilities has grown. More than 9 percent of college freshmen report having a disability. Many do not report having one. Freshmen reporting disabilities in 1994 were more likely than their nondisabled peers to be men, be older, express significant concern about financing their education; receive aid from Vocational Rehabilitation funds; be more interested in entering education and technical fields rather than business; be attracted to special programs offered at colleges and, finally, to have been influenced by a role model or mentor to attend college. Men are more likely than women to have learning or speech disabilities, but women outnumber men in every other disability category, according to Cathy Henderson, *College Freshmen with Disabilities: A Statistical Profile*, 1995, published by HEATH Resource Center of the American Council on Education.

Financial Aid for Students with Disabilities includes scholarship information and Department of Education terminology and resources, and describes the financial aid process. The "Selected Resources Section" lists the toll-free telephone numbers to call for technical assistance about federal financial aid: (800) 433-3243 (Voice) and (800) 730-8913 (TT).

In selecting the right college for yourself, you should send for appropriate college catalogues and scour them to see the type of courses offered in the field of your interest.

Does the college offer a major course of studies in the field of your interest?

Does it offer specialized seminars or advanced coursework?

Does it offer credit for fieldwork and/or internship?

Are you able to customize your program of study or are most of the courses required?

Are there a number of sections per course so that you can have flexibility in your schedule?

How many course hours per quarter or semester are required of a full-time student?

Are there financial aids for those with physical disabilities?

Does it offer a learning assistance center?

Are there plentiful accommodations for those with physical disabilities? Is it a specialized college or university such as Gallaudet, which serves individuals with hearing impairments or deafness? Is it a school well-known for its programs in your field of interest?

These and other questions can be studied by pouring over catalogues and related material you can request from a college. After you've narrowed the field, a visit to campus is in order to meet with advisors and/or professionals in your major field on a one-to-one basis. You can see for yourself what equipment is or is not available. If you can arrange to visit while class is ongoing, ask to observe a class or two. Is there diversity in the student body? What types of clubs and organizations does the school sponsor? Of course, the best source of information may be the student who is attending the college. Corner a student or two and ask questions. A fine source to consult to help you in your search for the right college is HEATH Resource Center's *How to Choose a College: A Guide for the Student with a Disability*, Washington, DC, 1993.

During the next few years, the staff of HEATH will continue to collect and to disseminate information concerning education after high school for individuals with disabilities. The staff will be responding by letter, fax, Internet, and telephone. The address is One Dupont Circle, Suite 800, Washington, DC 20036-1193.

You may also send for "CIDS Fact Sheet" and "Career Information Delivery: A Summary Status Report." The National Career Development Association can be reached at 5999 Stevenson Avenue, Alexandria, VA 22304-3300, or (703) 823-9800; send for *Guidelines for the Preparation and Evaluation of Career and Occupational Information Literature*. Each of the developers of CIDS provides information about its system, Write to Career Information Systems, National Office, 5258 University of Oregon, Eugene, OR 97403-5258, or (503) 346-3875. Another developer is VISIONS PLUS, Executive Plaza 1, 11350 McCormick Road, Suite 200, Hunt Valley, MO 21031, (800) 645-1992.

According to a recent article in *USA Today*, economic hard times have meant the virtual demise of the school counselor in many areas. Narrowly defined institutional self-interest must give way to a more enlightened, broadly based view of the opportunities available to students. Working with parent organizations, colleges can provide generic information on admission to students on all levels to encourage them to stay on track for higher education.

Adapting Technology on Campus

Career development staff may play an important role in facilitating the empowerment of students with physical disabilities. The staff can encourage students to develop the self-advocacy skills they will need in order to ensure that they receive necessary job accommodations. Students should practice explaining their learning styles and describing types of accommodations that help them overcome their weaknesses and capitalize on their strengths.

Career development specialists may also encourage students to participate in structured activities to help them enhance their career development skills.

The American Council of the Blind (ACB) took a strong stand on making campus computing accessible to students who are blind or visually impaired by adopting a resolution that states: "A minimum of one accessible computer should be provided in each computer laboratory on college and university campuses." One of the nation's leading advocacy organizations, ACB expects the resolution to help underscore the importance of providing computer access.

Because the use of computers and related technology is now imperative in educational settings, it is essential for educational institutions to ensure that appropriate access to computer equipment is afforded to students and faculty who are blind or visually impaired. Equipment to be provided in these labs would include, but not be limited to, screen-reading software and hardware, print enlargement equipment, Braille printers, and Braille displays. Personnel employed in these labs should be adequately trained to use the equipment so that students unfamiliar with it would be able to use the technology as well as their nondisabled peers.

The American Council of the Blind is an information and referral advocacy agency having 52 state/regional affiliates and 21 national special-interest and professional affiliates. For more information contact ACB at 1155 15th Street, NW, Suite 720, Washington, DC 20005, or call (202) 467-5081.

Technology and Disability, Volume I, Summer 1991, addresses the needs of persons with visual impairments, including low vision and blindness. Dr. Lawrence Scadden opens the issue with an overview of technology applications for those with visual impairments. Subsequent articles address specific technology applications, including four major methods used by persons with visual impairments to gain access to information. Also included are articles about the advocacy process, legislation, the funding of assistive technology, the historical perspective, and the development of electronic travel aids and electronic reading machines for persons with visual impairments. The "Case Study" section profiles people who use assistive technology. The issue of graphic user interface is addressed in the "Perspective" section. The journal concludes with a "Program Spotlight" on a computer access center. To obtain a copy of this publication or for subscription information, contact Andover Medical Publishers, Inc., 125 Main Street, Reading, MA 08167.

In 1995, employers recruiting at Purdue University in West Lafayette, Indiana, questioned the career services staff about communicating their companies' information to students via nontraditional methods. Employers were specifically interested in communication methods such as electronic mail and fax. In response, James A. Megathlin, assistant director of career services, circulated a survey in September of that year that surveyed 3 graduating classes of degree candidates. Megathlin questioned their access to e-mail, CD-ROM readers, the Internet, and fax equipment. Students were asked not only if they used various technologies regularly, but also where they used them—residence, computer lab or both. More than 2,000 survey forms were distributed. Almost 800 usable responses were received. Respondents represented eight academic schools at Purdue. Survey responses showed e-mail to be the most easily tapped technology among students at all degree levels; in fact, 82.5 percent of respondents used it regularly. Slightly more than half of the respondents used e-mail at both their residences and in computer labs. In some academic schools, such as engineering and science, more than 90 percent of respondents at all levels said they used e-mail regularly. Internet varied by degree level. Respondents at the master's and doctorate level used it more frequently than did students at the bachelor's level. Megathlin's survey also asked respondents if they used the Internet to find employment information. Almost one-half responded that they did use it in this capacity.

Slightly more than one-half said they used CD-ROM technology. Thirty-eight percent had CD-ROM readers available at a computer lab, while 35.1 percent used CD-ROM technology at their residences.

Respondents reported much less access to fax technology. Only 29.7 percent of the student said they could send and receive faxes. Slightly more than one-half of those students used a personal computer with fax capability.

Assistive technology plays a key role in advancing the independence of people with disabilities, but technology is expensive, hard to find, and difficult to understand. For this reason, United Cerebral Palsy Association of Chicago (UCPA Chicago) is spearheading a project called Infinitec, which will help people with disabilities access, acquire, and understand assistive technology. The Assistive Technology Exchange Network (ATEN) is administered by UCPA Chicago for the Illinois State Board of Education. It identifies unused equipment, from computers to touch-talkers, within school districts and special education cooperatives in Illinois. This unused equipment is then matched by ATEN with the needs of students anywhere in the state. It also solicits equipment donations from the business sector to further supplement technology available in schools. Eventually, ATEN will operate a warehouse to facilitate the transfer of technological devices among school districts and between the private sector and schools.

United Cerebral Palsy Association of Chicago helps people with disabilities, their caregivers, and health-care professionals to locate technological devices through ABLEDATA, an extensive database of information on more than 19,000 assistive technology devices. ABLEDATA can be used to locate both high- and low-technology devices available commercially and noncommercially from domestic and international manufacturers. ABLEDATA was developed by Macro International, Inc., and is funded by the National Institute of Disability and Rehabilitation Research and the U.S. Department of Education. For more information about ABLEDATA or to access the information in the databases, contact UCPA Chicago.

Optimizing Your College Experiences

On-Campus Organizations

After you are on campus, look around for other organizations or groups that may be dedicated to advancing the cause of people with physical disabilities. Beta Sigma Iota—the Order of Invictus, a Greek letter organization established at Nicholls State University in Louisiana—promotes the welfare of students with disabilities on college campuses. The general purpose of the organization is to provide social, intellectual, and leadership assistance for the good of all students on campus with disabilities. The society actively encourages its members to become leaders in promoting excellence in scholastic achievement and service and to celebrate the triumph of a courageous spirit over personal adversity.

The group also provides information on various student policies concerning such areas as federal, state, and local legislation; campus rights; financial assistance; and special needs for unusual circumstances. Beta Sigma Iota seeks to establish a voice in various student organizations. For information on establishing a chapter, contact Betty Elfert, Nicholls State University, Academic Success Program, P.O. Box 2043, Thibodaux, LA 70310, or call (504) 448-4108.

Cornell University has Access Alternative. Access Alternative was formed in response to the experience of a graduate student who is blind. T.V. Raman believed in a policy of gentle advocacy in searching for solutions to accessibility issues. Over time, members of Access Alternative met with representatives of various departments, including Public Safety and Life Safety and Risk Management. The organization now includes staff members with disabilities. A typical meeting is conducted as a forum to which the manager of a campus department has been invited. Programs begin with a short presentation by the invited guest followed by a sharing of concerns related to the department as presented by group members. Results have been dramatic and include the development of a Campus Safety Checklist and the redesign of construction barriers. For more information, contact Joan Fisher, Cornell University, Office of Equal Opportunity, 234 Day Hall, Ithaca, NY 14853-2801, or call (607) 255-3976 or (607) 255-7665 (TT).

Career Clubs

Although it is a fine idea to join a support group or a group aimed at those with disabilities, it is also important to join clubs based on your individual interests and on your career plans. You must see yourself in terms of abilities and discover that you can relate successfully to those without physical disabilities. Clubs based on subjects holding career interest for you may be foreign language clubs, an economics or accounting club, or a financial club. Another benefit of joining such a club is that they often have speakers of note address the group. It also affords you an opportunity to get to know the faculty sponsor on a more informal basis. No doubt you will eventually have him or her as an instructor should you decide to major in the sponsor's area of interest. Knowing an instructor in your area and enabling him or her to get to know you allows you access to an important source of information regarding a variety of career issues and may also stand you in good stead when you will be in need of a reference for a job application or during an interview.

Although it is important to receive special aids to keep you on a level playing field, you should not become an aids junkie. Career and vocational counselor David Schnell cautions that although aids such as notetakers may sometimes be advisable, it is important for you to develop the ability to take notes because note taking strengthens organizational skills. "If you want to compete in the everyday world upon graduation, do as much as possible to blend in with the student body." Schnell also suggests meeting with your prospective professors prior to or at the beginning of the first class or two to openly discuss your disability. "Don't ask for an accommodation unless it is truly needed."

According to Schnell, another area that can be overaccommodated relates to planning your schedule around those courses that are conveniently located on the campus. Schnell claims he has seen too many students accumulate sufficient hours, enabling them to graduate only to discover they have not taken a major appropriate to their career interests. What if you are confused about your selection of a major or which courses to take? Schnell says to speak with a career counselor all throughout the various stages of your college education. Another excellent source of career planning is the head of the academic department in which you are majoring.

Paid versus Volunteer Work

It's never too early to plan for your career. Engage in paid or volunteer work so you can demonstrate that you have successfully carried out significant assignments. It isn't always the pay that counts, but the experience. In your case, your time may be more valuable than your pay per hour because you have only so much time to devote before you are out of school and looking for a real job. Some volunteer jobs allow the time flexibility usually not afforded by a paid job, and many volunteer jobs can be tailored to your individual needs, interests, and talents.

An important distinction to keep in mind between volunteer work and work-for-pay is that in the former there is ordinarily a less hierarchical organizational structure in volunteer organizations. In most part-time work situations, there is a clear chain of command that relies heavily on the money incentive to assure that you perform your duties well. Usually, employers of part-time workers have many performers from which to choose so, if you don't work out to their satisfaction, there will be no hesitance in letting you go. There will be less tendency to take a personal interest in you as in the case of a volunteer group. In some cases, a volunteer job turns into a part-time or even full-time job. Many organizations, especially social-service types, like to employ those who have worked for them as volunteers, feeling that volunteers have learned the ropes of the organization and are truly interested in its causes and goals. This is true of the Girl Scouts Organization, which prefers to hire those who have had leadership experiences in the organization.

Community Colleges

The majority of students with disabilities who enroll in postsecondary education of any type enroll in two-year community colleges according to Lynn Barnett, editor of *Directory of Disability Support Services in Community Colleges,* published in 1992 by the American Association of Community Colleges. Community colleges in most states exist to serve those in the surrounding community by providing a low-cost education through a wide range of programs, including vocational and occupational courses. As part of their mission to serve the community, most community colleges have open enrollment—they admit all who wish to further their education.

A recent survey designed to monitor changes in higher education found that community colleges are experiencing the greatest growth of all postsecondary institutions. Nine out of ten community colleges increased their enrollment from 1988 to 1993. Another study found that undergraduate enrollment at community, technical, and junior colleges grew at twice the rate of four-year public colleges between 1980 and 1990. Additional information is found in Bill Reinhard's "Report Finds Community Colleges Topped All Sectors in Enrollment Gains during the 1980s" in the *Community, Technical and Junior College Times* of February 25, 1992, published by the American Association of Community Colleges.

In 1993, the HEATH staff reported in *Information from HEATH* on current trends and issues to be considered by prospective students. Community colleges, as is true of all educational institutions, are being affected by the fiscal crises that states are experiencing. Some consequences are increased class size and fewer sections, a freeze on hiring for regular faculty positions, and postponing the introduction of new programs.

Another important consequence is that in many states students are required to apply to such colleges earlier than in the past. In order to ensure a minimum number of enrollments, some colleges now require that students enroll by a specific date well in advance of the start of the semester. If the minimum number is not enrolled, the administration may cancel the class.

A second nationwide trend is the growth of assessment. An increasing number of states are requiring that entering students take placement tests before being admitted into degree-granting programs. In most states, if a student performs below a certain level, he or she will be placed in a remedial English, math, and reading class. On some campuses, these classes are noncredit. In order for the student to be eligible to enroll in for-credit classes, he or she must first pass the remedial classes.

Some states/community college systems make a distinction between a certificate and a high school diploma. In most states, students who are unable to fulfill the regular requirements of a high school diploma may graduate with a certificate. Different types of certificates exist in different states. A fair number of students with disabilities leave school with a certificate rather than a diploma. According to HEATH, in the school year 1989–1990, of all students with disabilities who left the public school system, 44 percent graduated with a diploma, 27 percent dropped out, and 12.4 percent graduated with a certificate.

Most community colleges have a true open admission policy. Texas, for instance, admits all students, regardless of whether they have a certificate, diploma, or a GED. An entrance exam is required for all students and based on performance on this exam, some students may be placed in classes to teach them basic skills or give them remediation.

Other states have different admission standards. Florida admits only those students who have a regular diploma or a GED. Although Florida does not admit those who hold special diplomas into its community college system, it does offer GED preparation, adult education, and remediation to those without standard diplomas.

Community colleges continue to be the schools of choice for most students with disabilities who decide to further their education. These institutions provide easy accessibility to a variety of courses. Prospective students and their advisors may inform themselves about some of the overriding trends in community college enrollment among students with disabilities as well as details pertaining to enrollment patterns and special services provided by specific campuses by reviewing the *Directory of Disability Support Services in Community Colleges*, published by the American

Association of Community Colleges. Single copies of the directory are available free of charge of HEATH. You may write to HEATH Resource Center, One Dupont Circle, Suite 800, Washington, DC 20036-1193, or call (800) 544-3284 (Voice/TT).

Internships

Planning for a career is not easy for anyone in these days of sudden ups and downs in our economy and current trends toward downsizing and increasing automation of business and industry. However, those with disabilities should realize that very few fields are closed to them, provided they have talent, willingness to do what it takes to succeed in the field, and proper preparation. Currently, it is a rather tough job market to enter even for college graduates. Increasingly, college graduates take internships with companies or organizations to make their theoretical college courses more applicable to the actual job situation.

It is no longer sufficient for a college graduate looking for a job, in the communications field, for example, to say he or she is qualified simply because of an appropriate degree. When I was in human resources for a small company, I received many calls from college graduates who were fresh out of college. One call I distinctly remember was from a young lady who told me that she had graduated with honors from a school that is well-known for its successful graduates. After she had finished speaking, I asked her what it was she could do.

There was a pause. "I graduated in communications," she offered.

Again, I repeated, "What can you do?," trying to prod her into explaining what transferable skills she could bring to our small communications company.

With obvious annoyance in her voice, apparently convinced I hadn't been listening, she said again, "I majored in communications. I can communicate."

"Can you run a video camera?"

A pause. "I ran one once in a television production class."

"Can you edit film?"

"Of course not."

Then, I tried to explain to her that our company had a need for those with very specific skills and because we were small, we didn't have the time or staff to train someone. Disgusted, she said she would try a large company. I realized then, that I had not been able to get across to her that having a degree is not sufficient—today's companies are hiring skilled people with experience.

Which brings us to the next question: If I can't get a job, how can I get experience? If I can't get experience, how can I get a job? There's no hard and fast rule how to get around this dilemma, but there are several routes to pursue. Volunteering, part-time jobs were already mentioned. The third route is internships.

Kris Conroy, coordinator of the cooperative education program at Harper College in Palatine, Illinois, echoes the importance of internships and student work experience in obtaining job interviews upon graduation. "I would definitely encourage any student to seek job experience in a field related to his or her major. The job situation is so competitive that cooperative experience is a distinct advantage in the job-search process." Engage in paid or volunteer work and activities during your college days so that you can demonstrate that you have successfully carried out significant assignments. These paid or unpaid positions are also good sources for references that you can use on résumés, on applications, or during interviews. Visit your college placement office, career counselor, or instructor and consult college bulletin boards to find sources for part-time work on campus.

Internships may be arranged through the department in which the student is a major. For instance, the head of the accounting department often has ties with local businesses that could result in an internship arrangement. No doubt the chairman has participated in an internship arrangement in the past and can now plug you into his network. An enterprising student could also assess some companies where he or she feels an internship would be especially valuable and then request that the chairman recommend him to the firm and assist in arranging for an internship or, perhaps, for part-time work. The college placement office is a natural to coordinate efforts in the arrangement of an internship.

A 1994 article in *Fortune Magazine* features Maury Hanigan, an employment consultant. He is quoted as saying that internships are becoming increasingly important, claiming that internships are where students learn the soft skills of working in a corporate environment. He warns that in many fields, internships are rapidly approaching the crucial status that they already occupy in medicine and law, where interning is practically a mandatory part of the training program.

Applying for an internship is similar to applying for your first job. You need to prepare an effective résumé and cover letter, and undergo a successful interview. For additional information, consult *Internships: A Directory for Career-Finders*, published by Arco in 1995.

Using *Internships: A Directory for Career-Finders* you can examine jobs in your career path and try out for exciting new positions in politics, the outdoors, or the entertainment business. You can develop practical skills you can't learn in college and begin to build your network of professional contacts. This network likely will serve not only in locating your first job, but throughout your career. The book is arranged according to fields of interest such as business and technology, communications, environmental organizations, and parks and human services.

There are even guides to internships in a specific geographical area, such as *The Complete Guide to Washington Internships*, second edition, edited by Jeff Parness and published by Bob Adams, 1990.

Statistics furnished by the National Society for Internships and Experiential Education show that internships are up by more than 30 percent in just 5 years. A candidate for an internship should start to market himself or herself at least a year in advance of the starting date of the internship. The candidate must be prepared to follow-up the original application at least once during the selection process.

NASA Internships

Some exotic internships are available. One is with NASA, the National Aeronautics and Space Administration. In the late 1980s, NASA's Technical Experience for Select Students (NTESS) came into existence as the result of a proposal made by Gallaudet University's Experiential Programs Off Campus. NASA's Goddard Space Flight Center in Greenbelt, Maryland, has one of the summer programs targeted to college students. It is specifically designed for eight undergraduates with a variety of disabilities. Accommodations are made by Goddard to ensure that none of these students is handicapped by a disability. The students are given three academic credits as approved by their home institution. For example, a voice synthesizer and a Braille printer were installed for an intern who is blind. For wheelchair users, the buildings on site were made accessible. Sign language interpreters are provided for interns who are deaf. Weekly class instruction in American Sign language is provided to the NASA employees. Telecommunication devices for the deaf or TDD and phone signalers are placed in the office of interns. Jeannie Desmarais from Tiverton, Rhode Island, while a senior at Gallaudet worked in the

Structural Analysis Section. Ho Josh Miele from Brooklyn, New York, and a senior at the University of California at Berkeley worked in the Astrophysics Section of the Pale Planetary Systems Branch.

In order to participate, a student must be an interested undergraduate with a disability and must be a citizen of the United States. The student must be majoring in physics, computer science, mathematics, or engineering and have attained a grade point average of 3.0 out of 4.0. For further information about NTESS, contact Experiential Programs Off-Campus at Gallaudet University, (202) 651-5240 (V) or (202) 651-5197 (TDD), or call the project coordinator, Dr. Vicki Kemp, at (202) 651-5313 (V or TDD).

If you're a college graduate or you will soon be and you have a severe mobility impairment, Shepherd Spinal Center in Atlanta, Georgia, may be able to help you explore a career in human resources through a paid internship program. Shepherd, which has been providing career planning and placement programs for those with spinal cord and brain injuries, is able to advise students, pay for the internships, and provide follow-up placement assistance as well as employer consultation, thanks to a grant from the Dole Foundation. The program, "Careers in Human Resources for Persons with Disabilities" offers funding for two years. The Dole Foundation is based in Washington, D.C., and was established by then-senator Robert Dole to provide grants nationwide to non-profit organizations that initiate innovative programs to promote the employment of America's fourteen million working-age citizens with disabilities. Anyone interested in participating in this program, either as an employee or an employer, should call (404) 350-7580 for further information.

Other Federal Programs

The federal government has addressed itself to finding a first step toward full-time employment through its Student Educational Employment Program. This program takes in both the Student Temporary Employment Program and the Student Career Experience Program. You are eligible if you are working at least half time for a high school diploma, general equivalency diploma, or for a vocational or technical school certificate or degree. You can apply throughout the year because it is an ongoing program. Both programs allow participants an annual leave and sick leave. Participants are eligible for training by the agency. Promotion is also possible. The usual appointment under the Student Temporary Employment Program is for 1 year, but the term can be extended in increments of a year as long as the person remains in school.

In the Student Career Experience Program your employment is directly related to your educational program and career goals. Under this program, you and your school work closely with the federal agency in setting up a program that combines work experience and school attendance. The agency is empowered to reimburse you for commuting expenses. To get into the program, your qualifications and suitability for federal employment are evaluated. One of the benefits of this program is that, without competing with others, you are allowed to convert your experience into a career or career-conditional job after receiving your diploma, certificate, or degree. Even though the program does not guarantee you a full-time permanent job with the federal government, it provides you with a head start.

For additional information, contact the Career America Connection at (912) 757-3000. Information also may be gained by using the Federal Job Information Touch Screen Computers located at various places in local federal agencies and by going on-line on the Internet.

Yet another program offered by the federal government may be of interest to you. The Presidential Management Intern Program is the most competitive of the federal government's entry-level career development and training programs. It is designed for students at the master's or doctoral level. It aims to attract men and women from diverse social and cultural backgrounds who show great promise for public service.

Experience counts, according to employers responding to a recent Job Outlook survey. Overall, respondents indicated that an average of 58.6 percent of their 1994–95 entry-level college graduate hires had co-op or internship experience. By sector the percentages were: Manufacturing, 69.95; service, 51.1; and government/nonprofit, 28. Forty-five percent of responding employers indicated that they offer co-op programs for college students, and almost 73 percent offer internship programs. About 37 percent offer both co-op and internship programs and, not surprisingly, manufacturing employers are more likely to offer such programs.

Not every internship is of equal merit. Some offer substantive work, while others are time-fillers. Industries such as film, television, music, and sports management have internships consisting of a lot of busywork or menial tasks. Find out what tasks you'll be expected to do before signing up for an internship program.

Internships vary by length of time, duties, academic credit given, and even levels of intellectual challenge. But the experience will show you that you are a contender in your chosen field. Qualified young people are hard to find. Corporations and agencies are placing greater responsibilities on interns and monitoring their performance more closely. Check with the communications department in your school for information on companies that offer internships. You can contact the American Association of School Administrators, 1801 N. Moore Street, Arlington, VA 22209, or call (703) 528-0700. Also, contact American Express—Travel–Related Services, American Express Tower, World Financial Center, New York, NY 10285. Or, contact the American Red Cross, 18th and D Street, NW, Washington, DC 20006.

A summer job in the federal government would be a unique experience. It is a long shot, however, because these jobs are in high demand. Without a doubt, the federal government is a pro-active affirmative action and equal opportunity employer so the fact that you have a physical disability will be a plus. For further information, write to the Office of Personnel Management, 1900 E Street, NW, Washington, DC 20415. Before contacting the office, you may wish to contact your U.S. Senator or local Congressman to inquire further and perhaps, you will net an endorsement on your behalf. It doesn't hurt to try.

Your decision to combine work with study may be more significant than you think. There appears to be a correlation between students who participated in experiential programs off campus (EPOC) cooperative internships while they were undergraduates at Gallaudet University and their satisfaction with their current careers. According to a recent survey of Gallaudet, 81 percent of the students with EPOC work experience were satisfied with their current careers versus 64 percent who had had no EPOC experience. Seventy-two percent of the respondents had a minimum of one EPOC work experience during their undergraduate years. Of that group, 89 percent reported that the EPOC work experience was either somewhat or very important to their current career. Those working in educational and nonprofit organizations rated EPOC somewhat to very important 74 percent of the time, compared to 100 percent for those working in government or in private businesses. The survey interpreters conclude that this shows the importance of experience in hearing work environments prior to their graduation.

William Banis, director of placement at Northwestern University, Evanston, Illinois, notes that in the early 80s the Big Eight accounting firms were starting to hire those with disabilities as cooperative students, and many of these students landed jobs with big firms such as Arthur Anderson and Price Waterhouse immediately upon graduation.

Roger Rotter, a graduate of Medill School of Journalism of Northwestern University, has managed to rack up some impressive internships despite having a serious hearing impairment. His first internship was at Access Living in Chicago where he helped those with disabilities find suitable transportation to and from their jobs. He was able to apply his journalism training to his internship position at *Inside Sports,* a magazine published in Evanston, Illinois. He served as a production assistant and helped with layout and proofreading. He also enjoyed an internship with Leo Burnett Advertising where as a corporate relations intern, Rotter wrote articles and edited a monthly newsletter for employees. He also wrote press releases. Rotter currently is an intern for Edelman Public Relations and is writing press releases and creating media lists. The company provides him with a phone that makes it easier for him to hear. Although he realizes that getting a position in journalism or public relations is difficult for the recent college graduate, he feels that this series of internships has given him a good feel for the positions he is seeking and will give him a plus on his résumé.

Internships: A Directory, written by Sara D. Gilbert, and published by Macmillan, 1995, gives complete information on interning. Each entry in Gilbert's book mentions the location of the organization, its activities, the number of internships offered, the type and function of the internship, its schedule, any stipend or pay, academic credit offered as well as eligibility requirements, and how to apply. In writing a cover letter for an internship, be sure to have the correct address as well as the sponsor's name and title. Mention in the first paragraph why you are writing the letter and express your sincere interest in the position. Don't forget to be specific as to how you may be contacted. Include address, phone number, fax number, if any, for the purpose of having the organization contact you for an interview.

A sample entry is the American Management Association (AMA), 135 W. 50th Street, New York, NY 10020. Under general information, the listing states that the AMA is a nonprofit membership-based organization providing a wide variety of services and training in the fields of business and management. It says it has 300 employees. It lists one AMACOM book intern and one marketing intern position and gives the job duties in detail. For the book intern, responsibilities include assisting in the production, proofreading, editing, and layout of publications, re-search and management analysis. For the marketing intern, responsibili-ties include research and compilation of marketing information. The candidates should be marketing, economics, or statistics majors, proficient in WordPerfect with excellent communication skills. Knowledge of Lotus 1-2-3 is preferred. The wage per hour is listed as well as enumeration of benefits, such as formal training, opportunity to attend seminars and workshops, and reimbursement of travel expenses. The sponsor declares it is willing to complete any necessary paperwork required for an intern to receive educational credit. Possibility of full-time employment is mentioned, as well as placement assistance in the form of letters of recommendation, names of contacts, and job counseling.

Another good source of information on internships is *Peterson's Intern-ships*, 1995, which features more than 35,000 opportunities to get an edge in today's competitive job market.

If all else fails, consider the temporary services. The drawback here is that, although employees of temporary services do not work on a permanent full-time basis, the hours for most assignments fall within the 9 to 5 range and are usually set for seven and a half to eights hours within a single day. If you have a class schedule that allows for a free day or days within each week, such as Tuesdays and Thursdays, you may attempt temporary work. But, you will be limited to short terms. The recent trend in temporary work is toward fairly long assignments.

Another possibility is to take an unusual shift, such as weekends or the night shift. Some agencies that advertise for actors and others who have unusual schedules may be a good bet for a student. In any case, register only with an agency that places jobs in your nearby area. Some-times, these agencies have work assignments you can perform at home so that the hours you are available would not be a major issue.

The internship began as an interesting introduction to a career field. In many careers it has become de rigor. As noted earlier, some professions such as medicine and teaching have always had some form of internship, but the modern trend in business is to hire those they know can do the job because they've seen them do it. Employers like to hire the people they've already met. The experience of applying for one parallels the experience of actually applying for a full-time job, and, thus, the expe-rience in itself is valuable even if the goal of getting an internship is not actually attained.

Here again, your assistance center for disabled students, your guidance counselor, your teacher, and heads of major departments may be able to help you.

CHAPTER FIVE

FINDING YOUR IDEAL WORK ENVIRONMENT

Ready, set, go—the job search and how to get started! In these days of fierce competition for jobs, any job, do not expect to sit back and let someone else do it all for you. You are the one responsible for getting a job you will enjoy. By placing responsibility entirely on someone else— an employment agency, for example—you may get a job but not the job you really want. The person who works for an agency takes orders for jobs and must fill those orders within a reasonable time with a qualified applicant; if not you, then someone else. He is not working exclusively for you—he is working for the agency who employs him and for the company who has retained the agency to fill a specific job or jobs. You are the one who is marketing you.

Local Industries and Other Employers

Career and placement services of colleges are becoming more sophisti- cated, especially those on the junior college or community college level. Community colleges are eager to help local industries meet their employ- ment needs by listing their openings and by informing qualified applicants in the college of these openings. For example, the College of Lake County in Grayslake, Illinois, provides several job-search resources to its students, alumni, and Lake County residents:

- A weekly jobs bulletin that lists all positions employers have placed with the service during the week.

- Computerized individual job matching in which a student completes an application form that then generates information on job openings. This information is then sent directly to the student's home.

- Information on all aspects of the job search.

- A variety of employers throughout the year engage in on-campus recruiting, and each year nearly 100 area employers recruit for a wide range of jobs.

- The career and placement services provides a center for occupational reference material.

William Rainey Harper College's Career Transition Center supports job search with:

- Computers with laser-jet printers

- Software programs, such as Resume Marker, WordPerfect 5.1, Horizons, Harris Corporate Search

- Job opportunities listings, both full- and part-time

- Newspapers, directories, periodicals, and career books and also fax, telephones, and a copy machine.

More than 1,200 job listings come to the center each week.

Many community colleges are attempting to ensure that their programs meet the needs of local businesses for trained employees. For instance, Waukesha County Technical College in Wisconsin is assessing the level of employer and graduate satisfaction relative to the Office Aide, Custodial Services, and Food Service Helper programs. As a result of the needs assessment, programs will be developed and improved. With the assistance of the associate dean of special needs, outreach coordinator, special needs instructors, and the manager of cooperative education/student placement, additions and modifications to services were identified and proposals have been submitted to the Department of Education and to the State of Wisconsin–Division of Vocational Rehabilitation to fund some of the planned new activities. Newly developed services would provide increased assistance in preparing for a job search and would also assist the student in securing an internship prior to permanent placement on a job. Another goal was to develop, offer, and evaluate a multisession workshop to improve employers' understanding of the ADA.

The North Iowa Area Community College Career Placement Project has as its number one goal to develop, revise, offer, and evaluate modules of curricular offerings in career exploration, job readiness, job-seeking skills and job shadowing/cooperative education experiences for vocational students with disabilities. A Job Replication book has been included as a resource with Sigi Plus. Two of the six students participating in the project completed a shadowing experience with one student shadowing in two businesses. Another goal was to offer workshops and sensitivity training to college staff to increase their awareness and sensitivity in working both with students with disabilities and with the accommodations available to those students.

Mott Community College in Michigan recently developed a survey that was sent to 277 students who were identified as having a disability by the college's Disabilities Services for Students Office. From the 57 responses, certain trends emerged. The majority of respondents were planning to complete a degree program at the college. Also, approximately one-half of the respondents had used the career center and/or placement services in the past and almost all of the respondents were planning to look for a job after graduation. The majority of respondents indicated that they did not feel they understood how the ADA protects their rights when they are looking for work. This last concern was addressed by the delivery of information and training sessions to disabled students and graduates related to ADA issues. A part-time staffperson was hired as a liaison between the Disabilities Services office and the Career and Job Placement Center. Stuart Munro called each student and spoke with the student individually concerning career interests. He assisted with any requests for information. He secured the use of a TDD for the center and used his considerable network of information to advocate for students and graduates with disabilities. Many of the individuals that Munro contacted by phone later came into the center and were assisted with the use of the DISCOVER and MOIS Systems and have conducted career research on a variety of occupations.

What Employers Want

Now that you think you know what you're looking for, what are employers looking for? What do they really want? According to Burton Nadler, director of career services at the University of the Pacific, as quoted in *Employment Review*, April 1996, organizations in the past were looking for college graduates with potential. Now they are interested in people with a sense of focus. "They are picking and choosing. They aren't looking for generalists with potential, but for people with a focus on job and career."

When Nadler was a campus recruiter for Merrill Lynch, he perceived that the students he interviewed knew the company and knew themselves, but they didn't know the job. "They weren't tying together the nature of the job to their skills." If you are interviewing for a research analyst position with an investment bank, give examples of how your skills fit the position. "Don't leave it up to the interviewer to make these connections."

Be careful not to become so focused on a certain field or occupation that you get tunnel vision, however, your value may be viewed differently according to the interviewer and/or the company the interviewer represents. Bill Corwin, assistant director of career services at Princeton, is quoted as saying that many graduate students are looking over the academic fence at nontraditional jobs in corporate America. Those with refined skills who are working on advanced degrees in fields ranging from astrophysics to electrical engineering are in great demand at major financial institutions.

Some experts recommend having a portfolio. According to a recent survey by Michigan State University, employers found that the most useful materials in personal career portfolios were résumés, transcripts, lists of courses completed, job descriptions, job performance evaluations from co-op and internship experiences, descriptions of prior leadership positions held, a historical work experience perspective, and projections of career goals for the future.

If you lack focus, don't reveal this lack to the interviewer. *Employment Review* staff writer Brian Caruso sums up his article on what employers are looking for by saying that getting on the right career track and joining the right company is based on a lot more than your skills. You need to be motivated, show initiative, and even get creative to be considered by the firms that are having a hard time finding you.

Published Materials

The first step is to know what's available. You should research your career options through published materials. You need to learn to use library resources to locate books and computer database information. While you're in the library, read trade and professional journals, newspapers, and bulletins.

Spread the word among your friends and acquaintances that you're about to begin the search of the century. Advise everyone you know and everyone who crosses your path that you are on a job hunt. Discover professional associations, chamber of commerce groups, and clubs related to your area of interest, and then arrange to attend their meetings, workshops, and seminars. Be sure to get a spot on the mailing list of these organizations. Keep a résumé in your back pocket when you attend gatherings.

Even though getting a job is a full-time job, don't neglect other parts of your life. Take a break for social activities. Keep in touch with friends and family. Think positively. You have skills, talents, and experience that someone out there needs and wants. It's just a question of discovering your spot in the sun.

When you think of libraries, don't limit your thinking to public libraries. Although public libraries are trained for research along a broad number of areas, they do not specialize in careers. That's where you have an advantage in asking for help from within a career center of a college or university and/or a trade association or a specialized library within a school itself. For example, the library within the John Marshall Law School of Chicago contains invaluable information on foreign companies and export-import information of interest to any whose career depends in whole or part on international trade. Any number of private libraries within certain large business organizations and companies house vast collections of information pertinent to the industry represented by the company and information as to the company itself and companies that pursue similar interests and missions.

While visiting a private library, don't hesitate to read the bulletins and notices put up in the library and other sections of the building pertaining to job openings. If the company seems of interest to you, why not inquire as to where human resources is located and pay a visit. Or try to contact a person in the department of your interest, such as accounting, and schedule an exploratory interview. If the executive has the time then, don't hesitate to discuss career opportunities in a broad sense. Watch your time, 10 to 15 minutes shows interest on your part and respect for the executive's busy schedule.

What are some key books to get you started? *Dictionary of Occupational Titles* provides a brief description of more than 20,000 occupations. This reference book is helpful in locating job titles and skill words that are associated with specific jobs. Occupations are indexed alphabetically.

The *Enhanced Guide for Occupational Exploration*, compiled by Marilyn Maze and Donald Mayall and published by JIST Works, 1995, describes more than 2,800 of the most important jobs that comprise more than 95 percent of the work force. Its listings are based on information from the U.S. Department of Labor and other sources.

There are 12 major interest groups with 66 more specific work groups and 350 subgroups. The grouping of jobs by increasingly specific clusters makes it easy to find a specific job, beginning with the major interest areas in which the job is located. The Table of Contents is used to identify the major areas of interest and to find the more specific work group or subgroup. Specific job titles may also be looked up in the alphabetized listing contained in Appendix A.

For example, under GOE: 07.01.44 "Financial Work": a real estate closer coordinates closing transactions in a real estate company. The closer receives and deposits escrow monies in established accounts and disburses funds from each account. He or she reviews closing documents to determine the accuracy of information and the need for additional documents. The closer contacts courthouse personnel, buyer and seller, and other real estate personnel to obtain additional information. Then, there are listed credit analyst; escrow officer; mortgage clerk; mortgage loan closer; real estate clerk; securities clerk; supervisor, real estate office; supervisor, statement clerks; underwriting clerk and vault cashier. It also furnishes the alternative title of vault supervisor.

"To prepare effectively for the job search, you need to know as much as possible about the organizations that interest you," says Karmen N.T. Crowther, a business librarian at the University of Tennessee–Knoxville, writing in the *CPC Annual: A Guide to Employment Opportunities for College Graduates, 1992–93*. She urges job seekers to try to uncover the following information about the company: age, services or products, competitors within the industry as a whole, divisions and subsidiaries, location/length of time established there, size, number of employees, sales, assets and earnings, new products or projects, number of locations, and foreign operations.

First, visit your career center and locate recruiting literature provided by individual companies. Check company profiles for those companies hiring in your major in a volume of the *CPC Annual* or *Peterson's Annual Guides*. Then consult other reference books such as *Standard and Poor's*

Register; this contains several volumes with information on industry classifications, geographic locations, names and profiles of company executives, and company addresses.

When you have considered all available materials, turn to the business reference section of your campus or local library and continue your search.

Publicly owned companies are easier to find information about than privately owned ones. Corporations as a whole are generally easier to find information about than their subsidiaries or divisions. Large, nationally owned corporations are always easier to profile than local or regional ones. No single library is likely to hold the key to everything you need. By using library computer software, you may be able to locate material in other libraries; this material could be sent to your local library. Remember there are college and university libraries, information to be furnished from the chamber of commerce or from government offices. You may call or write to trade associations in your search for company information.

The main sources of information on businesses are:

- *Moody's Manuals* published by Moody's Investor Service. Volumes in this series cover companies listed on U.S. stock exchanges. Information includes a brief corporate history, business and products, a list of subsidiaries and properties, officers, comparative income and balance sheet statistics, and securities data.

- *Standard and Poor's Corporation Records* are similar to *Moody's Manuals.* S&P's contain both financial and narrative profiles of publicly owned U.S. companies.

- *Value Line Investment Survey* reports on approximately 2,000 stocks in 90 industries on a rotating quarterly basis. Data for each publicly owned company's stock is presented as a one-page summary, including 10-year statistical history of key investment factors plus future performance estimates.

- Corporate annual reports to stockholders contain current financial statistics and other information about the firm's operation. Many libraries keep files of these reports.

- 10-K reports are financial disclosure reports that are annually submitted to the U.S. Securities and Exchange Commission by publicly owned corporations. These reports are available in many libraries and contain a variety of financial data.

- *Everybody's Business* published by Doubleday in 1990 offers a be-hind-the-scenes look at about 400 companies.

- For company history try the library catalogue. Company histories will be listed under the name of the respective company. You might also try a history of the industry.

Small Employers

According to Constance J. Pritchard, assistant dean of students for career planning, placement, and orientation at the University of South Caro-lina–Aiken, the growth in employment is with small firms. She cites a recent survey that found that during the past few years, almost 40 percent saw their small firms increase the number of professional positions. Almost one-third of small employers said that more than half of the positions in their organizations were professional in nature.

Which types of small employers have the largest percentages of employees in professional professions? Those in the education, financial services, and government sectors.

What's the first step in finding small employers? Look for them where they're looking for you. Personal referrals tops the list of hiring methods, followed by classified ads and referrals from employees. Effective network-ing is an important strategy to find opportunities with small employers.

Small employers hire as needed, so timing is all-important. Pritchard suggests approaching multiple small employers to uncover opportunities. Small employers place more emphasis on how you work than on your academic credentials, so be sure to stress your accomplishments and your desire to achieve and to follow-through in your résumé and during your interview. Doers and team players rank high in recruitment by small employers so expect to do a lot from the beginning of your employment with a small firm.

James W. Botkin and Jana B. Matthews are the authors of *Winning Combinations: The Coming Wave of Entrepreneurial Partnerships between Large and Small Companies*, published by Wiley and Sons, 1992. They say, "With the ever-accelerating pace of technological change that we are experiencing today, it has become increasingly difficult for emerging entrepreneurial firms, acting alone, to accomplish in a timely manner what is needed to be successful. Add the factor of globalization to tech-nical complexity and the managerial problems are exacerbated." Botkin and Matthews believe that partnering between large and small companies, if done correctly, can be an especially creative and innovative strategy. So, while you are toiling away at a small firm, a larger firm may be eyeing your firm as a potential partner, and you will suddenly be on the new wave of this partnership and, hopefully, benefit from the flexibility of small business and the stability and higher wages of big business.

How do you find your way into small business? Small business has traditionally put up signs in store windows and depended on employees to spread the word around the community that a job is available. That was before cyberspace. As companies are becoming used to using on-line computers for general business purposes, they are turning to the idea of on-line recruiting. *Inc.* magazine of November 1995 profiled a small business that recruits in cyberspace. Clam Associates in Cambridge, Massachusetts, decided to post help-wanted ads on the World Wide Web. Kathy Santos, Clam's "Webmaster" put up a Clam home page on the Web last January. Job listings were added in March. After a few fits and starts, Santos rewrote her ad after being bombarded with résumés from inappropriate candidates. While the company still uses traditional methods such as newspaper ads, Santos is quoted as saying that candidates who respond to the Web listing "are much more educated about our company because all the information is right there on the Web." Clam's Web Page contains information about its products, services, and business partners, as well as the mission statement of the company. Santos predicts that on-line recruiting will fill 16 positions in the next several months.

"How do you find that elusive small company?" asks Kenneth M. and Sheryl N. Dawson, co-authors of *Job Search: The Total System.* In a number of ways. Call the local chamber of commerce in the area in which you would like to work. Make the rounds of the networking clubs, whose specific purpose is to provide marketing leads. Participate in professional trade associations in your functional area. Contact vendors for the industry in which you are interested. Read trade publications and other business newspapers, particularly local business journals, for leads. Speak with lenders that specialize in assisting small firms. Use your school's alumni directory to find some of your best networking contacts. Consider family, friends of family, neighbors, members of clubs, and other organizations to which you or your family belong, church members, and professionals who serve your family such as doctors or dentists.

Before intruding on these contacts, develop a script. Begin with a brief statement describing your degree and work background and then an explanation of how you came to call this particular contact. Next, prepare a series of questions, asking how the person was successful in attaining his or her present position. Ask for assistance. The authors advise, "Take the time to develop your networking skills and you'll discover the best jobs available among the best small companies."

The On-Line Search

Internet electronic job search has been exploding in popularity according to William Banis, director of Northwestern University's Career Service. Banis claims it is difficult to keep up with the expanding sites on World Wide Web and other electronic systems. At Northwestern all of the job listings go on-line 24 hours a day, seven days a week. Northwestern professors who are disabled use voice interpreters attached to the computer. "World Wide Web allows you a more multimedia application and puts a whole new spin to career search."

Banis believes that the old approach can still give pretty good results, if the direct mail campaign is handled well. But, he explains that with the new method a lot of applications can be quickly prepared and targeted anywhere. After job openings are found, they can be downloaded to a disc with the appropriate contact person listed. Then, a mail merge can be done. A student is able to do 20 to 30 individual résumés with mail merge and have them off and running in a matter of minutes whereas in the old days it took two or three months to work up such a volume. Banis recalls the effort it took for him in his first job search conducted the old way with individually typed letters and a look up of dozens of companies before a list could be formed of appropriate company targets. "Internet is an essential job search skill for the 90s," he concluded.

Of course, gaining facility with on-line databases takes some practice and there are fees connected with usage, including sign-up fees and telephone charges. Even though the systems strive for accuracy, just as there are mistakes in printed materials, there may be errors in on-line information. Every database has a separate access code, and every vendor system speaks a different language. If you are using a database in a library, school setting, or career center, don't hesitate to ask for basic instructions.

Cynthia Shockley in "Sources, Strategies, and Signposts for Information Professions," *Business Information Alert,* January 1996, comments on the fact that in 1995 Internet use doubled, as it has every year since 1988.

Dow Jones New/Retrieval's Text Library has expanded by 67.5 percent. When an article is retrieved from any of the thousands of sources represented by the Information Access Company (IAC) databases, it will be labeled as coming from the IAC and not from an individual database. Other sources contributing to Dow Jones's growth include the Federal Document Clearing House, which provides complete coverage of developments in the federal government. Sometimes you can get a head start on your competitors by surmising possible openings before official announcements are made.

The Internet service will run in parallel with Corporate Profound, Profound, and Profound Business Facts on the Microsoft Network. For more information, contact Profound at (212) 750-6900 or connect to the home page at http://www.profound.com.

Company profiles, some 25,000 of them, can be located at Avenue Technologies home page (http://www.avetech.com/avenue). A subsidiary of Data Times, Avenue Technologies compiles company information from a number of sources, among them the Data Times newspapers. For more information, contact Avenue Technologies at (415) 705-6971.

The new Business & Industry database (File 9 on Dialog, BIDB on DataStar) will join the Knight-Ridder (KR) OnDisc family of CD-ROM databases. As with other KR OnDisc products, searchers can choose between full-blown Dialog search software or simplified Easy Menu approach.

Shockley recommends Business & Industry as a good choice for end user searching by both students and businesspeople because of its emphasis on facts and numeric data.

Whether you majored in computer science or you have passing familiarity with a keyboard, you cannot afford to pass up the new job market provided by accessing the electronic age. Writing in the *Electronic Job Search Revolution*, published by John Wiley & Sons, 1995, Joyce Lain Kennedy and Thomas J. Morrow describe a technological revolution that is reinventing the ways that people and jobs meet. Résumés zap across cities or countries by telephone lines. Help-wanted ads flash on home computer screens. Vast databases of résumés match people to jobs. Résumés are optically scanned, organized, stored, and pulled out in a wink. CD-ROM and videoconferencing are used for interviewing. Electronic marvels make it easy to customize a blue-ribbon job hunt.

The Guide to Internet Job Searching, by Margaret Riley, Frances Roehm and Steve Oserman and published by VGM Career Horizons, 1996, shows how to uncover hundreds of leads using on-line resources.

Kennedy and Morrow claim that this new technology is taking some of the burden off of harried human relations staffs who each time a job opening for a good position hits print, are set upon by hoards of job seekers. They cite an example of a major employer in the Midwest who received 10,000 résumés in a one-month period. The human resources staff tried valiantly to cope with skyscrapers of paper by holding "résumé parties." During these parties, a dozen or so people worked in a conference room late into the night, eating sandwiches, and sorting résumés. After the staff had found 172 viable candidates, they stopped sorting.

If you decide to send your résumé electronically, you can be assured that you will quickly hear back from the receiver that your message has gotten there. After your résumé becomes part of the software technology world, it will have a broad audience. You will need to bone up on keywords so that by keying the right words into your résumé, you will snag the appropriate job openings. If a fairly large company tunes into your particular résumé, it might sort you into more than one job category. Perhaps, you have as a keyword, "mathematics modeling," and you also have "statistics" as a keyword. Your résumé may be forwarded to a department looking for someone skilled in mathematics or predictions as well as a department looking for someone in statistical analysis. This type of sorting is rarely done when it comes to handling of paper résumés.

Human resource specialists have an easier time weighing factors across résumés when they work with computer systems than with the traditional résumés. For example, an order may have been placed for a secretary. That is a broad job category. Reading through the job description provided by the person who wants the secretary and, then, discussing the implications of the position with the person who placed the notice, the personnel specialist can add factors to the job title, such as specific skills in shorthand and typing, level of computer competency required; and on what software. If the human relations executive cannot come up with a candidate who matches all ten points of the job description, by weighing the factors, the executive can make a shrewd choice among the less-than-perfect candidates.

The fact that the volume handled by electronic screening systems is so great, the best of the best are usually chosen for interviewing. To increase your chances of being interviewed, you must use other systems of contact as well.

You may consider on-line information services. Most of these services operate on a pay-as-you go basis, although there is an initial sign-up fee.

Most commercial services have full Internet access. No single on-line information service has the resources of the full Internet.

Business America on CD-ROM offered by American Business Information, Inc. lists more than 10 million businesses in the United States, including retailers, wholesalers, professional firms, and service companies. With Business America on CD-ROM, you can locate key names of officers and executives, addresses and telephone numbers of companies, number of employees in a company, and annual sales volume, along with other needed information. American Business Information can be reached at 5711 S. 86th Circle, P.O. Box 27347, Omaha, NE 68127.

Corporate Jobs Outlook analyzes sales figures, earnings of the company, salary and benefit ratings, financial stability, industry outlook, and estimates of job opportunities as well as listing information about key executives. This service contains the complete text of *Corporate Jobs Outlook!*, a newsletter covering career opportunities at leading corporations. Corporate Jobs Outlook may be reached at P.O. Drawer 670466, Dallas, TX 75367.

Duns Million Dollar Disc is a CD-ROM produced by Dun and Bradstreet Information Services. This product contains information on more than 200,000 public and privately held companies in the United States. It includes commercial, industrial, and business establishments. Full details on locations are included. The names and business background of key management personnel are given. The disc can be searched by industry, location of business, and by other criteria.

Finally, The Business Elite offered by Database America provides in-depth information on 500,000 of the largest corporations in America's business-to-business marketplace. The database yields company name, address and telephone number, stock exchange, business description, sales volume, employment size, as well as executive names and titles. Database America may be reached at 100 Paragon Drive, Montvale, NJ 07645.

Specialized Databases

More and more electronic databases are being developed each month. But few are dedicated to specialties other than business. The Trustee Center for Professional Development's Barterbase is maintained by a consortium of liberal arts colleges to help their graduates. Hartwick College in Oneonta, New York, was a leader in creating the consortium and now coordinates its efforts. Each of the participating colleges contributes to the database. Hartwick College supports a database for private schools with teacher fellowship programs. Hamilton College maintains a database of law firms that hire paralegals. Oberlin College compiles a database of publishers who hire editorial assistants. St. Lawrence University specializes in environmental employers, while Colby College lists those who hire in the performing arts and museums. Students at member colleges can obtain a computer disk with the relevant information or they can tap into the system via a modem-equipped computer and directly request information on-line.

Martindale-Hubbel is specialized for the legal profession. It is offered by Reed Reference Publishing Company. Identified are 800,000 plus lawyers and law firms, more than 1,000 corporate law departments, and 6,500 services and suppliers to the legal profession worldwide. Employment opportunities may be searched by state, county, city, as well as by name of client, name of attorney, college, college year, law school, and legal services, among others. This service is usually available to law libraries, university libraries, and large public libraries. It is updated quarterly on CD-ROM and throughout the year on Lexis/Nexis. Lawyers and legal assistants should be able to locate alumni of their schools or colleges and use this to compile a list of possible people for exploratory interviews.

Some databases make it easy to search for pertinent information on big business. Business ASAP on InfoTrack is provided by Information Access Company. The CD-ROM database has the complete text of 350 titles indexed in Business Index, Business and Company Profile, and general Business File. The subjects include business and industry, trade, and management. Business ASAP on InfoTrack is provided by Information Access Co., 362 Lakeside Drive, Foster City, CA 94404.

In addition to using the same sources that are used by people without disabilities, you should also be aware of the URL List of Disability-Related Links on the World Wide Web. Here is a surfing guide:

Evan Kemp Associates: http://disability.com/cool.html

All in one search page (26 engines): http://www.albany.net/~wcross/all1www.html

Disability International: http://www.escape.ca/~dpi/publist.html

Index of employment info/job listings: http://copper.usc.indiana.edu/~dvaslef/jobsearch.html

Index of IRC channel Pix & FAQs (frequently asked questions), purpose of each standing IRC channel: http://www.uni-karlsruhe.de/~Urs.Janssen/irc/channels.html

Netree, a graphical directory of continuously updated stories: http://www.netree.com/

Yahoo's url for their disability links page: http:/www.yahoo.com/Society_and_Culture/Disabilities/

More job listings, Government Web sites & mail listings: http:/www.gnn.com/gnn/wic/bus.toc.html

Global Network Navigator's disability index (humungous): http://www.gnn.com/gnn/wic/med.toc.html

NCSA's Computing for the Handicapped access info: http://bucky.aa.uic.edu/

On-line services offer a variety of menus. You are able to reach employment-related databases and bulletin boards that are exclusive to on-line subscribers. You can also receive information about job openings offered by electronic job ad companies and nonprofit organizations. Costs vary. Be sure to check regarding a monthly subscription fee, a connection charge, a software start-up kit fee, and other charges that may be added.

A premier service is America Online. America Online offers articles on careers as well as the World-Wide Talent Bank, which is a résumé database, a cover letter library, self-employment service, and the Federal Employment Service. America Online, Inc. can be reached at 8619 Westwood Center Drive, Vienna, VA 22182.

CompuServe Inc. should be looked into for company data. CompuServe has databases for Value Line financial statements, Standard & Poor's company information and Investext investment analyst research reports. These databases are not so easy to come by. In addition, if you become a member, you can search for jobs in CompuServe's classifieds area. CompuServe Inc. can be reached at (800) 848-8199.

Dialog Information Services offers more than 400 databases. It's easy to research using your occupational field category, such as biology, biotechnology, economics, humanities, law, science and technology, or social sciences. In addition, Dialog Information Services has abstracts of more than 50,000 journals with some in full text. Newspapers such as the *Boston Globe* and *USA Today* and Business Wire databases contain full-text coverage. Dialog Information Services can be reached at 3460 Hillview Avenue, Palo Alto, CA 94304.

Prodigy Services Co. provides access to on-line classifieds and a careers bulletin board. The board allows for informational interviewing. You contact people in your job field of interest and ask them to talk about the field in general or to answer some of your questions regarding work conditions or salaries to be expected. You may also find this a good way to get referrals. Members may leave messages about occupations in which they are interested, requesting other members of the service who are engaged in the occupation to make contact.

You may reach Prodigy Services Co. at 445 Hamilton Avenue, White Plains, NY 10601.

Federal Government Openings

For those interested in careers with the federal government, Access is an on-line service of Federal Outreach Service, Inc., which publishes federal career employment announcements in printed form. The on-line service is updated every weekday. The service is available 24 hours a day. Criteria such as level of job, location, agency, or occupational specialty can initiate a search. You may reach Federal Research Service, Inc. at 243 Church St., N.W., Vienna, VA 22180.

Also check out the Federal Job Opportunities Board operated by the Office of Personnel Management. This bulletin board includes current job openings as well as expected future job opportunities. After dialing into the system with a PC/model/communications software, directions will be given. The board operates on a menu-driven format, which means it leads the user step-by-step. The database is updated every night. Using a job series number or job title, you can search the entire database for every federal job opening and potential job opening by specific positions. When you are logged into the system, you can activate the "help" feature to view all the occupations and their corresponding numbers. If you are unfamiliar with the job series system of numbering, you can employ the help feature to view all the occupations and their respective numbers.

Another on-line service to consider is the Network World Bulletin Board System. Computer and computer networking specialists make thousands of calls monthly to this service, which reflects the job ads appearing in *Network World* magazine. The on-line job ad service is at no cost to job seekers, except for the cost of the telephone service. The board has a full-month's worth of ads from the magazine, and also information concerning the corporate background of the company placing the ad. Networking Careers On-Line accepts résumés electronically and faxes them to employers. There is also a career forum for sharing information and advice concerning careers and employment subjects.

On-line computer services can be commercially or college-campus run. Either type lists information concerning employers. However, an on-line database usually permits only one-way conversation. A few systems are interactive, permitting job candidates to inquire of recruiters and receive answers from the recruiters. But, CD-ROM (which stands for "Compact Disk-Read-Only Memory") is not interactive and cannot be updated by the user. Some database services dispense information on $5^1/_4$" or $3^1/_2$" computer diskettes that are readable by most PCs. The database service updates information on a regular basis by issuing a new, inexpensive diskette.

Trends

Information Interviews

Information interviewing is one of the most useful skills you can acquire, but it is time-consuming and can present logistical problems for those with physical disabilities. William Banis, Director of Northwestern University's Placement Bureau, suggests that if information interviewing is too energy-draining for those with physical disabilities, they should consider substituting the phone for the face-to-face visit. This has the plus of saving time for the interviewer and for the person being interviewed.

Marcia R. Fox, writing in *Business Week's Guides to Careers*, gives information these attributes:

Permits students to obtain information about a company or industry

Helps uncertain students to decide upon a career path

Helps locate industries that are booming during difficult economic times

Helps students become adept at interviewing techniques

Increases self-confidence when dealing with people.

What is an information interview? Fox defines it as a dynamic conversation with a purpose. Yet, unlike a job interview, which takes place in a tense competitive framework for the purpose of getting a job offer, the information interview occurs in a context of extraordinary freedom and control for the person doing the interviewing. "The entire process from identification of the interview purpose to the selection of key resources and, finally, to the interview stage itself, is an excellent vehicle for practicing important and transferable analytic and interpersonal skills."

Here are some sample questions:

How did you decide on this career and what were the steps you took to get a job in the field?

What do you like about your job?

Describe a typical workday.

What is a typical entry-level position?

Is this field expanding?

Are you aware of people with physical disabilities succeeding in this field?

Do you have anyone to refer me to who is working in this field and has a physical disability?

What are some of the related occupations I might investigate?

Be sure to watch your time limits and write a follow-up thank-you note. If a reference given to you during the interview proved valuable, write a letter or pick up the phone and thank the person who gave you the reference during the information interview.

Self-Employment

According to *Recruiting Trends*, 1995–96, published by the Collegiate Employment Research Institute of Michigan State University, fewer full-time employment prospects for new college graduates will be available.

There will be more contract, consulting, temporary, and part-time job opportunities. Graduates may need to start a career in a job that does not require a college degree and then work into a degree-required position.

Wasn't it better in the old days when students went right to work after high school and were trained on the job? Those that needed more advanced training or were interested in liberal arts or general learning then could take college courses or work toward a degree and even have their tuition paid by the current employer? Now, thousands of dollars later and a degree in hand, you are asked to start at the bottom of the ladder with no great expectations for spectacular advancement, especially in view of the fact that the market for middle managers is ever-decreasing.

Recruiting Trends also speculates that there will be more privatization affecting government hiring. More graduates will be selling their services on a job-to-job basis. There will be more self-employed, self-directed individuals.

The same survey predicts that prospects for telecommuting is expected to increase during the next 3 to 5 years. This will create more manufacturing space and less office space with more flexible work arrangements both in terms of time and of place.

The August/September 1995 *Business and Economics* said old rules are gone and the sooner today's workers understand the new rules the better off they will be. "Everyone is a contingent worker, not just the part-time and contract workers. Workers need to regard themselves as people whose value to the organization must be demonstrated in each successive situation in which they find themselves. Workers need to develop an approach to their work and a way of managing their own careers that is more like that of an external supplier than that of a traditional employee."

Search Firms

People with physical disabilities do not usually go to job search firms. Ray Kaehler of Esquire Personnel believes that this is because they have not been provided with information as to how to go about contacting and using such services.

The executive search firm is the high end of the job search firms. These firms generally deal with people qualifying for jobs in the $30,000-plus range, so if you are entry level do not consider this as a source. If you feel you qualify, be sure that the executive search firm you locate through the yellow pages or through a friend engages in the area of specialization that matches your job search. Each of these firms have access to the hidden job market: jobs listed only with executive search firms or even exclusively with one firm. You gain the advantage of less competition for each job and also have the chance to try for a job that you would otherwise never hear of. Each search firm has its own list of corporations it deals with locally, regionally, and nationally. Keep this in mind, and hook up with agencies that serve the area in which you wish to find employment.

You might try more than one search firm. Do not expect firms to acknowledge having received your résumé. A firm will contact you when it feels it can offer you an appropriate job match. Be assured that the executive search firm will search your background thoroughly. If the background matches an opening, the firm will call you; if the call goes well, a face-to-face interview will be scheduled. One advantage of using a search firm is that throughout the search process, detailed feedback is shred with the client, and the client is offered a variety of interviewing tips. All fees are the responsibility of the company, not the candidate.

Employment agencies work for their client companies in filling job orders that the companies place with the employment agency. In turn the employment agency will work with job seekers to find workers to fill these posted openings. There are more than 15,000 employment agencies in the United States, so there is probably one within a commuting distance from your home. Each has its own market or specialty. Some generalize over a wide number of jobs and companies, while others specialize in accounting or in office staffing. Generally, their listings in the yellow pages will describe whether they are specialists or, if not, will present the array of positions or industries in which the agency makes placements. Many times the terms, "accounting," "financial," "medical," "office," or "computer" will actually be a part of the agency name. On the whole, employment agencies start with entry-level and secretarial positions and handle hourly paying jobs on up to lower-level management positions. They do not cater to blue collar workers, high school dropouts, or upper management people. "Save yourself a trip if you happen to be one of these," advises Michael Latas, author of *Job Search Secrets*, published by Job Search Publishers, 1993.

If you're not sure what types of positions are filled by the agency, call ahead and discuss your ideal position with a staff member. Trust the agency to know whether it can be of help with your particular job search. If so, you will be asked to come to visit the agency and to fill out an employment application. This application should be filled out neatly and completely. Most firms operate on an employer-based fee, but a few firms also handle applicant-paid fees. A counselor will conduct a brief prescreening interview to qualify certain points and to fill in any area not completely covered on the application. One of the key questions you will be asked is your availability for interviews upon short notice and the minimum salary you would consider. This type of prescreening is a help because it eliminates firms that will not match your expected salary. Also, if you have an obvious physical disability, it will be seen, and the counselor will be able to handle some of the disclosure issues that you would have to face alone when independently applying for a position.

Temporary Employment

What kind of jobs does temping offer? According to the National Association of Temporary Services (NATS), approximately 63 percent of temporary workers are hired as office support staff clerks and receptionists. Fourteen percent involve light and heavy industrial skills assembly line work, janitorial services, or product demonstration work. Twelve percent require technical and professional skills. Eleven percent are in the medical area, including registered nurses, therapists, and lab technicians for hospital staffing and home health services. According to the National Association of Temporary Services, temporaries have gained new skills, especially in computers; 86 percent of temporaries have computer skills. Other interesting statistics include the fact that 44 percent provide the main source of income for their household, and 54 percent have been asked to continue as a full-time employee at the firm or company where they were assigned. The former statistic means that wages in the temporary field can be quite good. The latter statistic is encouraging, especially for those with disabilities because temporary work success shows that you are capable of doing the job.

There is usually a conversion fee charged by the agency when the temporary employee becomes a full-time employee. For the most part, the fee is paid by the company doing the hiring. But, make sure you find out whether there is a fee and who is responsible for paying it—you or the future employer. A vice-president of the national firm, Snelling and Snelling, advises that popular jobs for those with physical disabilities are assistance at conventions and product demonstrations. Such demonstrations may require cooking or food preparation. If you want to convert to full-time employment based on temporary work, apply to a firm that offers both temporary and permanent placement.

In a large survey of temporary placement firms I conducted by telephone recently, I discovered that very few firms actually had placed people with physical disabilities. The counselors at the firms assured me that this was not due to the fact that they would not accept those with disabilities as clients, but that very few had contacted them. Esquire Placement of Chicago welcomes referrals from Chicago Lighthouse for the Blind. All candidates referred were placed. Ray Kaehler of Esquire Placement suggests that those with physical disabilities take a pro-active stance and call up to inquire about openings and how to apply to a temporary or permanent placement firm.

What are temporary services looking for? Debbie Zurinski, area vice president of Snelling and Snelling, headquartered in Dallas, Texas, says, "We place people who have skills." A hot area of placement is answering the telephone, using a switchboard, using word-processing packages such as Excel, WordPerfect, Lotus, graphics packages, Power Point, and Harvard Graphics. In the temporary industry, according to Zurinski, it makes no difference who the person is, it's the skill that's used. Being good in math and having the ability to file are important skills for placement in temporary office positions.

Zurinski does not trust to luck when she screens people. She has each person demonstrate a set of skills. If the person is applying for a job that requires legible handwriting, she inspects a handwritten sample. As she interviews a person for a people position, such as receptionist, she makes certain the person has a pleasant smile and a happy face. For a filing position, candidates are asked to demonstrate filing technique by actually sorting files according to alphabetical and numerical sequence. To see a person's facility with a particular computer or word-processing program, Zurinski asks the person to do a task or two on the computer. What is important to Snelling and Snelling is performance testing.

Zurinski observes that it is an advantage to try different positions and companies for those who are not quite sure of what they wish to eventually settle on as a career. She says temping allows people to find jobs without committing to the company for a long time. If they don't want to go back to a particular company, according to Zurinski, they just have to say so. It's been her experience that temping is a two-way street, offering benefits to employee as well as employer. And, she adds, "A lot of our temporary jobs lead to full-time employment because most people like to be familiar with a person and his or her abilities before offering a full-time job."

Other Sources of Help

Often overlooked sources of employment are public employment services. This usually means a state agency. In addition to providing for unemployment compensation benefits, the agencies assist with counseling and location of suitable jobs. The counseling services often screen individuals for employers who list with the public employment agency. This is a good source for entry-level jobs. Other services offered are self-assessment and job search workshops as well as job banks whose purpose is to match skills and experience with available job vacancies. And the job search service is now on-line. A few simple instructions will get you started with the state's computerized job search program. The Illinois computerized system segregates suburban jobs from city of Chicago jobs, this saves a lot of useless inquiries because the Chicagoland area is large, posing many transportation difficulties for those with physical disabilities. The mass transit system that serves Chicago proper is outstanding for its concerns and accommodations for those with physical disabilities.

Career counselors who charge to assist you with every aspect of your job search are available. They include marketing services to combine job search and executive search functions. Be prepared to pay a lot for this latter service.

You may decide to use a résumé service. But, before you do, get referrals as to the quality of the firm's service. Remember a résumé service merely prepares résumés. It may also send them out. It does not offer job placement in the broader sense.

Professional associations usually provide placement assistance. They may list vacancies in their publications and at annual conferences. By advance planning, a job candidate can obtain a reference that may lead to an interview with a company member of the particular association. In-person networking at association-sponsored conferences can be invaluable as a prelude to an actual interview. Conferences will also expose the job seeker to many companies he or she was not even aware of.

Job Fairs

Use your time at job fairs constructively. Try to bring a companion so you can cut your job in half. Visit as many booths as you can, but do not stay long at each or you won't accomplish your mission. Be sure to take along a card index file or an electronic notebook to record the viable contacts you make along with comments on follow-up and scheduling an interview. Have adequate copies of your résumé for any company that expresses an interest in you. Pick up any and all literature on any company that draws your interest. Such information may clearly indicate how the company is set up and describe its latest products and services. Ask questions of the person manning the booth, especially questions as to which departments are expanding, what types of people in terms of skills, background, and attitude the company favors, and how you can access the current job openings of the company. Prioritize the companies in terms of your interest and the probability of finding work.

Make an A list and promise yourself that companies on the A list will be contacted with the next 2 weeks. Companies on your B list might be contacted via telephone. You may engage in a few minutes of questioning regarding possible positions of interest to you or clarifying some factor that relegated the company to your B list, such as failure to list benefits on its company information sheet. By so doing, some of the B companies might make your A list. By working with another person, follow-ups to companies on your "B" list can be shared. Being on an A list requires a personal contact from you.

By interviewing directly at a job fair, you will reveal an obvious disability automatically when you come to the interview. You will not have to go through the process of worrying as to when to reveal it. You can relax and simply have its appearance as a natural part of the interview. The employer representative is there to hire qualified people, and he is spending his precious time interviewing you, so it is unlikely that he will dismiss your candidacy simply because of your disability. If there is a question as to whether your disability will interfere with the essential duties of your ideal position, this is a time to discuss it openly. It will also give the employer time to figure out how accommodations can be made for you within his workplace, so that when your interview at the actual company site is scheduled, the employer will not have to fret about how you can be accommodated, and the interview will be spent discussing your unique qualifications for the proposed job.

Networking

"If you could chose only one method to get a job, choose networking," advises Michael Latas in *Job Search Secrets*. Latas feels that because people like to help others, you should give them the chance to help you. But, he warns, never get trapped in negative conversations while you are networking. Search out people who can help move you into a positive situation. He tells an interesting story of checking out a job in a grocery store. When he was in a long line at a grocery store, the woman ahead of him said, "I'm an efficiency analyst; maybe I should see the manager?" The man in back of him responded, "I know him—he's over here stacking the racks." The man then promised to introduce her. The two left the carts full of groceries in the checkout aisle and went over to the manager to plead her case for a job. The manager told her that if she could help him schedule his employees' time to meet the flow of customers, he would hire her.

If you are unemployed, you should take advantage of contacts to be made in various self-help organizations such as Business-People-Between-Jobs or job search groups sponsored by local churches. The Lutheran Church of the Atonement in Barrington, Illinois, operates a Career Center that provides weekly speakers and information on how to locate jobs, prepare for interviews, and compose effective résumés.

Many of these job search organizations work with temporary agencies or consulting and telemarketing firms. For instance, Ray Kaehler has had clients referred to his agency from Lighthouse for the Blind. Those who are unemployed can share news of openings as they themselves check out various firms. As you go to a firm, share openings with members of your group. Unemployed people are often close to the company where they used to be employed and can pass on openings from their former employers. Sharing job hunt adventures develops a spirit of can-do camaraderie and also pools valuable information as to state-of-the-art job seeking. Sharing war stories also enables job seekers to get more inside information on their targeted industries and broadens their knowledge of what jobs are out there, sometimes in niches they previously had not thought about.

"Your networking should begin the day you decide to look for work and should not conclude until you have secured the position," according to Michael Latas. And, please don't simply be a taker, be sure to write thank-you notes. I remember years ago contacting an executive in a well-known search firm whom I had come to know through being on a committee he chaired for the Executives Club of Chicago. Bill Billington listened to me for more than an hour, outlining my job search. He asked me many probing questions that helped me to better narrow my search scope. He told me that although his agency did not handle the type of position I was seeking, he advised me as to which agencies might be of help. As I thanked him profusely for his valuable time and advice, he said that he was not doing anything more for me than that which was done for him years before when he had just started out. But, he said, "Be sure to help someone else with his job search as soon as you have succeeded in yours."

Government Jobs and Training

The Job Training Partnership Act of 1982 was the federal government's largest job-skills training act. It is aimed at educationally disadvantaged minorities, persons with disabilities, and disabled veterans and other veterans. It replaced the Comprehensive Employment and Training Act (CETA) of 1973. The legislation requires states to provide such services as client assessment, basic education and remediation services, job training, and placement services free of charge.

Although the federal government is also undergoing a period of considerable downsizing, including the elimination of entire departments, the total percentage of those persons with disabilities employed by the federal government has remained at 7 percent since 1980, according to a report by the Office of Workforce Information. Several special noncompetitive appointments are available for people with physical disabilities. Managers can hire individuals under special appointment in just days as compared to the several months usually required under the competitive process. The federal managers must meet "critical job elements" for ensuring diversity in the workplace. By law, all agencies must develop an outreach effort to identify qualified job candidates who have disabilities. For example, agencies have direct-hire authority for Schedule A and the 700-hour trial appointment. To find out what this entails, contact an individual federal agency that interests you.

Applicants with a handicap must be considered fairly for all jobs in which they are able to perform the duties efficiently and safely, according to the Equal Employment Opportunities (EEO) *Federal Register* 29 Code of Federal Regulation (CFR). The Agency for Human Resources Management encourages federal managers to give people with disabilities full and fair consideration and to make accommodations when necessary.

Those who are severely disabled are eligible for 700-hour trial appointments, which give an individual appointed the opportunity to demonstrate ability to perform the duties of the particular appointment. The applicant must meet minimum qualification standards or be certified by a state vocational or Veterans Administration (VA) rehabilitation counselor as being capable of performing the duties of the position. Applicants establish eligibility by meeting the experience and educational requirements in the qualification standards, including any written test requirement or by certification. The Office of Vocational Rehabilitation (OVR) certification option permits agencies to waive the established qualifications. Employment usually begins with the 700-hour temporary trial appointment. This appointment is for a period of about 4 months. If the applicant does not meet the qualifications required, the agency asks for a certification letter from a OVR or VA and a medical report.

If the trial period proves satisfactory, the agency may convert the trial appointment to a permanent appointment excepted appointment. No further documentation is required for the conversion. If an agency decides to permanently appoint a person with a disability within a trial period, OVR or VA certification is mandatory, regardless of whether an applicant meets qualification standards.

Office of Vocational Rehabilitation counselors should decide any limitations regarding the position, suggest job or work site modifications, and provide any current information that could help in evaluating the applicant and making a sound judgment. For key personnel and issues in federal hiring and the disabled, contact *Ability Magazine*, Jobs Information Business Service, 1682 Langley, Irvine, CA 92714, call (714) 854-8700 or (800) 453-JOBS.

Excepted Schedule A applications are available for people with severe disabilities who have successfully completed a 700-hour trial appointment and have been certified to participate by a state vocational rehabilitation (VR) or Veterans Administration (VA) counselor. An individual appointed under Schedule A may be noncompetitively converted to a competitive appointment on the recommendation of his or her supervisor. The requirement for conversion is successful completion of the trial period and satisfactory performance must have been demonstrated for a 2-year period.

The excepted service is in such agencies as the CIA, FBI, National Security and about a dozen other agencies. There is a student intern program and a physically impaired program. Excepted service employees are not eligible to transfer to other agencies for noncompetitive reinstatement that is afforded to competitive service employees. When appropriate, the Office of Personnel Management can use special examination procedures to assess the abilities of applicants who are physically disabled.

Such special procedures include the use of readers; examinations conducted in Braille, tape, or large-print for visually-impaired; interpreters for
test instruction, and also modification of parts of tests for hearing-impaired competitors. Federal agencies are mandated to provide interpretive
services for hearing-impaired and to use readers for visually impaired, to
modify job duties and/or restructure the work site, to alter work schedules,
and to obtain special equipment or furniture for those employees who
have physical disabilities.

People who have disabilities can make special arrangements to take
any required federal job test by calling (202) 606-2528. Federal Job
Information for the Deaf can be accessed by calling (202) 606-0591.

Not all people with physical disabilities obtain their jobs through
excepted service. The majority compete for them in the same manner in
which nondisabled persons compete. Thankfully, quite recent changes
brought about by attempts to simplify government have resulted in making
the government as an employer easier to access for information about job
openings and easier to apply to after an opening has been uncovered.
Hiring for government jobs has been decentralized. Now, the job applicant is expected to be pro-active and to call and/or visit a local governmental agency of interest in person. Network with government agency
personnel just as you would network with executives in private industry.

In 1993, the Vice President Al Gore presented the National Performance Review. This review recommended broad changes in governmental hiring practices and protocol. The trickle down for the job seeker is
to make it far simpler to become qualified and it has also become easier
to obtain information about where the jobs are.

First, the traditional application form, Standard Form 171 (SF171),
was analyzed. Information required on this form was condensed and
transformed into a new optional form referred to as Form 612. This new
form can be tailored to fit an announced job. However, SF 171 has not
been phased out. Therefore, you have a choice of using the old SF 171
or the new Form 612. If, after examining samples of both, you find you
don't care for either, the government has given you a third choice. You
may now prepare a résumé, although you need to include in a résumé all
the information that is asked for on Form 612.

Computers are used to scan thousands of résumés for keywords. These
keywords are always in the form of nouns, not verbs. The computers neatly
file applications by job possibilities in multiple electronic in-boxes. The
applications are whipped out in response to a specific job announcement,

and a few are sent on for serious evaluation for the specific opening. The competition for federal jobs is stiff.

A new trend of interest is for some federal workers to work from home or a telework center for part of the workweek. Certain jobs, such as technical writer or budget analyst, are particularly suited to this arrangement. The Department of Transportation, because of its mission to save energy and cut down on commuting, has taken the lead in this endeavor.

Where do all the federal employees work? About 75 percent of all full-time civilian employees work in the Executive Branch, Defense, Treasury, Veterans Affairs, and Health and Human Services. The area with most federal employees is the Washington, DC region, spreading around Philadelphia; New York; Norfolk, Virginia; Portsmouth and Baltimore. But, a great number of openings are in other places throughout the country, mostly in major cities. There is some opportunity in small cities.

Regional centers of the Office of Personnel Management offer federal job information. These job hotlines are TDD accessible. The Washington, DC area job hotline number is (202) 606-0591. The Northeastern area is (617) 565-8913. The Northcentral area is (816) 426-6022. The Southeast area is (919) 790-2739. The Mountain area is (303) 969-7047.

SF 171 and Form 612 have a section for Veteran Preference. Five points are added to your credit rating if you were honorably discharged from one of the branches of service. Ten points are added if you are disabled. In some cases, credit is also given to spouses, widows, and widowers and mothers of a disabled veteran.

A form of temporary employment is also available to students. The temporary appointment is for a period of up to 1 year, but the agency is empowered to extend the appointment in increments of 1 year as long as the student remains in school. However, the duties of the temporary position do not have to relate to career goals or to academic courses. As long as you are in a temporary position, you cannot be converted to noncompetitive. You must compete for it and demonstrate in your application that you have the qualifications and credentials.

Whatever job you intend to apply for, be sure to get the exact information regarding the agency, job code and classification, person to whom to apply, and qualifications because candidates who do not qualify will be rejected automatically. Also, be sure to note geographical location; many locations may be unattractive to you.

Although some parts of the hiring process have been simplified, the classification system remains complex. There are 459 job series or kinds of work with 15 grades or levels of difficulty. Each trade has ten steps. Each of these little boxes has its own specific salary. More than 50,000 are employed within the personnel department to figure out and administer this classification system.

Federal blue-color workers are generally employed as civilians working for the armed forces. These blue-collar workers are paid according to local hourly rates under the Wage Grade (WG) pay system. Grades range from WG 1 to WG 19. For further information, consult the *Guide to Federal Technical, Trades, and Labor Jobs Resource Directory*, available from Suite 301, Executive Parkway, Toledo, OH 43606, call (800) 274-8515. This directory specifically lists blue-collar jobs and nonprofessional jobs that do not require a college degree.

The following occupational categories represent the largest categories of jobs that are offered by the government, according to "working for the U.S. in the 1990s" issued by the U.S. Department of Labor, Bureau of Labor Statistics in the 1993 issue of *Occupational Quarterly:*

GS 000—Miscellaneous

GS 100—Social science, psychology, and welfare

GS 200—Personnel management and industrial relations group

GS 300—General administrative, clerical, and office services

GS 400—Biological sciences

GS 500—Accounting and budgeting

GS 600—Medical, hospital, dental, and public health

GS 700—Veterinary medicine

GS 800—Engineering and architectural

GS 900—Legal and kindred groups

GS 1000—Information and arts

GS 1100—Business and industry

GS 1200—Copyright, patent and trademarks

GS 1300—Physical sciences

GS 1400—Library and archives

Search for government openings by:

Interviewing federal and local government officials for information concerning announced jobs vacancies

Preparing résumés and locating application forms

Finding out where the government offices routinely post their job openings

Keeping accurate records

Following up with any contacts you have made.

A student of mine in the Infinitec program of United Cerebral Palsy did not allow his physical disability to prevent him from hobnobbing regularly in the Cook County Building and in the Daley Center, two government buildings in Chicago. Through his gradual chatting with employees, he was able to get a luncheon date with a government official through the auspices of a newfound friend, an employee in the state government. Although the luncheon did not result in an immediate job offer, it paved the way. A few weeks later, he received a call that a job opening that might be of interest to him was about to be posted. He acted on the tip immediately and was able to obtain the job.

Be sure to call the contact person to get a copy of the full job announcement and any supporting documents. Send in your application to the personnel office as listed on the announcement and be sure to send it in enough time for it to be received before the official closing date. Some allow for faxing, but be sure to confirm whether or not this is permitted for any particular position. Don't forget to send a short cover letter with your application addressed to the proper official.

To access Federal Career Opportunities on-line for thousands of up-to-date federal job openings, you can subscribe by calling (703) 281-0200. You will need an IBM-compatible personal computer that has a 2400-baud Hayes-compatible modem.

A Quick and Easy Federal Job Application Windows 3.1-compatible system is offered by Data Tech Software. DataTech Merged Word is a comprehensive system for obtaining a federal job. The new optional forms are included along with the original SF-171 application. The software program includes a word processor with spell check to help manage the new optional forms, a résumé, and the original SF-171. The kit also includes a condensed version of the *Book of U.S. Government Jobs* that is designed to be searched by keyword commands.

The *Federal Times*, a newspaper containing thousands of ads for federal jobs along with trends in employment in the federal sector, can be found at most libraries or can be subscribed to by writing to 6883 Commercial Drive, Springfield, VA 22159. Ads for federal professional and technical positions are listed in the business section of *USA Today*, *The Washington Post*, the *Wall Street Journal*, the *New York Times*, and in selected local newspapers.

Federal Jobs Digest provides a biweekly job listings. The digest is available through Breakthrough Publications, P.O. Box 594, Millwood, NY 10546. There are thousands of General Schedule and Wage Grade job listings. It also contains display ads.

Federal Agency telephone directories may be obtained from the Government Printing Office, Department of State or Department of Defense in Washington, DC. The *Occupational Outlook Quarterly* is available from the U.S. Department of Labor, Bureau of Labor Statistics, Washington, DC 20402, or from the Government Printing Office.

If you are a veteran, you may send for free fact sheets regarding the Veterans' Reemployment Rights Statute, "Reemployment Rights for Returning Veterans and Job Rights for Reservists." Write or call the Veterans Employment and Training Services, Department of Labor, Washington, DC 20210.

As the number of federal jobs shrinks, the competition for these jobs increases. According to Paul Maraschiello, writing in the *Federal Jobs Digest* of March 8, 1996, a few years ago there were 4,000 vacant jobs every week. As of this writing, there are a little more than 1,600 vacant jobs listed in the computer data banks at the Office of Personnel Management.

Maraschiello is the president of the largest résumé writing company in the Washington, DC area and specializes in assisting people find federal employment. He personally evaluates the federal employment potential of applicants and provides counseling. He has developed a Federal Résumé copyrighted software program that prepares answers to Knowledge, Skills, and Abilities (KSAs) and Ranking Factor Questions and provides referrals to federal jobs. Contact Maraschiello at 100 East Street, S.E., Suite 101, Vienna, VA 22190.

Maraschiello says, "I am now seeing well prepared SF171s and federal résumés that tell the whole story. I am being sent material that has been compiled by people who have read and understand what I mean when I say 'be thorough!'" He counsels that after you have prepared a really good SF171, or federal résumé, you need to locate the jobs and apply, apply, apply. It often takes 3 months for an application to be processed. To be successful, you need to be diligent in your search for vacancies, calling to have a copy of every announcement that is of interest to you. When you receive the announcement, read it carefully and critically evaluate your qualifications in light of what the government is seeking.

He observes that in almost every federal job application he has seen in the past few years, there have been a series of questions, usually between three and six, that must be addressed separately. These questions are called for example, Ranking Factor Questions KSAs, or Selective Placement Factors. Pay particular attention to these questions because they address particular skills that are required to perform the job.

The two new optional forms and an information flyer called "Applying for a Federal Job" replace instructions and questions on the SF171. The Office of Personnel Management plans to make the flyer available in Braille, large print, audiotape, and computer disc. The forms are officially titled Optional Application for Federal Employment (OF 612) and Declaration for Federal Employment (OF 306). OF 612 asks personal questions, such as citizenship and questions regarding experience, education, and skills. A section of OF 306 asks about court martials, felonies, loan defaults. Even though these forms are optional, agencies could request you to complete the form at any time during the hiring stages. But the idea is to offer the form only to the final few applicants for a specific position. Whatever form you submit, all information asked for on the flyer and in the job announcement must be included.

If you choose SF171, you do not have to answer the questions on Page 4 of the form. You may respond N/A for other personal questions on SF171, including Questions 3 through 5, which inquire as to date of birth and birthplace and your sex. It is probably good to answer questions on availability for travel and the hours you wish to work.

Some categories such as Professional Nurse may use the Telephone Application System. In this Telephone Application System, responses are computer-rated against the qualifications standard. For a few positions, respondents may be able to complete OPM Form 1203, an optical scan form.

There are many ways of accessing career opportunities in the federal government. Career America (912) 757-3000; CIA (800) 562-7242; Department of Interior (800) 336-4562; Federal Jobs Information Center in Minneapolis/St. Paul Area (612) 725-3430. Then, there are publications such as the *Federal Times*, 6883 Commercial Drive, Springfield, VA

22159 or call (703) 750-2000; *Federal Jobs Digest,* Breakthrough Publications, 310 N. Highland Ave., Ossining, NY 10562 or call (800) 824-5000.

In most cases, with the exception of those with severe disabilities who can short-circuit tradition procedures, applicants for GS2, GS3, and GS4 jobs must take the clerical exam, which is offered by OPM directly or by appropriate agencies, if no OPM is in the area. Some areas test weekly while some test intermittently, but at the least once every several weeks. Candidates should visit or write their local OPM and schedule a date to take the exam.

Some areas such as New York and Huntsville, announce testing dates a few days before they occur. Other areas, such as Boston and Washington, D.C., offer the exams on a weekly basis. Individuals who do not live near an OPM should write to the closest one and request test scheduling and site information for the clerical exam. The following are OPM addresses:

ATLANTA

Office of Personnel Management
Richard B. Russell Federal Building
75 Spring Street SW, Suite 940
Atlanta, GA 30303

CHICAGO

Office of Personnel Management
John C. Kluczynski Federal Building
DPN 30-3
230 South Dearborn Street
Chicago, IL 60604

DAYTON

Office of Personnel Management
U.S. Courthouse & Federal Building
200 West 2nd Street, Room 507
Dayton, OH 80225

DENVER

Office of Personnel Management
12345 West Alameda Parkway
PO Box 25167
Denver, CO 80225

DETROIT

Office of Personnel Management
477 Michigan Avenue, Room 565
Detroit MI 48226

HONOLULU

Office of Personnel Management
300 Ala Moana Blvd., Box 50028
Honolulu, HI 96850

HUNTSVILLE

Office of Personnel Management
520 Wynn Drive, NW
Huntsville, AL 35816-3426

KANSAS CITY

Office of Personnel Management
601 East 12th St., Room 131
Kansas City, MO 64106

NORFOLK

Office of Personnel Management
Federal Building
200 Granby Street, Room 500
Norfolk, VA 23510-1886

PHILADELPHIA

Office of Personnel Management
William J. Green, Jr., Federal Building
600 Arch Street, Room 3256
Philadelphia, PA 19106

RALEIGH

Office of Personnel Management
4407 Bland Road, Suite 200
Raleigh, NC 27609-6296

SAN ANTONIO

Office of Personnel Management
8610 Broadway, Room 305
San Antonio, TX 78217

SAN FRANCISCO

Office of Personnel Management
120 Howard Street, Room 735
San Francisco, CA 94105

SAN JUAN

Office of Personnel Management
Federico Degatau Federal Building
Carlos E. Chardon Street
Hato Rey, PR 00918

SEATTLE

Office of Personnel Management
700 5th Avenue, Suite 5950
Seattle, WA 98104-5012

TWIN CITIES

Office of Personnel Management
Federal Building, Room 503
One Federal Drive
Ft. Snelling, MN 55111-4007

WASHINGTON, DC

Office of Personnel Management
1900 E Street, NW
Room 2458
Washington, DC 20415

After applicants pass the clerical exam, they can take their test results card to any agency and, if they qualify for the position, be hired to fill a vacancy. After an applicant takes the exam, he or she is rated and placed on a clerical register. Consequently, after you pass the clerical exam, you have a choice: you can wait to be called off the register or you can contact various agencies in your area directly to determine which agencies are filling openings.

Some agencies in addition to OPM, have authority to give the clerical exam. This is called direct-hire authority. If a candidate makes contact with an agency with direct-hire authority, he or she can be hired on the spot without having to go on a register. This direct contact approach is clearly faster. After an agency receives a candidate's name from a register, the agency sends him or her an SF171 or OF 612 to document education and experience. If the documentation proves to be satisfactory, the agency may set up an interview. Other agencies and positions work in a way similar to that outlined for the clerical position.

CHAPTER SIX

MAKING THE BEST IMPRESSION: RÉSUMÉS, COVER LETTERS, APPLICATIONS, AND INTERVIEWS

Résumés

Make no mistake—a résumé is a formal document. It cannot be taken lightly. A résumé is your ambassador. It represents you. It is often sent on to the employer before the job candidate has a face-to-face meeting or contact by phone. If your résumé isn't attractive, neither will be your job candidacy.

In the space of this single document, you, the job seeker, must span three time frames. As reflected in its original Middle English meaning, the résumé is a source of beginning again or resuming where one has left off. Thus, a résumé should not read like a tombstone, flatly listing one's milestones. Rather, it must weave (1) the past experiences and bring into focus (2) the up-to-date current person represented and, (3) give indications of accomplishments to be made in the future. In the 1800s, the French adopted the résumé as a summing up, and résumé became attached to the world of jobs as a "brief" written account of personal, educational, and professional qualifications and experience.

In the word *brief* lies the challenge—to sum up pertinent past accomplishments, relating the past as prologue to future accomplishments while giving a profile of the job seeker in his or her present state. Tricky, yes, but it can be done!

There are other uses for a résumé besides an invitation for an employer to grant you an interview. It can complement a letter of application for a particular job, or it might be designed to appeal to employers across a broad field such as children's retail stores. It is also useful when an interview is scheduled. Always bring a copy of your résumé to your interview, whether or not you have sent it on ahead. Your interviewer may have mislaid your original résumé. Perhaps, unknown to you at the time of sending it in, more than one copy was needed. Because you have your résumé in hand, you may make another copy in an instant. It also affords you a chance to regroup your thoughts while you are sitting in the outer office awaiting your interview.

Of course, the résumé should reflect you and tell your story. But, above all, the résumé must speak to the needs of your potential employer. The résumé says, in effect, "I know your needs, and I am here to help you. My résumé can vouch for the fact that I have had past experiences and accomplishments that you can use. I have education and training that is just waiting to be of service to you." Remember that as John L. Munchauer, author of *Jobs for English Majors and Other Smart People*, says, "When an employer needs a candidate with specific knowledge and/or experience, the résumé should reflect that specific need." He gives the example of an employer needing a biologist to do gene splicing. To respond to this need, the résumé should not only indicate a degree in biology, but also should elaborate by listing courses, skills, and experience relating to gene splicing. He goes on to observe that many employers offering nontechnical jobs in fields like sales, journalism, merchandising, and finance need, most of all, well-educated people they can train on the job. Thus, on a résumé, education, activities, sports, and experiences can portray a bright person with relevant interests and aptitudes.

The most common type of résumé lists work history in reverse chronological order. Accurate dates must be used both by year and by month, except for certain experiences such as a summer job, which may be listed as the summer of 1994, or in the case of certain jobs such as student teaching or teaching, which are clustered in terms of quarters or semesters or years, such as "taught at Lincoln Grade School for the years 1993 to 1995." This presumes the fall of 1993 to the spring of 1995. You may include a brief description of job duties under each position or specific accomplishment in the section that covers your work history or experience history.

While it is not mandatory to include a section on education, it is always a plus to list any degrees, formal courses, workshops, or training experiences you have had that are pertinent to the job for which you are applying. For instance, if you are applying for a position as a woodworker, listing a B.A. degree in history is not nearly as impressive as mentioning that you were an outstanding student in vocational education in a vocational high school, having taken several special courses and workshops in various areas of woodworking and having won student design awards. This latter experience shows that you are able to perform the principal duties of the position.

In these days of corporate downsizing, many people are actually overqualified for the jobs they are seeking, and their résumé while impressive may not show job skills relevant to the position applied for, or they may be outdated in terms of when the person actually used them. This is particularly true in the case of a person who has risen rapidly through the ranks and has just been laid off from a middle-management position. Now he is applying as an electrical engineer. When was the last time he actually did wiring? So, you as a recent high school graduate or college graduate often have an advantage in that you have up-to-the-minute knowledge and job skills in the area of your choice, and you don't expect to start at a top wage. Therefore, what you lack in years of experience should be balanced in your work section history by elaborating on the specific job duties you were assigned in your previous job or jobs.

If you have had no paid jobs, then use volunteer positions or internships. For example, if you are applying for a general clerks job, mention the total range of your skills, quick and accurate mathematical computation, payroll accounting functions, filing, both alphabetical and numerical, keypunch operation, and the like. By specifically listing your skills, one or the other is sure to be a skill or duty match with the requirements of the job for which you are applying. And why not mention a school that has a good reputation or a school directly geared to your intended profession, such as a person looking for a position as a mathematics instructor listing in his résumé that he is a graduate of the Illinois Academy of Math and Science.

List volunteer experiences, beginning with the experience most closely aligned to either the type of organization to which you are applying and/or the position you seek. For example, you are applying for intake in a hospital. Volunteer positions of being a hospital tour guide are important as is being a volunteer at the admissions desk of a local crisis center. In the first case, the site of work matched the intended future site of work; while the latter patched the type of job being applied for along with the pace being similar to that required in the future job. Both a crisis center and hospital are fast-paced. Both see people who are in a highly charged emotional state and usually not at their best. Quick thinking, calmness, and fast action are transferable skills from the volunteer position to that of the paid position.

Don't skip activities and hobbies. But, observe caution. You might enjoy coin collecting, but it is not a particularly relevant hobby to list when applying for a sales job. However, listing a hobby such as coaching little league lines up with sales work because it incorporates leadership, organization, ability to inspire, persuade, and convince, as well as a liking for working with a diverse group of people.

To include references or not to include them—that is the question! When I was involved in human resources, many résumés came across my desk with a short statement at the bottom of the résumé to the effect that references were available upon request. This always struck me as being redundant because the job applicant ought to be sophisticated enough to realize that either during the time he or she is to fill out an application or during an interview, the applicant will be asked for references. Still, this shows that the applicant is conscious of having to produce references at some point, and that the references will be favorable. However, in a few cases employers may consider a résumé to be incomplete if references are not included. If you have a particularly outstanding reference, try to simply list the name, address, and telephone number of the reference along with a brief indication of the relationship with you—supervisor, coworker, friend. Do not list a relative. The exception is when your main work experience has been in the employ of a relative. Even then it might be wise to list the relative's company, but give a nonrelative employee or supervisor as a reference.

The use of active rather than passive verbs is recommended. Compare the following: "I was in charge of 25 employees" with "I trained, supervised, and motivated a staff of 25." Contrast "I was a productive employee" with "I consistently turned out more letters than the quota allotted to my job" or "I sold more cars per month than any other trainee."

Create a word bank of powerful verbs to get across your message and to avoid repetition in your résumé and cover letter. Here is a start toward words that make a strong statement:

accessed
adapted
administered
advised
analyzed
appraised
arbitrated
assessed
assigned
authored
calculated
categorized
communicated
completed
conducted
constructed
consulted
coordinated
counselled
created
defined
demonstrated
discovered
edited
encouraged
enforced
established
estimated
evaluated
expanded
expedited
facilitated
gained
generated
implemented
improved
increased
initiated

innovated
instructed
investigated
liaised
maintained
managed
mediated
merged
monitored
motivated
negotiated
operated
organized
participated
planned
presented
produced
programmed
projected
realigned
reengineered
reorganized
researched
reviewed
scheduled
selected
self-motivated
serviced
streamlined
structured
substantiated
suggested
supervised
supplemented
supported
trained
volunteered

Before deciding on a final version of your résumé, make lots of notes under each portion of the résumé. For example, what should you state as your objective? Get a good job? Too vague. Get a job that suits my abilities and experiences? Incomplete. Why not add to that the specific abilities and experiences you wish to apply toward your next job? For example, you may have had job experiences in which you were asked to train as well as handle your own office work. Are you now seeking a job to expand on your training skills or do you wish to find one in which you can master more of your own skills and go on up in the organization? You must be able to articulate your goal and not expect the human resources person to be your guidance counselor.

Keep in mind that résumés are used not to select people, but to reject most people. Only a select few are saved for the possibility of going the next step forward in the selection process, which is generally the in-person interview, although there has been a considerable trend toward a preliminary phone screening and then based on the results of this screening you will or will not be scheduled for an in-person interview. Phone screening cuts down on the time of the interviewer.

Despite the fact that you are your own best cheerleader during the job search process, your potential employer is not interested in seeing that you receive a job. Rather, the employer is self-motivated to fill a job opening that he has with a candidate most closely matched to the requirements of the position and within the salary range of what the employer has preestablished as the pay rate for the position.

From the candidate's point of view, the job search is personal. Whether or not he gets the particular job affects his ego and his paycheck and, possibly, his choice of career. Whether or not this candidate gets the job offer is of no personal concern to the employer. The employer has a job order to be filled and his sole interest is making a good match. He is screening a large number of candidates just to get down to the one person to fill his need.

Résumés can take many forms because they reflect individual strengths. A résumé should stress your work history if you are not a recent graduate and/or you have worked for one or two employers for a significant period of time and the job and work situation you now seek is parallel to this experience. If not, you might stress your academic strengths and volunteer experience and hobbies and activities.

An alternative to merely stating you have references should they be requested is to simply submit letters of recommendation. If you go this route, be sure that the letters of recommendation are typed on company letterhead stationery and signed by the person writing the letter. If the résumé and letters of recommendation are mailed to an employer, a cover letter should accompany them.

Carol Kleiman, the Chicago Tribune Jobs Columnist and an authority on career planning, parted with "Hints on how to get a résumé ignored" in her Tribune Column on Thursday, February 1, 1996. Kleiman claims that job seekers often are in the dark about what happens after they send in the résumés. How carefully are the résumés read? What do people who read résumés look for? What do they care about?

According to Kleiman, one manager who frequently advertises and is inundated with résumés gives us a look into what turns off a potential employer. The mistakes are: a company-metered envelope; sloppy-looking résumés; words misspelled and skills that don't match the ad. If a person uses company postage, won't he/she use my company supplies, if I hire him/her? Some résumés come in wrinkled, some on fax paper, some are printed off-center. Some people forget to include a cover letter so they are quickly forgotten, too. Do people just send out résumés blindly and expect a response? The neatness and accuracy of the envelope often is more important to this manager than the résumé itself. "After all, the envelope is your first impression."

While it is always safer not to use fax until it is more generally used, many companies are inviting applicants to send faxes because it speeds up the process. Nowadays, recruitment ads often list a fax number where résumés can be faxed. If in doubt, call the company regarding its fax policy on résumés.

Nicole Kraemer in *The Washingtonian* of March 1996 gives résumé tips. Claiming that a résumé is an advertisement, Kraemer urges the résumé writer to sell herself or himself on paper. She quotes Nicholas Lore of the Rockport Institute, a Rockville, Maryland–based career-consulting firm as saying, "People buy the best-advertised product more often than they buy the best product." The theme of the article is that with a stellar résumé, you may get a better response than someone having better credentials.

Career consultants seem to agree that your résumé should be tailored to each job for which you apply. Ask yourself what qualities the company is looking for, then highlight these in the work experience section. Résumés created on a personal computer are far easier to revise than those typeset by professional services or those done on a typewriter. Matthew Greene, author of *Winning Résumés*, advises that only a few words or lines may have to be modified, usually in the job objectives and skills summary.

Before sending out the résumé, check your name. Is it spelled correctly? Did you use a nickname when a more formal name would be more businesslike? What about your address—is it current? If it is temporary, indicate when it will become permanent or, if you are not certain, mention that you will contact the company should it change between the time the letter is received and the move occurs. Be sure to include your phone number. Career counselor Phyllis Martin, who wrote *Martin's Magic Formula for Getting the Right Job*, published by St. Martin's Press in 1987, says that you double your chances for a call if you also leave a number where a message can be taken for you. If you can leave a fax number, so much the better. Don't forget a crisply written job objective. Have you highlighted your education, including not only the basic information of name and address of institution, but also any honors or noteworthy awards or other information that might help to lift you above the educational credentials of rival job seekers? Be sure your work experience is highlighted. Include work for which you were not paid if it strengthens your case. Finally, mention any other qualifications that makes you a superior candidate for a particular job. Martin states that the following individual items mentioned under special skills and attributes in a résumé won a coveted job interview for the person listing it:

Knowledge of a foreign language with the language specified such as Spanish

Knowledge of sign language

Knowledge of procedures for federal grant requests

Knowledge of a computer language with specific language cited

Ability to type 60 words per minute

Knowledge of shorthand

Knowledge of cardiopulmonary resuscitation.

Should you disclose the fact that you have a physical disability as part of the résumé? Most of the career books that touch upon this delicate subject are not in favor of making a disclosure at the time of writing the cover letter and résumé. As Gibson of Preferred Staffing expresses it, "The object of the résumé is to get an interview. There's no sense in revealing a disability before the interview is scheduled because disclosure might give a potential employer a reason not to schedule an interview." Yet, a few authorities maintain that disclosing an obvious physical disability in a résumé offsets a possible surprise should the candidate appear and the interviewer is startled because he did not expect to meet a candidate with a physical disability or he has never interviewed a candidate with the particular physical disability you have and so the interviewer becomes ill at ease. The focus of the interview then can become distorted and focus on the disability rather than the ability. Most authorities feel the subject should be brought up sometime before the actual interview, perhaps mentioned on the application or perhaps in a telephone call after the interview has been set up or in the same phone call as long as the interview date has been established. If the physical disability is not easily noticed, many authorities counsel not to bring it up until after the hiring is complete or, perhaps, not at all if it doesn't affect job performance. But, if it appears to the interviewer that you have been deceptive in not bringing it out in the open, the employer may not trust you and so may decide not to make a job offer.

Some résumé writers like to put personality into their résumés by including a description of themselves either under a heading such as "Personal Traits" or "Personal Characteristics" or by seeding hints of personality throughout the résumé. Personality can be put into the job objective itself. Instead of blandly stating, "My objective is to use my talents," a job seeker who is applying for a job requiring a high-energy level such as sales work might say: "My job objective is to put my high spirits into a productive outlet," or "My job objective is to use my natural leadership ability to supervise others," or "I want to combine my overriding interest in modern music with my job site so I am looking for a similar position to the one I now hold, but in a record company or an entertainment agency." Under "Work Experience" you can add an adjective or two to the duty such as "careful preparation of sales letters" to the plain vanilla of "I wrote sales letters" or you can add an adverb "I cheerfully assisted customers in the complaint department." Because that is a feat in itself, you would probably be hired in a complaint department for that reason alone.

Whatever you write in your résumé, make sure it's accurate and fairly representative of the facts. Never give a false reference or be too generous in inflating your job description. I remember reading a résumé that stated, "I was promoted to head of my department just a year after I was hired." When I interviewed this young lady, I asked about the size of her department and I learned that she received her promotion in a two-person department when the other person retired. Bruce Jacobs writing in *Indus-try Week* on "Catching Résumé Cheaters, Simple as a Phone Call," says that 80 percent of résumés investigated contained inaccuracies and about 30 percent either misrepresented or fabricated academic credentials. Other authoritative sources say that due to the tight job market, there is a substantial increase in forging degrees or in upgrading a state school to an Ivy League school. Remember, if you're caught, you're out, and you'll have a gap in your employment history that will be really difficult to deal with.

A résumé that had as its job objective a position that requires commitment and ability to handle a wide range of responsibilities had a particularly effective handling of duties. Under her first position of executive administrative assistant, the applicant bulleted the following:

- Hired to provide both secretarial and administrative support for the president

- Prepared all correspondence to customers and to the parent company in Australia in addition to interoffice communications

- Handled domestic and foreign travel and accommodation arrangements for president

Handled in this way, the specific duties do not leave room for guessing on the part of the human relations person who has only a minute or so to scan the résumé.

Cover Letters

A cover letter is an art in itself. A cover letter is the first document that introduces you and the content of your submittal. In this letter, attempt to show why you are interested in the particular company and/or the position being offered. Thinking of the three time zones of the résumé; that is, past, present, and future, how can the cover letter take you from the present and whisk you into a new arena of employment? Let's say you have been a receptionist and have skills in running a PBX board, and your work history demonstrates that you have had steady employment at one company and regular raises. Your cover letter might indicate that, while you have enjoyed being a receptionist, you now feel you have mastered the skills of this position and are now ready to use your newly acquired computer skills to apply for a job that requires the handling of multiple tasks, will challenge your ability to organize, and serve as a step up in a company. Never give a negative reason for applying for a new job such as the present company does not appreciate my star quality, or I have learned everything I can possibly learn about my job, or I am bored.

To convey sincerity regarding your interest in the potential employer's company, do a bit of homework. You can call the library or visit the library and research the target company in *Dun and Bradstreet, Everybody's Business, Ward's Business Directories, Reference Book of Corporate Managements, Macrae's Blue Book, U.S. Manufacturers.* Mention a fact or two about the company and how its goal meets yours.

Gregory Brennan, author of *Successfully Self-Employed*, gives tips on cover letters that cover the subject well. Brennan insists that job seekers use a simple format that prompts recipients to read the résumé and then to be eagerly awaiting a call from the writer of the cover letter. He urges the writer to advise the prospective employer that the writer will be calling soon to set up an appointment. Brennan suggests addressing your cover letter to the actual hiring authority for the position that you seek. Next, recognize that the purpose of a cover letter is to compel the hiring manager to read your résumé as an advertisement for your abilities and potential. He says you need write only four paragraphs, each with a specific purpose:

1. In the first paragraph, introduce yourself and describe your connection to the decision maker. "I just read your advertisement." Or "My friend who works in your department advised me of a possible opening."

2. Use the second paragraph to explain your expertise and how the company will benefit from hiring you.

3. In the third, briefly describe one or two of your successes in your current or previous job that demonstrate your qualifications for the position you seek.

4. In the last paragraph, mention when you intend to call to seek an appointment.

When finished, Brennan says, your letter should be powerful enough to make recipients eager to learn more about your qualifications and happy to accept your follow-up call. Other brief tips:

Print your letter on high-quality paper.

Keep paragraphs short, between two and four sentences each.

Don't be wordy.

Single-space the document and proofread carefully. Check spelling, grammar, and punctuation.

Make sure you spell the recipient's name correctly and use the person's proper title. If you aren't certain, double-check with a company receptionist or the assistant to the decision-maker.

Send your résumé by 2-day delivery to be efficient and to show you are indeed serious about the job opening.

The cover letter should highlight what the résumé presents in detail. The cover letter needs to indicate that the enclosed résumé will demonstrate that the writer of the résumé has all the essential skills and level of experience necessary to successfully perform the job to which the résumé is targeted.

Your cover letter should state a few short words who it is that you are and what your objective is. Refer to any previous phone contact you have made with the prospective employer and incorporate that into your letter such as "Thank you for inviting me to send in my résumé as of our telephone conversation last week." Be sure to thank the reader for his time and for considering you as a candidate. You may say you are looking forward to an interview.

A final word on spelling and grammar. Use your spell check or grammar check on your computer, if you have one available. But, be sure to follow a spell check with a visual inspection. Spell check cannot distinguish between "it's" or "its" and okays a word as being spelled correctly as long as it's a recognizable word. For example, "I was torn on April 6, 1977." "Torn" will not be refuted by the spell checker because it is a correctly spelled word. Unfortunately, not the correct word. If you are not a good proofreader, find someone who is.

Applications

If résumés seem difficult to master and cover letters are tricky, applications contain even more pitfalls. In a résumé, you have some control over what will be revealed and how it will be revealed. In an application, this is not true. What is asked must be answered. Even a question such as "Have you served in the military?" must be answered with an "N/A" meaning it's "not applicable." Unanswered questions or blanks definitely go against the applicant.

Why are job applications so unfriendly? They were made that way. Job applications have been designed to collect negative information to screen people out of prospective positions. Job applications separate the men from the boys. Perhaps the only consolation is that each of your rivals for the position will have to overcome the same hurdle.

The first thing you will see on most job applications is the company's name and address, as well as the names and addresses of any subsidiary or affiliated companies. Often, just under this information, the application will indicate that the company is an equal opportunity employer. That is good news for a person with a physical disability. Of course, every job application will ask you to provide your name. Give your first name first and last name last if the form does not state the order. I myself, being used to writing my name in this order, have been occasionally tripped up when an application asks for last name first, so read carefully or fill out in pencil before putting down an error in ink. Some experts recommend filling out applications in invisible ink. Be sure you know your social security number, and it is a good idea to bring your card with you. Some applications combine home and mailing addresses. Many applications use a separate line for each, asking an applicant for present address or temporary address, followed by a line asking for permanent address. If both are the same, so indicate.

Remember, never leave a blank on an application. Many forms will ask for home phone and alternate phone. Do not give out your business phone if you have not yet given notice; a coworker or, worse yet, your supervisor might just come walking along while you are chatting to your prospective employer. Keep in mind the new regulations allowing employers to listen in on employees' calls. Don't do a superficial job of listing an emergency contact; it can come back to haunt you in a real emergency. List someone who can be reached at a definite phone number throughout most of the day. If you are subject to accidents or are especially unlucky when it comes to reaching someone in a hurry, put down two names and numbers. Note that many applications mention that all persons, upon hiring, must verify U.S. citizenship status.

Put down the type or title of the position for which you are applying. If you are responding directly to an advertisement for a specific opening, copy what the ad calls for; for example, supervisor of data processing department. Never put "open" under position applied for. This makes you appear desperate or so lacking in skills that you don't know where you would fit.

Be sure you know the right date. Don't shout across the room, "Hey, what's today's date?" It only leads the employer to think you're the type of candidate who doesn't know what time it is.

Be sure to note who or what referred you to the company. If you are answering an ad, write the specific newspaper in which the ad appeared. The human relations executive will give you plus points. Also, knowing which newspapers drew applicants helps plan future media campaigns. If a friend referred you and the friend works for the company, mention the name of the friend and his or her department, unless you know that the friend is not well respected in the company. Usually, companies are happy that their employees recommended others. It shows that employees are satisfied with their companies and, of course, saves recruitment money. Another big advantage to having been referred by someone inside the company is that companies prefer hiring someone known to them.

If you are not particular as to whether you wish to be hired part-time or full-time, but really want to be hired, check both and then explain during the interview. If you want to work part-time, you must be willing to work year-round. If you only intend to be a seasonal employee, check summer. If summer is not the season you need to work, then strike "summer" and insert the season. As to "shift preference," be sure to check only the one or ones you can handle well. Some people cannot handle the graveyard shift and almost fall asleep at the wheel trying to drive back and forth during the early hours of the morning. Are you willing to travel? Be honest and mention whether you would be willing or unwilling to drive. Willing or unwilling to fly?

Salary required is tricky. If you put a salary considered too high, you will be passed over. If you put too low a salary, you just may receive it or, alternatively, be overlooked as not confident enough of your abilities to ask for the going rate. How to find out? Search books and current magazines that present salaries across a wide range of jobs. You could also check advertisements in the newspapers that list rates for comparable jobs. You could also call a friend who is employed in the type of position you are seeking. But make sure you're not comparing a general clerk's salary who works in a top national corporation with a clerk's salary who works in a nonprofit organization. You might make a guess based on the minimum salary you would consider or need to retain some measure of independence and then mark a plus such as $7.50 plus per hour, if the job is entry-level and, thus, probably based on wages per hour. This would probably be the case for entry-level jobs in the hotel industry. Jobs considered as supervisory jobs may or may not be listed as hourly rates. Many times jobs such as supervisors of hotel housekeeping are listed as hourly rates. Managerial jobs such as a management trainee job would be expected to be listed as per month or per year.

Listing a range is always safer than just taking a stab in the dark. If your college placement office advised you that junior accountants were averaging $1,500 per month, you might put down a figure of $1,500 to $1,600 a month. If you learned that engineers were generally starting at $30,000 per year, it would make no sense to list a starting salary of $25,000 or of $35,000 unless you were either underqualified or very qualified for the position and had a choice of job offers. Remember, that during the interview you can always adjust a bit up or down, and you have the opportunity to inquire about raises and merit pay or bonuses, all of which would affect the angle from which you viewed a starting salary. Promotion policy also directly impacts salary.

When you're asked "When can you start?," do not say as soon as possible. This seems to reflect desperation. Even saying, "immediately" is too much, and if you are already employed, it suggests that either you intend to give a very short notice, you have already given notice, or you have been given notice. It is far better to write down a date some 10 to 14 days later than the present date. Or, you may say within 2 weeks of receiving an offer from your company. This makes you seem self-confident and in control of your affairs and well-organized, all of which appeal to an employer.

Most job applications ask you for hobbies, special interests, and activities, often mentioning that you should omit references to organizations or activities that have racial, religious, or sex identification. The intent of this is to avoid discriminating against a candidate on the basis of religion, sex, or other factors. However, don't let this provision turn out to be reverse discrimination. For example, if you held a leadership role in the National Association for the Advancement of Colored People (NAACP), not listing this information results in a missed opportunity to display your leadership skills. Again, many women belong to associations for women only, such as the Association of Business and Professional Women. Not to be able to note membership and leadership activities within this organization is a disservice to you as an applicant. If you have had leadership experience in a church group, rather than list the specific church or denomination, try to give a more general listing such as "served as social director for an auxiliary of a large urban church."

If you're asked for your geographic preferences, you should state where you currently live, such as Atlanta, Georgia, if you do not wish to be relocated. Relocation is expensive and in today's business world, jobs are not as lasting as they were in the past. So if you are transferred to Baltimore, Maryland, chances are you will know no one. I do not recommend relocation unless you have an unusually high-paying job or your area really does not hold much promise for jobs in your field. In the American workplace people are tending more and more to stay put, so you will hardly be alone for preferring not to be uprooted.

Many forms are very specific under the heading of "Foreign Languages in which you are fluent." Fluent means written or spoken with ease. Many forms further delineate fluency along the lines of ability to read, write, and/or speak. If you have had fairly good training in language, such as 3 years of Spanish, you might be fluent in the language and you can brush up quickly. Speaking and listening to Spanish being spoken will quickly get you into gear. Remember, too, that conversations between guests and hotel workers are, in general, brief, and guests will be most likely pleased with your attempts to speak their language. For applications that are not so detailed or applications that do not refer to language ability, you may list your second or third language under "Special skills" and then give an indication of your ability level such as fluent in reading and speaking, but not fluent in writing.

Many application forms also have extended space for information regarding past experience in working for the same company. If you had worked for this organization before, be sure to cast your reason for leaving in the best possible light. If you were let go because of substandard work, you should not be applying to the same place of business because your reference can easily be checked. Reason for leaving could be: "Hired on a temporary or seasonal basis," "Returned to college," or "Left to get high-paying job."

With regard to employment history, always begin with the present or last job rather than in the reverse order. The exception can happen, though, and at times a form will instruct you to proceed in reverse chronological order. Always follow the instructions on the form to the letter. Do not deviate. The employer calls the shots, not the applicant. Note that many forms ask for the month as well as the year. There is never a need to be so specific as to the exact day of the month you began and the exact day you stopped unless you have the turn of mind of an accountant and are applying for a very detailed position. It will not go against you, but it is not necessary to go into more detail than month and year.

It is important to list the name of your supervisor. If the person has left the company or you have become aware of the fact that the person is now deceased, note this fact. Perhaps, you can substitute the name of another superior, for instance the head of your department, even though you usually reported to your immediate supervisor. You may also give the name of a coworker or anyone who is familiar with the quality of your work. Before going to a site to fill out an application, do your homework and check that the reference firm's address and phone number are still the same.

Some students in my class were confused when an application asked whether or not they had been bonded. Well, if they had, they would have remembered. Bonded means you have a back up in funds to replace any money or funds you may be required to handle as part of your job. A driver of a Brinks truck has to be bonded. The next question asks whether the applicant has been convicted of a felony. If you have been convicted of a lesser crime than a felony, you can honestly answer "no" to this question. Furthermore, if you have ever been arrested for a felony and have not been convicted, again "no" is the proper response. Some applications ask whether you have ever been arrested. This is no longer a legally admissible question. You only have to report convictions, not arrests. Some people have balked at this question, thinking they have to explain every traffic ticket they have ever received.

Women who are married must be careful to note whether or not previous work was performed under a maiden name. If so, it is important to note that you worked under a maiden name under each company for which you did so. If you have shortened your name or you have used an alias, be sure to note when and where so your records can be properly checked and credited. This also holds true for high school and college transcripts. I once lost out on a valuable interview because the college that issued my bachelor's degree could not send my transcript. I had forgotten to mention my maiden name and the college had no listing of my married name, which I had used to sign the letter requesting my transcript.

Every application asks for military information or history. If you are a woman, just list N/A unless you have indeed served in the military. Many men have not served in the military and the N/A applies.

The best applications I have seen are written in simple language and the questions are straightforward. These forms allow sufficient space in which to write without having to cramp your style and subsequently have points taken off because your finished application appears messy. Well-designed applications also afford applicants the opportunity to provide appropriate personal touches. For example, some forms encourage applicants to include additional information that might be pertinent to their employment. If you are lucky enough to be given this opportunity, don't ignore it. In the space provided, write something positive about your personality or experience. Don't leave this section blank!

Always read carefully any preemployment statement that you are asked to sign. Note that many "Preemployment Statements" require you to sign that you understand a drug test and a negative result therefrom are required as conditions of employment. Don't squawk later that you do not wish to submit to a drug test—you've already indicated your permission by having signed the form.

When an application form asks you when you will be available to start your new job, think of the actual date you could begin work. If you are not certain as to the exact date, you could list August 6 to 8, 19__. Application forms that simply state "When can you begin work?" leave themselves open to a vague response such as "as soon as possible" or "anytime." Such an answer reflects poorly upon the applicant. If he or she hasn't as yet given notice, then it would be unethical for the person to simply walk off the present job. A thoughtful person gives at least a 2-week notice so that the company has time to hire a replacement. Never sound desperate or needy, even if you really are. Keep up a confident front. If you don't have confidence in yourself, other people will not have confidence in you.

In "Education Information," many forms begin with high school. Be sure to list the zip code with the address of the school. Applications that don't specifically ask for the address of the school but that allow space for such information should be filled out with the complete address of the school. This makes it easier for the human resource expert to check on any information regarding your schooling. Always list the type of degree you have earned and the field in which you earned it. Not just B.A., but B.A. in history. Don't overlook Special Certifications and Publications. Before you go job hunting you should delve into your scrapbook or your drawer of special achievements to gather together a complete list of any honors, awards, special projects, and papers that you have amassed. Make a list of them and take the list when you apply for a job. Not every project, of course, will be relevant to the job for which you are applying. That's why carrying the full list will allow you to select those special projects that are important to this job application.

Disclosure and Testing

Perhaps, the question of disclosure is the most vexing problem encountered in the job-search process because disclosing a disability immediately might turn off a prospective employer, but failing to disclose it at all will result in the employee not getting accommodations that may be necessary or at least greatly helpful. But, no matter, when you choose to do so, make the disclosure with candor and forthrightness, adding a touch of humor or philosophy to help the interviewer in identifying you as a person—a person apart from the disability. An easier way out is when a third-party makes the disclosure. As Pat Gibsen of Preferred Staffing puts it, "As a liaison between the employer and the job candidate, I am not at liberty to disclose unless I have been given written permission from the applicant." In the event that a translator would be necessary in the interview, Gibsen would let that be known to the potential employer and Gibsen would assist, if necessary, in locating a translator. When a third person is speaking for you, it is an affirmation of the fact that you can do the job for which you're applying. And in the case of the private employment agency, the agency does not make money unless it places you. So, why would an agency spend its time on a candidate it thought could not do the job? Gibsen reminds his job candidates with disabilities to use positive phrases throughout the interview such as "I have," "I will," "I can," rather than "possibly," "maybe," or "sometimes." Don't speak in a weak voice. This conveys the idea that you are not a healthy, strong person. Speak with energy and vigor to reflect your energy to accomplish whatever is asked of you on a job.

Russ Conte, job counselor at the Chicago Private Industry Council, says that those with physical disabilities must be fully prepared if they expect to be successful in a job search. Have professionally prepared résumés. He cites an actual example of a woman who submitted a résumé, citing within it her experience with a carnival in Wisconsin. For years of experience, she listed 7,000 and wondered why she was not getting replies to the résumés she had sent out. Also, says, Conte, you'd be surprised at the number of candidates who never get a single reply from a résumé because they fail to list their return address or list an improper one or a former address.

Testing

Do not be surprised if you are asked to take a series of tests. Many tests are aimed at sampling your skills. You may be asked to type a certain letter or copy a form while being timed. Or, you may be asked to produce a document according to certain specifications while using Windows. Once when interviewing candidates for a 10-key adding machine for a bank position, I actually had finalist candidates demonstrate their ability in front of me using the actual machine they would be working on. In addition, if you are in a field such as art, architecture, public relations, or advertising, prepare a sample book so that you can bring it to the initial and/or subsequent interviews.

Do not be surprised if you are asked to take a math test, spelling test, or reading test. Applicants for positions in medical facilities are often given a test to determine the degree of their familiarity with medical terms. Legal secretaries may be tested as to their familiarity with legal terms. Every employer values someone who can read and comprehend and who can do simple arithmetic. You will not be given geometry, trigonometry, and calculus tests unless you are applying for an actuarial or pure mathematics position. But office work clearly requires the ability to add, subtract, multiply, and divide with accuracy and a fair amount of speed. You may be tested on competency in working with decimals and fractions. All you probably need to do is to get a grade-school or high-school math book and review. If you feel nervous, you might take a quick brushup course or hire a tutor. People who can do math in addition to being able to read take precedence over those who cannot figure. Also, when math is required as part of the job description, a higher salary is usually indicated. So it makes sense to brush up on math.

If you are scheduled for a test, try to get a book from a book store on test taking or GED preparation.

Profiles

For individuals who have severe disabilities, a profile can serve as an enhancement to résumés. A vocational profile paints a composite picture of a potential employee's skills, experiences, available supports, preferences, needs, and living situation. Information contained in the vocational profile differs from that obtained through more formalized vocational assessments. According to Caven S. Mcloughlin, Ph.D. et al, editors of *Job Development and Training for Persons with Severe Handicaps*, published by Paul H. Brookes Co., 1987, the vocational profile consists of already existing information rather than information developed solely for the purposes of evaluation. The profile is used exclusively as a guide for matching an individual to an appropriate job and is not intended to exclude a person from a certain job.

The use of the profile frees the applicant from the necessity of taking standardized or norm-referenced tests as a means of proving his or her readiness. Readiness to begin work is assumed of all applicants. Information is presented from a person's entire life and not from one or more brief samples of "work" performance. The use of a profile indicates a belief that a person's skills, experiences, available supports, preferences and needs, and living situation are not captured accurately or comprehensively on a standardized checklist. A format composed of open-ended categories allows each person to be described in a unique manner. Implicit in these statements is a belief that there is a danger lurking in any effort to determine systematically the best job for an individual. Many researchers and practitioners have noted that traditional assessment/matching procedures simply do not work for persons with severe disabilities.

The Interview

The interview is still another test of your ability to win that coveted job offer. Don't blow it! While you cannot ensure you will be the chosen one, you can do a lot to increase your chances of success.

You have only one chance to make a first impression. The day before your scheduled interview, decide what clothes you will wear. If you have time to make a dry run to the place where you will be interviewing for a peek at the styles, fine! People tend to like people who look like themselves. The interviewer will think that you fit in. You want to strive for good business taste. When in doubt, stick with a traditional dark or neutral-colored suit. Be concerned with colors. Bright colors are high-energy and will be fine if you are applying for sales or creative work, but if you are applying as a financial analyst or computer repairer, you need to appear more businesslike. Gray, black, or a conservative blue are colors that will reflect a businesslike you. Beards are iffy. Some companies approve of beards, but many shy away from anything but the clean-shaven look. To be sure, it's best to stay away from beards or mustaches until you land the job. However, if you feel that it's your trademark, your style, your "you," then go ahead. You may never fit in with this particular company. It is better to know that fact now before being hired as beardless and being unhappy. You will spend most of your day at your work so you must be comfortable about your personal appearance.

Be sure to have your face well-scrubbed and your hair attractively groomed. If you've worn your hair the same way since junior high, now may be the time to consult a stylist. You wouldn't frame a beautiful painting in a plastic frame. Then, why present a nice face in a dowdy frame? Your hair literally frames your face. If you haven't much hair left, you should still go in for a consultation on how to make the best of what you have. Is there anything businesslike about a balding man tieing his hair in a long, gray ponytail fastened by a rubber band? Avoid heavy make-up, but do make up. Be sure you have brushed your teeth and taken a breath mint or two. Bathe either the night before or take a quick shower in the morning. Be fresh. Avoid chewing gum, your tongue, or your nails, even if nervous. Certainly, don't smoke prior to your interview. Most smoke lingers and many companies now view smokers with some disfavor.

Attitude is all! If you had to work 8 hours a day, 5 days a week, 12 months a year next to someone who complained all day, talked loudly to his friends, answered all your questions with sarcasm or a grunt, would you want to work next to him or her, regardless of how skilled the person was? No, you would not. Then, why not be the person you would like to work next to? A pleasant smile can deflect a coworker's hesitancy or fear of approaching you. A twinkle in the eye attracts people because it signals happiness and goodwill. Laugh and the world laughs with you is no idle statement. With the trend toward violence escalating in the workplace, no one wishes to hire a hostile person seething with rage. There has been a renewed interest in teamwork within the workplace. Teamwork requires a positive, constructive, cooperative attitude. Team-work requires listening creatively. People with chips on their shoulders tend to have their ears blocked also. The only time a nasty attitude may help is if you are applying for the job of repossessor or warrant server.

Watch your speech. Because of your type of physical disability, your speech may not be as clear as you might like. For that reason, be sure to speak at an average rather than fast rate. Speaking more slowly allows a person to speak more distinctly. If it takes you a while to form your words, don't become flustered or say "um" or make odd vocal sounds. Just pause until you can gather your thoughts. After all, you are not engaged in a public-speaking contest. Under the stress of interviewing, many people tend to rush, and their speech begins to suffer. Take your time. You worked hard for this interview, and the interviewer will give you sufficient time to formulate your thoughts. Speaking too quickly or too fast in response to a question may make the interviewer believe that you give answers off the top of your head and that you are not a person to make a thoughtful, considered judgment. Better to think before you speak.

What if you didn't understand the question or the implication of the question? Don't take a wild stab at an answer. Simply ask the interviewer to repeat the question or suggest that you are not certain where the question is leading. If he or she is a good interviewer, he or she will recast the question for you. Besides, it will give you additional time to contemplate your answer.

Be prepared for the interviewer to ask how you heard of the company. This is an open invitation for you to praise the company. "I have always used your products." "I know Joe Smith in the Purchasing Department. He's my neighbor and often talks highly about the company." "I read your annual report and I was very impressed with. . . ." "Your stock has shown a steady increase over the years." You should have looked up some information concerning the company before you applied. If nothing else, while you sat in the waiting room for your interview, you could have looked through any available company literature. You could have asked questions of the receptionist, if all else failed. I remember an interview with a company that was new to the area and I hadn't been able to get any information about its products before I was scheduled for an interview. When the interviewer peered over his glasses at me, asking how I had heard of the company, I took a calculated risk. Looking him straight in the eye, I said, "Hasn't everyone heard of your company?"

Of course, it goes without saying that you must be on time, preferably a bit early on the day of your interview. This is difficult for anyone who must rely on public transportation, which is unreliable or on an agency vehicle or van. What you cannot closely control, you will have to make wide allowances for. Leave twice as early as you think you should. For instance, if in the best of times you can make it to a particular location in about an hour, allow 2 hours. Murphy of Murphy's Law is just around the corner. This will be the one day that the bridge across the river gets stuck in the "up" position, or the agency van blows a tire, or the bus breaks down or rushes past you without stopping. Don't let the strain of trying to make it on time get you up into such a lather that you cannot project a calm, confident exterior. No one wants to hire a harried employee who is out of breath and wild-eyed.

It is not your position to interview. You are to be interviewed. This means that you must take your cues from the person interviewing you. Allow the person to complete his question or statement before you intrude with your comments. Stick to the point of what he or she is asking. For instance, if he says, "Tell me a little about yourself," make it a little. He has already seen your résumé and application. Starting with the story of your birth will fail to grab his attention. Tell about yourself in relation to the position for which you are applying. For example, keep your senses alert before and during the interview. If you see or hear a busy office, start your story by telling how you enjoy doing multiple tasks and like to work around busy people. If, on the other hand, the office is quiet and subdued, talk about how you enjoy concentrating on your tasks at hand and are very self-directed, although you enjoy relating to fellow workers during lunch and on breaks.

This may also be a good time to bring up the question of your disability. You might say, "I am a very patient person. When I had my accident which caused my paralysis, I knew it would take much time and effort to improve and to reach a level of self-sufficiency, but I realized there were dedicated people to help me and with determination and some pain I was able to improve to the point where I felt I could handle my job and compete with the best of them." Or, you might say that because you've had your disability from birth, you have learned not only to accept your disability but emphasized your ability. Because your sight was always weak, you made a special effort to protect your hearing and learned how to listen to people.

Because the interviewer is not allowed to ask you direct questions about your health, it is always effective to get in points about your good attendance and punctuality at whatever point in the interview you can stick in this information. Certainly, you can mention this when you are asked whether you think you can do the job or you are asked, "Why should we hire you?" Sometimes, toward the end of an interview, you are asked, "What else should we know about you?" That's another good time to put in a good word about your health and your strength. You might say that "because walking isn't my strong point, I've learned to organize and plan carefully to save steps." You might also say words to the effect that "if

I weren't in general good health, I wouldn't have the strength and energy to put up with my condition."

Interview Questions

Study the following interview questions. They are quite typically encountered regardless of the position applied for:

What are your goals for 5 years from now? Ten years from now?

What do you consider your greatest achievements?

What are the tasks you most enjoy in your job? Which would you rather not do?

What type of boss are you comfortable working under? Would you object to working for a woman boss?

What are your three weakest points? (Be careful here. If the position is a demanding one, answer that you tend to work too hard or you don't take your breaks or you rush through lunch.)

What motivates you?

What do you like to do in your leisure hours? (Don't mention anything dangerous or anything that might be considered odd such as being in a flying saucer study group or learning Latin or collecting sand.) Reading, watching television, or seeing old movies are fine, if you can't think of anything on the spur of the moment. Volunteering is a very good answer, especially in big business which is presently committed to having its employees engage in volunteerism. Besides, volunteering makes you appear to be empathetic to the needs of others and a team player.

Are you furthering your education or do you look forward to additional training? This question should be answered in the affirmative. Be sure to mention any recent training you've undertaken even if it's a one-night lecture in a field related to your occupation.

By all means, try to be yourself during the interview. What good will it be to get the job under false pretenses? I remember a friend of mine who had lost his job and had been applying for several months before he was able to snag an interview. The company to which he applied and was granted an interview was well-known for its reliance on workers who were willing to travel at a moment's notice and who didn't mind working overtime. My friend got nervous on airplanes and liked to eat his meals at regular times and to keep a regular bedtime schedule. But, desperate for the job, he said he didn't mind a flexible schedule—in fact, he looked forward to it. And he got it. But, 3 months into the job he knew he had had it. His health was affected. He couldn't sleep well, and he was beginning to lose his temper with customers. Before long, he and the company had a mutual parting-of-the-ways, and then he was worse off than before. Not only was he without a job, but now his last job reference would not give a good recommendation, and when he had to list the period of his employment, some 6 months, it stood out like a sore thumb on his résumé.

The interview is a mutual selecting process. If you like the company, chances are it will like you. If you see red flags during the interview, you are alerting yourself to danger. Your subconscious is telling you that danger lies ahead. Have the confidence to listen to your inner self. It is you and you alone who must hold this job and face your boss and coworkers hour after hour, day after day. What is someone else's cup of tea may turn out to be your vial of poison. Remember, the fact that you have now been offered an interview means that you are doing something right—you must be submitting an attractive résumé and cover letter so it stands to reason if you have one interview, others will soon follow. Keep up your confidence. If you could join an informal or formal group at a YMCA or church or nonprofit organization that was composed of unemployed people or set up your own support group, you would see that rejection is just part of the normal job search process. By sharing your troubles and triumphs with others in the same boat, you will keep up your spirits and rise to the next challenging interview. If you lose hope, you will most likely project a lack of confidence on your next interview and your lack of confidence will rub off on your interviewer. Remember interviewers like to hire winners not losers. If you lose hope, you may be tempted to take the next offer. You can only accept one offer. By taking the first to come along, you may miss out on a truly good job offer that is tailor-made for you and your talents. Whenever the students in my career course finished an interview and had not received a job offer, I would always tell them it doesn't make a bit of difference except to your pride to have been turned down a hundred times. You only need one good offer!

In times of fierce job competition, it takes time to find the right job—a lot of time. The average for middle managers who have lost their jobs to find another job is from 3 to 6 months. If you are aiming for an entry-level job, it will probably, but not necessarily, take less time because companies are outplacing senior talent to be able to save money by offering lessor salaries to relatively inexperienced employees. The type of job for which you are searching makes a difference as to time you will need to find the right employer. For example, the largest category of employers, which is the service industry and the area of general office workers and clerks, has continual job turn-over, in addition to the fact that this type of employment absorbs thousands upon thousands of workers. But, if you are headed toward a field where many are called but few are chosen, such as museum work or zoology, you may have to wait your turn with greater patience. While I do not advocate studying for careers that employ the most people, there is merit in considering which fields are growing and which are stagnating as one of the factors in overall career planning. The next chapter is designed to explore the hot spots in the employment picture.

Mock Interviews

Many programs for those with physical disabilities stress mock interviews. Enrollees in the United Cerebral Palsy Infinitec Training Program in Chicago, Illinois, were given a minimum of three mock interview sessions. Students took turns interviewing as well as being interviewed. The instructor often took the position of interviewer. Interviewing practice began as soon as the student had completed his or her résumé and had been coached in interviewing skills. After each practice interview, which was held at a conference table in the training classroom, the students not being interviewed were asked to comment on the one being interviewed. What could be improved? Sometimes, it was speaking too softly. Other times, the one being interviewed had failed to answer the question asked, going off in a different direction instead. One student out of nervousness tended to roll her eyes and look all around the room. The only place the student didn't look was at the interviewer. This student, after having heard this criticism, began to practice more direct eye contact during each subsequent interview. Another student brought a clunky purse to her practice interview and almost hit the interviewer as she swung around, trying to find a place to set down her purse. She was advised to bring a smaller purse or a briefcase to her real interview. Other students found it difficult to answer questions concerning what role they saw for themselves in 5 years or 10 years. They were asked to write down a few of their goals and look at them often so as to be prepared to answer questions relating to their future work aspirations.

Some students were stumped when the interviewer turned over the question period to the interviewee. What was it that the interviewee wished to ask the interviewer? Here's where you need to have a few stock questions such as:

What type of advancement might I be offered if I successfully perform this job?

What benefits does your company offer?

What type of training programs do you have?

Do not directly inquire about insurance because the interviewer might then believe that you will be a big benefit drain on the company. Many interviewers already believe that those with physical disabilities will be costly in terms of company insurance so you don't wish to fan the flames.

If the interviewer dances around the question of insurance, you might mention that you have supplementary insurance or that your spouse has an insurance policy that covers you or that on your last job you never needed to use insurance.

Never ask about sick days because some employers believe that those with physical disabilities tend to use many sick days going to the doctor or the therapist or because they are sickly. Don't play into this prejudice by asking questions pertaining to health benefits or days off.

Some employers may fear hiring a disabled individual because of concern about a higher-on-the-job injury rate than other employees, despite good safety training. Be sure to mention that ergonomic research can make all workplaces accessible and safer for both disabled and nondisabled workers. Further, second injury funds provide financial relief to employers who otherwise would be unfairly forced to bear the burden of a claim. To qualify, the employer must establish that it meets the statutory requirements, which often include the employer's knowledge of a preexisting condition.

Before going on an interview, you should be aware that Congress encourages the hiring of several disadvantaged groups of employees through incentive programs to employers. For example, the Job Training Partnership Act provides subsidies to employers up to a specified percentage of wages for on-the-job training of eligible individuals. Similarly, the Internal Revenue Code provides employers of "targeted employees" a tax credit, calculated as a percentage of the employee's wages, subject to a cap.

Mark Matthews, professor of human development, University of Kansas, gives these tips. Convey to the employer the skills you have and the things you are capable of doing instead of just listing job titles or positions. For those who are young and for that reason have not had job experiences, list the things you've done, skills you've used in volunteering, things you've learned, difficult tasks you've accomplished and how you have learned to accommodate for those things that might be viewed as a disability by a potential employer.

Although you should be concerned with your clothes and other aspects of your appearance, you needn't make a fashion statement. "Well-dressed" in the context of a job interview means "understated," according to Jeffrey G. Allen, author of *Successful Job Search Strategies for the Disabled,* published by John Wiley & Sons, 1995. Allen says you can minimize the visual effect of your disability if you know the business uniform and wear it proudly. Select clothing that works with your disability: comfortable, durable, with simple lines tailored to your body contours.

Many people with disabilities don't have a lot of money to spend on clothes; these job seekers should frequent high-quality resale shops and Goodwill stores. Clothes can be altered to your disability; they don't have to be custom-made. Those companies that specialize in clothes for people with disabilities include Avenues at 1199 Avenida Acaso, Suite K, Camarillo, CA 93012. Some organizations provide shoes for those who require only a single shoe and foster exchanges to pair people with the same size shoes so they can split a pair. Others sell singles outright at greatly reduced prices.

Tom Thomson of Harper College gives two general principles for disclosure: 1. Don't disclose during the interview. There is time to disclose after an offer is made. 2. Whether to disclose or not to disclose is related to whether or not you will need an accommodation to accomplish your duties. Obviously, if you do not disclose, your employer is under no obligation to provide accommodations you may desire or need.

Furthermore, Thomson says that for those whose disability is noticeable, you must be prepared to deal effectively with questions or reactions arising out of the appearance factors of the disability. The use of humor is always effective. By displaying a sense of humor and a positive attitude toward your disability, you show the employer that you have come to terms with your disability and are ready to discuss the really important thing—your ability to do the job under consideration. By being at ease with your disability, you set the interviewer at ease, and the interview can proceed toward your abilities. If you require an interpreter on the interview, you should ask where the interpreter should sit, and it would also be helpful for you to mention to the interviewer whether the interviewer should speak to you or to the interpreter or to both of you. Try to discuss your disability in an off-handed way and, as soon as possible, get back on the track of why you are there: that is, to discuss why you should be chosen for the job. Your disability should not be the focus of the interview.

Generally speaking, Thomson says that if you must disclose your disability, wait until after the offer is made. Remember you are a pioneer in blazing the trail for others with disabilities. For that reason, you must be prepared to work harder, at least at the beginning of the job, until you are fully accepted as a team member. You are breaking new ground. You do not have to perform as a superperson, but you do have to be a bit better. You should be psychologically prepared that people will be checking you out. Be assertive, beginning with the interview.

The Workbook: A Self-Study Guide for Job Seekers, published by the Epilepsy Foundation of America, has a thorough discussion of the advantages and disadvantages associated with the timing of a disclosure. For instance, on a job application, if the employer is covered by the ADA or Rehabilitation Act, the request for information is voluntary. If covered by a state law, such questions may be legal. Advantages offered by disclosure on a job application are honesty and peace of mind. Disadvantages listed are that it might disqualify you with no further opportunity afforded to present yourself and your qualifications and it offers the potential for discrimination.

What about disclosure during an interview? *The Workbook* cites the same advantage as during a job application and adds that disclosure during an interview provides an opportunity to respond in person to specific issues related to the disability and can give you a chance to raise issues of accommodations you might need or to state that your disability does not interfere with your ability to perform the job. But, disadvantages are that it puts the responsibility on you to handle issues related to your disability in a clear nonthreatening way. Too much emphasis placed on the issue indicates a problem. You may take away from a discussion of your abilities to a discussion of disability.

How about disclosing after the interview when a job has been offered but prior to your start date? Again, honesty and peace of mind are the advantages. In addition, if the information disclosed changes the hiring decision, and you are sure of your ability to perform the job, there is legal recourse. But, it might lead to distrust with the personnel department and your eventual supervisor who is sure to hear about it.

Should you disclose after you begin work? This is an opportunity to prove yourself on the job before you disclose. It allows you to respond to questions regarding your disability posed by coworkers. Disadvantages are possible employer accusation of falsifying your application and the possibility of having difficulty such as a seizure before your coworkers learn how to react. It could change your interaction with your peers.

In the case of epilepsy, should you disclose following a seizure on the job? This gives you the opportunity to have proven yourself prior to the disclosure. If seizure affects employment status, but the seizures do not affect your ability to perform your job or do not affect your own safety or the safety of others, you may be protected by law. Here, again, you face possible employer accusation of having falsified your application and again there is the possibility that your coworkers will not have the knowledge to be able to react to your seizure. Then, too, epilepsy myths and mis-understandings may be perpetuated. If you choose to never disclose, the employer can't respond to your epilepsy unless you have a seizure. But, on the downside, you may increase your nervousness and fear of having a seizure on the job and if you have a seizure, you might be hurt by inappropriate first aid and, again, failure to disclose may perpetuate epilepsy myths and misunderstandings. Also, if you do not disclose a disability, your employer does not have to provide a reasonable accommodation for it.

In conclusion, a good résumé can get you in the door, but the interview is your chance to get the job. *Washingtonian Magazine* asked human resources directors at area companies their advice regarding tips on interviewing. The results, reported in the March 1996 issue of the magazine, are highlighted here:

- Winder Heller of System Planning Corporation in Arlington, Virginia, advises job seekers to follow up the mailing of a résumé with a phone call a week or so later to request an interview. He estimates that fewer than 5 percent of job applicants do this.

- Bill Barker of Techmatics, Inc. emphasizes the importance of researching the prospective employer. "Libraries are a good place to start, as are stock brokerage firms, which have databases on publicly traded companies. You can request the company to send an information packet. Then, after reading the information, compile a list of questions to ask during your interview. You'll be one of the few to take the time to do so.

- Karen Wall of BTG, Inc. says that even if the company's dress policy is casual, wear neat business attire. Your appearance shouldn't attract more attention than your credentials. "We're looking for someone who has the judgment to know what to wear," she said. She also advises getting the name of the interviewer correct. She counsels people to find the place before the day of the interview so you don't get lost and arrive late. Showing up 10 minutes ahead of scheduled time is ideal.

- Joel Itskowitz of Troy Systems, an Alexandria, Virginia, information technology company, tells interviewees to listen carefully to questions. Employers are looking for signs of intellectual curiosity. Have your questions tag on to what is said. Don't make them seem scripted or canned. Employers want confident, self-motivated people who will fit into their culture, according to Itskowitz. "Make eye contact . . . and smile. Project your enthusiasm for the job. Think of the interview as a conversation, not an interrogation. And don't forget to send a thank-you note."

CHAPTER SEVEN

TARGETING GROWTH INDUSTRIES FOR THE FUTURE

In the past, when the college degree was there, the jobs were there. For the past decade, this has been far from true. Education, mathematics, protective services, architecture, and communicative technologies majors will have to work diligently to find jobs. Students majoring in arts and letters will continue to find that opportunities are scarce. Many will then choose to go for advanced degrees as a result of not discovering a job to their liking.

Engineering, nursing, computer and information services, sales, and physical sciences will continue to have a good supply of jobs. Health careers over the next decade will offer enormous opportunities. This occupational area has the potential for the most rapid growth. According to the U.S. Department of Labor, the second fastest-growing occupational area requiring skill is the computer specialist, which has spin-off applications in other employment areas, such as accounting and engineering.

An area that is often overlooked is sales. Sales has tremendous potential for the right personality, regardless of major. A good salesperson is always in demand—in good times or bad. For example, sales positions alone are expected to generate more than 700,000 new jobs in the 1990s.

Gallaudet University in Washington, D.C., conducted a survey regarding the Class of 1993. It indicates that a major shift in employment-sector hiring began in 1992. For many years the federal government was the largest employer of Gallaudet graduates, who are deaf and hearing-impaired. But the downsizing of government has resulted in fewer new hires. Between 1991 and 1993, government positions held by Gallaudet respondents dropped from 30 percent to 11 percent.

Jobs in private, nonprofit, and educational institutions have shown steady increases. Full-time employment was down, and graduate school enrollment was up. Further education in graduate schools has shown a steady increase during the last several years, reflecting a national trend, while full-time employment within the first year of graduation slipped slightly to 56 percent, according to the survey. Part-time employment was high at 19.2 percent; 38.8 percent of the survey respondents enrolled in graduate or further education programs at 18 different colleges and universities. Of those in graduate school, 24 enrolled in education majors: deaf, sports, English, technology, elementary, and environmental; 5 in counseling: school, rehabilitation, mental health; 2 in administration and supervision; 3 in social work; 2 in psychology; 1 in public administration, and 1 in human resource management.

Those who were working full-time took jobs within the area of their majors. Placement varied—from accounting and biochemistry to computer science and education. The survey also inquired about job satisfaction. A 76 percent job satisfaction rate was recorded. The highest levels of satisfaction were reported from graduates working in government and private business. Eighty-one percent said they believed they were appropriately qualified for their jobs.

Author Jeremy Rifkin in his address at the opening session of the California Career Conference of November 1, 1995, declared that there will never be enough jobs in the new "knowledge sector" to absorb the millions let go in the manufacturing and service sectors. We will need only the cream of the crop—software will handle the rest of the work. Rifkin sees us moving toward a two-tiered society, with the top 20 percent operating in a cyberspace economy and the bottom 80 percent operating in marginal occupations or, at the very bottom, in prison.

He suggests redeployment of people to work in the nonprofit sector with the government providing retraining and income vouchers to help bring the income for their work to a decent level. Another solution he offers is a movement to a 30-hour workweek with the government providing financial incentives to employers.

American industry is rapidly fragmenting into three distinct economies: the Networked, the Kluge, and the Provincial, according to David Friedman, writing in *Inc.* magazine, February 1996. The Networked economy consists of densely packed concentrations of entrepreneurs and companies in urbanized areas that generate virtually all of the nation's globally competitive, high-wage industries. These highly specialized companies flourish because they can rapidly team up to manufacture products for world markets. Some examples are the small-scale, world-beating exporters and technology developers in California's "Silicon Valley" and San Diego, the Research Triangle biomedical centers in North Carolina, auto-production specialists in the Midwest.

The nation's Kluge economy—the concentration of public-sector bureaucracies, universities, and closely aligned private companies in government-related industries, like utilities or defense, exists virtually side by side with the Networked economy. Kluge, which is pronounced "klooj," is software programmers' slang for code that is an ill-assorted collection of poorly matching parts, forming a distressing whole or mess.

Watching from the sidelines in the growing southern and intermountain western regions of the country is America's Provincial economy—the back-office service providers, lower-wage earning, lower-skilled producers, and urban corporate refugees whose interests now dominate national politics.

The Networked economy, according to Friedman, is where a company wants to be. Of the three sectors, only this one offers the high wages, profits, and skills that improve our standard of living. The Provincial economy trades technological prowess and upward mobility for relatively rapid job growth in lower-paying, less-skilled activities. And the Kluge economy, built as it is on an increasingly shaky, discredited public-sector foundation, is the least likely place for a company to flourish in the 21st century.

The *Wall Street Journal* of January 23, 1996, cautioned those who plan to escape corporate downsizing by playing career lotto: "Not all start-up companies offer a clear path to riches or satisfaction." Here are the *Journal*'s tips for start-up dreamers:

Be realistic about the potential rewards

Bet on smart, experienced managers, not sexy technology

Get your finances in shape and make sure your family can handle what's ahead.

1994 to 2005 Employment

Nonfarm Job Growth

James C. Franklin, economist in the Office of Employment Projections, Bureau of Labor Statistics (BLS), has studied the employment outlook for

1994 to 2005 in terms of industry output and employment projections. Total employment is expected to grow at a much slower pace than the 1983 to 1994 rate. However, the service-producing sector is projected to lead employment growth among virtually all nonfarm wage and salary jobs.

All of the projected growth in nonfarm wage and salary employment at the major industry division level occurs in the service-producing sector, with the exception of employment gains in construction on the goods-producing side of the economy.

Even within the service-producing sector, employment growth is highly concentrated. Slightly more than two-thirds or 12 million of the 17.8-million job increase for the service-producing sector is in the services division. The addition of job growth for the retail trade at 2.7 million and government at 1.9 million to the services division accounts for 93 percent of the job gains in the service-producing sector. Just two industry groups—business services and health services—account for more than one-half the growth within the services division.

The transportation division is expected to add 476,000 jobs from 1994 to 2005. The trucking and warehousing industry accounted for more than half or 575,000 of those jobs. High productivity growth is also expected in the air transportation industry as air carriers adopt strategies to lower employment costs and increase plane load factors. During the 1983 to 1994 period, air transportation gained 293,000 jobs at an average annual rate of 4.6 percent. During the 1994 to 2005 period, employment in air transportation is expected to grow from 748,000 to 870,000 for a gain of 122,000.

Employment in communications reached a 1.4 million peak in 1982. Most of this employment was in telecommunications. Since 1982, employment for all of communications remained flat at around 1.3 million. The telecommunications share has gradually declined. The future shape of the telecommunications industry is highly uncertain. The communications infrastructure is built on rapidly changing computing technology. Having been highly regulated in the past, the communications industry is looking forward to less regulation, but the extent of deregulation remains unclear. Both the evolving technology and the unsettled regulatory issues make projecting output and employment quite problematic. But demand for information and communications will continue to be vital to our economic interests, no matter how the issues of deregulation are decided. Even with the expectation of productivity growth, employment is expected to decline slightly by 70,000 from the 1994 level of 1.3 million.

Both wholesale trade and retail trade, with the exception of eating and drinking places, are expected to have healthy productivity gains. The productivity increases are traced to applications of inventory control and computerized order systems and from restructuring of the sales work forces. Wholesale trade is projected to gain 419,000 jobs from the 1994 level of slightly more than 6.1 million to reach slightly less than 6.6 million in 2005. Jobs in retail trade, excluding eating and drinking places, are projected to increase by 1.6 million from the 1994 level of 13.4 million to the 2005 level of 15.0 million. The projected job growth is significantly less than the growth of 2.8 million during the 1983 to 1994 period. On an average annual basis, the projected employment growth rate is 1.1 percent. Output for retail trade is projected to grow at an average annual rate of 2.7 percent.

Real output for eating and drinking places is projected to grow at an annual rate of 1.1 percent between 1994 and 2005. Productivity is expected to remain flat, while employment growth is projected to pace output growth for a job gain of 1.0 million during the 1994 to 2005 projection period. This represents a slowing of employment growth for eating and drinking places as compared with the 1983 to 1994 period when employment grew by 2.0 million jobs.

Depository institutions such as banks, credit unions, and savings and loans are expected to have high rates of productivity growth through the projected period. Mergers and consolidations in the industry will continue, resulting in employment loss. Unprofitable branches will be closed, and operations will be combined and centralized. Additionally, banks will continue to expand their use of automatic tellers and other computerized means of providing customer services, instead of hiring additional employees. The real output of depository institutions has a projected annual growth rate of 2.0 percent, while employment is projected to decline at an annual rate of 0.9 percent. The number of jobs declining in depository institutions is projected at 190,000. Thus, we have another example of automation replacing people. Productivity through automation results in an industry needing fewer human employers.

The security and commodity brokers industry has higher-than-average projected rates of growth for both output and employment. The projected annual growth rate for employment is 2.8 percent and for real output, 7.0 percent. This makes the securities industry one of the fastest-growing industries in terms of real output—second only to computer manufacturing. The projected rate of growth, however, represents a slowing of the 10 percent rate of growth during the 1983 to 1994 period. Similarly, the projected 2.8 percent of employment growth is a decline from the 4.8 percent rate during the 1983 to 1994 period. The gain in jobs for the security and commodity brokers industry is an expected 182,000, rising to 700,000 from the 1994 level of 518,000.

Employment for insurance carriers is expected to increase by 82,000 to slightly more than 1.6 million in 2005. Output is expected to increase at an annual rate of 1.9 percent, slightly slower than the 2.2 percent rate for total output. Employment in the industry for insurance agents, brokers, and service is projected to increase only slightly, from 686,000 to 702,000 for a gain of only 16,000. Output is projected to grow at a rate of 2.6 percent.

Employment in the real estate industry is projected to increase from 1.3 million in 1994 to 1.5 million in 2005—an annual rate of 0.7 percent. This is a significant slowing of employment growth compared with the 1983 to 1994 period, when employment grew at a 2.9 percent annual rate. Computer applications such as on-line multiple-listing services will con-tribute greatly to this industry's productivity increases.

The Services Division

Employment growth in the services division is overwhelmingly the most important result of these projections. The services division is a subset of the service-producing part of the economy, consisting of businesses that supply services, excluding transportation, finance, insurance, real estate, and retail and wholesale trade. Of the 16.8 million increase in total nonfarm wage and salary jobs in the projection period, the services di-vision is expected to account for 12.0 million of these jobs. Employment in the services division has a projected annual growth rate of 3.0 percent or more than twice that of all nonfarm wage and salary jobs. As a share of total nonfarm wage and salary employment, the services division jobs accounted for 21.4 percent in 1983; 27.2 percent in 1994, and is projected to have a 32.0 percent share in 2005.

Within the services division, most of the projected job growth is in business services, with a job gain of 3.8 million, and health services, with a gain of 3.1 million. Together, these industry groups account for 57 percent of the job growth in the services division. The industry group with the third largest projected job gains within the services division is social services at 1.4 million. Together, these three industry groups account for

69 percent of the job growth in the services division and almost half or 49 percent of the total nonfarm wage and salary job growth.

The BLS has developed projections for more than 500 detailed occupations. The growth rates range from an increase of 119 percent for personal and home care aides to a decline of 71 percent for letterpress operators. Employment change is analyzed from the projected rate of growth for an occupation and the size of the numerical change. The employment of occupational therapy assistants and aides is projected to grow very rapidly (by 82 percent) between 1994 and 2005, but will increase by just 13,000 jobs. In contrast the employment of secretaries, which is expected to grow by only 12 percent, will increase by 390,000 jobs.

The fastest-growing occupations after personal and home care aides and home aides is that of systems analysts, computer engineers, physical and corrective therapy assistants and aides, electronic pagination systems workers, occupational therapy assistants and aides, physical therapists, residential counselors, and human service workers. The next grouping is occupational therapists, manicurists, medical assistants, paralegals, medical records technicians, and teachers in special education.

Patterns of Change

A review of the patterns of occupational change from 1983 to 1994 and those projected for from 1994 to 2005 reveals several noteworthy developments, according to Ronald E. Kutscher, associate commissioner, BLS Office of Employment Projections, writing in *Monthly Labor Review*, November 1995. Over the historical period, significantly faster growth and a resulting increase in the share of employment is noted for the executive, administrative, and managerial occupations; professional specialty occupations; marketing and sales occupations; and service occupations. In contrast, several occupational categories increased very slowly. Included in the latter are agriculture, forestry, fishing, and related occupations; precision production and craft occupations; and operators, fabricators, and laborers occupations.

Two groups—technicians and related support occupations and the administrative support occupations, including electrical—increased at a rate about equal to that of the overall economy. Their share, consequently, increased only modestly. An important element of the composition of changes by major occupations during the historical period was the increase of occupations requiring postsecondary education or training, except for service occupations. Further, occupations requiring the least education and/or training had significant declines in their shares of overall employment.

Three groups show important changes from their most recent past:

1. The group with the most significant change is administrative support occupations, including clerical. It employment shares increased very modestly during the 1983 to 1994 period, but is expected to decline 1.7 percent points during the 1994 to 2005 period, despite a projected slight increase in employment. This important change reflects the expected impact of office automation on many clerical occupations.

2. A modest departure from past trend is expected for the executive, administrative, and managerial occupations. While this group's employment share will increase during the 1994 to 2005 period, the increase is projected to be much smaller than that from 1983 to 1994. This slowing reflects that an important segment of downsizing has been and is expected to be directed at managerial occupations. It is offset in part by the shift in employment to services where smaller establishments require relatively more managers than do larger enterprises.

3. Another occupational group with a notable departure from its 1983 to 1994 trend is the professional specialty group. This group gained employment share during the 1983 to 1994 period, but its projected growth during the 1994 to 2005 period is twice as fast as that in the overall economy. As a result, its share of employment will increase more rapidly than in the past. The growth reflects, in particular, expected employment increases in the teaching occupations and professional health care occupations, a result of expected increases in school age and in older populations that demand these services.

Projected changes in the other major occupational groups are expected to more closely mirror their 1983 to 1994 pattern. One group, which includes agriculture, forestry, fishing, and related occupations, is projected to decline absolutely, attributable to a very modest decline among self-employed farmers. This affirms that the fastest-growing occupational group, except for service occupations, are those requiring more education. The two occupational groups projected to have the largest absolute increases in employment are professional specialty and service occupations, groups at the opposite ends of the spectrum in terms of educational requirements and earnings.

William Goodman, an economist in the BLS Office of Employment and Unemployment Statistics, reports in the August 1995 issue of *Monthly Labor Review* that employment growth in the day care industry since 1972 has been much more rapid than the growth of most industries. Overall, the number of day care jobs has grown by approximately 250 percent or 375,000 jobs. Unlike most industries, child day care continued to expand vigorously during the recessions of 1973 to 1975 and 1990 to 1991.

Employment in the day care industry as estimated from the BLS survey includes not only employees directly caring for children, but all employees of day care companies. According to the BLS Occupational Employment Survey, 8 percent of the child care industry's employees are managers or administrators; 15 percent are clerical workers; 33 percent are teachers, and 25 percent are child care workers. The remaining 19 percent are widely scattered among a variety of other occupations.

Recently the population of children has not only increased, but has accelerated in growth. Although future trends of most of the forces that have driven employment in the industry cannot be predicted with confidence, extensive population projections from the Bureau of the Census show a pattern of deceleration followed by a decline in the population of young children.

Federal child-care spending on certain major programs jumped by 84 percent in 1991 after expansion of JOBS Child Care, Transitional Child Care, and Head Start programs and creation of "at risk" programs and the Child Care and Development Block Grants. Since then, the combined funding of these programs and Project Head Start has been increasing by about 20 percent annually. But in 1995, their combined funding grew by only 3 percent.

The number of workers in the private day care industry has more than doubled since its employment was first estimated in 1972, increasing by nearly 400,000 jobs. Growth in the U.S. population of young children will decelerate in the next 5 years, and this population will start to decline by 2003. As a result, the industry is unlikely to sustain the rapid growth it has experienced since 1972.

Training

One advantage of working in large companies is that you are much more likely to receive employer-provided training according to results from a new survey from the BLS, as reported by Harley J. Frazis and others in *Monthly Labor Review*, May 1995. Interest in the role that training plays in the economy has grown in recent years. Concerns about the competitiveness of U.S. labor in the globalized economy, the weak performance of labor productivity since 1973, and the widening gap between the earnings of high school graduates and college-educated workers are among the reasons behind the movement toward increased training in the work force.

Employer-provided training is formal training planned in advance that has a defined curriculum. The training can take place in a variety of settings, including the classroom. In contrast, a spontaneous demonstration of a job skill to answer a question posed by an employee to a supervisor would be considered as informal or on-the-job training.

The data covered:

Orientation training, which provides information on personnel and workplace practice and overall company policies

Safety and health training, which provides information on safety and health hazards, procedure, and regulations

Apprenticeship training, a structured process by which an individual becomes a skilled worker through a combination of classroom instruction and on-the-job training

Basic skills training, which means instruction in reading and writing and arithmetic and basic English language skills

Workplace practices training, which is training in policies and practices that affect employee relations or the work environment

Job skills training that upgrades employee skills, extends their skills, or qualifies workers for a job.

The BLS survey was mailed to nearly 12,000 establishments. The sample size was 11,068. A typical questions asked was, "During 1993, did your establishment provide or finance formal training in basic reading, writing, arithmetic, or English language skills for any of its employees?"

The provision of formal training varied somewhat across industries. Slightly less than 60 percent of all construction establishments offered such training in 1993, compared with roughly three out of four establishments in each of the following industry groups: finance, insurance, and real estate; services; and transportation, communications, and public utilities.

The three types of job skills most commonly taught through formal training programs were:

1. Sales and customer relations skills

2. Management skills

3. Computer skills.

Establishments used a variety of methods for selecting employees for formal skills training. During 1993, more than one-half of all establishments that provided formal job skills training made the training available to all employees. About one in four reported having employees volunteer for training, and a similar percentage chose those with potential for promotion. The proportion of large establishments that chose employees who had deficiencies in various skills was nearly twice that of all establishments.

The evidence regarding the relationship between training and the size of the establishment indicates that employees of large firms are more likely to receive job training than are employees of small firms. One reason given is that large firms are more likely to train because of economies of scale. The average per-employee costs of developing and conducting formal training declines as more employees participate. Another theory is that large employers are more likely to take risks and are more willing to train many employees, including those that are likely to quit after training. Some sociologists have suggested that large firms train their workers because they have more problems creating cohesive work environments than do smaller firms. The proportion of workers in a company who work part-time may have an effect on training because the payoff to training is less with workers who would use their skills for fewer hours each week.

Change and Synergy

In the modern marketplace, no company big or small is immune to significant change. During 1995, according to James A. Belohlav, an associate professor in the Kellstadt Graduate School of Business, De Paul University, Chicago, and writing in *Business Horizons*, March–April 1996, about 5 percent of the companies appearing in *Fortune*'s listing of largest businesses had not been there the previous year. During the past decade, the *Fortune* listing shows an average rate of change that has been quite consistent—about 5 percent per year. The competitive effects of the global marketplace, information technology, and the work force revolution have combined to produce change so continuous that it has come to be viewed as a normal part of business life.

Belohlav explained, "To be competitive, a business needs to know what is changing. To remain competitive over the longer term, a business needs to know how and why change is occurring. Corporate strategy of the future is reinventing business itself in search of competitive essence."

According to Belohlav, competitive differences will come as a result of synergy. Synergy is a condition in which the whole is greater than the sum of its parts. In a synergistic relationship, something more or extra is created. A corporation is a system consisting of main effects and interactions. The main effects are the functional activities such as marketing, operations, and finance. Today, companies are trying to maximize the main effects within their organizations. This results in increased employment opportunities in these business areas. Belohlav notes that being more efficient in any single function is no longer a competitive advantage because more companies are capable of doing so. He says that success in the future will be based on an ability to understand the interactions among the main effects of the organization and interactions with the environment. It is not enough to merely survive—a company must adapt. Now more than ever, employees within large corporations must learn to adapt to ever-changing market conditions. Their survival in the company may be determined by how fast they learn and how fast they adapt to new conditions, even though large companies due to their size cannot react as quickly as small corporations or businesses. The question for you is: Would you rather be on an ocean cruiser or a sailboat?

In big business, quality management has been the cry since the 1990s. The learning organization appears to be emerging as the direction of the future. To be successful, companies must train people to do the best job now and educate them to be the people the company will need in the future.

How will the enabling traits and requisite skills become incorporated into existing firms? Jean-Pierre Ergas, former chairman and chief executive officer (CEO) of the world's largest packaging company, American

National Can, is quoted as saying that the role of business functions will diminish at the corporate level. Within the world-class enterprise of the future, the most important roles at the corporate level, according to Ergas, will be given over to cash management, reengineering, auditing, and human resources. He claims that emphasizing human resources will ensure that the most important asset of the organization, its people, are properly used as individuals, within teams, and as part of larger groupings.

Competitive pressures of the 1980s and 1990s have been felt more strongly in the major industries that are dominated by very large firms. Large U.S. corporations were the first to feel the impact of international competition and to suffer its devastating effects. Because of the competitive pressures created by Japanese companies, quality became a competitive weapon in the 1980s in most industries. Its role in economic life seems to be attaining a new level in the 1990s. In some industries, such as the automotive industry, quality is no longer merely a competitive weapon, but rather a prerequisite to survival.

Quality is as important for small businesses as it is for large corporations. One reason is that some small companies have been competing directly with foreign firms for a long time. Some have suffered the same fate as large companies, while others have prospered from the competition. Many large firms rely on a number of small companies for parts and services used in producing the products of the larger company. Quality-conscious corporations are demanding continuously higher quality in the goods and services they purchase from small businesses. At the same time, though, big companies are reducing the number of vendors. This downsizing of vendors is just beginning to impact the bottom line of the small business, so the job seeker should be careful to check that a small business that seems inviting is not locked into a single source for its business. Should that force let go of the lifeline, the small company's boat is sunk.

Health Care Industry

According to Laura Freeman, an economist in the BLS Office of Employment and Unemployment Statistics, *Monthly Labor Review*, March 1995, the home is now the choice for certain types of health care, and one of five jobs in the nonfarm economy since January of 1988 has been in the health services industry. Health services are always in demand, and the health care industry is known for its strength in bad times as well as good.

For example, during the most recent employment recession of June 1990 through February 1992, employment in the health services industry grew 7.5 percent, while employment in the total nonfarm economy fell by 1.7 percent.

Since 1988 home health care has had the largest relative employment increase, 168 percent, while hospitals have had the smallest relative increase, approximately 18 percent, but the largest number of additional jobs, approximately 580,000.

Home health care is currently the fastest growing portion of health care. At the same time, employment in the medical instruments and supplies industry increased 17 percent during the 1988 to 1994 period, compared with a loss of 6 percent in total manufacturing.

Home health services as defined in the *Standard Industrial Classification Manual 1987* consist of "establishments primarily engaged in providing skilled nursing or medical care in the home, under the supervision of a physician." The services provided may be as fundamental as help with the basic activities of daily living. The services also may be as complicated as caring for patients needing specialized care for AIDS or cancer chemotherapy. Home health personnel work days, evening, or weekends, depending upon the needs of the patient. The time spent with a single patient may range from one hour a week to round-the-clock care.

Home health aides account for 31 percent of the industry. Various professional health providers make up 32 percent, of which 20 percent are registered nurses and 7 percent are licensed practical nurses. Other specialized personnel may include physical therapists, occupational therapists, social workers, and speech pathologists.

The home health care industry is expanding and being redefined by changes in employment trends and the occupational distribution in the hospital industry. It is taking on responsibility for more complicated health problems.

"Drugs Manufacturing: A Prescription for Jobs" by economist Stephen Heffler, writing in the *Monthly Labor Review* March 1995, attests to the fact that the job market in many manufacturing industries has shrunk during the past 50 years. He points with great expectations to the drugs-manufacturing industry, which has shown healthy gains year after year. "Not only are jobs being created in this relatively small industry, but many are high paying, high skilled, and research oriented. The industry surged through four recessions with remarkable profit margins and substantial job growth."

The mid-1960s marked a significant turning point for the drugs-manufacturing industry. While growth averaged just 2,000 jobs per year in the decade before 1964, the industry added more than 4,000 jobs per year on average from 1964 to 1986. The primary reasons for the changing pattern in growth was increased third-party health insurance coverage provided by employers and the implementation of Medicare. Both drugs-manufacturing and total manufacturing employment grew during the 1987–1989 period. However, from 1990 through 1993, the drugs-manufacturing industry added 8,000 jobs per year, on average, a marked difference from the average loss of 347,000 jobs per year across all manufacturing industries. The accelerated employment growth was due to a variety of factors, including rapidly rising drug prices, increased access to export markets, and the large number of patent-protected products.

While the trends in the large pharmaceutical preparations segment reflected those in the drugs-manufacturing industry as a whole, two smaller components grew more slowly. The diagnostic and other biological products segment grew by nearly 25 percent from 1980 to 1993. The medicinal chemicals and botanical products segment grew much less quickly than the other two components of the drugs-manufacturing industry during the past decade.

In 1993, a worker in the drugs-manufacturing industry earned wages averaging $944 per week, about $320 more than the average for the whole manufacturing sector. Even workers involved directly in production earned more than their counterparts across all manufacturing industry. The lesson here is that the boat of wages rises with the tide of the industry in which the wages are earned.

Employment in drugs manufacturing has registered steady growth primarily because the demand for pharmaceutical products has increased in bad times as well as good. Drug companies have been able to raise prices to keep profits high. Thus, they have avoided the downsizing and restructuring common among manufacturing industries in recent years. However, red flags have been raised. The pattern of employment growth in the drugs-manufacturing industry during the past three decades may not continue. New challenges have appeared. Both the BLS and the Department of Commerce expect employment to continue to grow in the industry during the next 5 to 15 years. The share total employment in the industry held by professional and technical occupations is expected to increase as well, with research and development taking on added importance. However, the BLS projects the industry to grow into the next century at less than half the rate it grew during the 1979 to 1992 period. Newly-emerging factors, such as health care reform and international competition, will challenge the industry and its historic pattern of employment growth.

Small Businesses

Just what is meant by small business in today's economy? Most attempts at a definition of small business have relied on a quantifiable characteristic such as how many are employed or the volume of sales. One classification scheme interprets small business as a firm having fewer than 500 employees. A more detailed classification further segments small business into very small, from 1 to 19 employees; small, from 29 to 99; and medium, 100 to 499 employees. Any company with more than 500 employees is tagged as big business.

According to the Small Business Act of 1953, a small business is independently owned and operated and not dominant in its field of operation. The Committee for Economic Development identifies a small business as a firm in which:

Management is independent

Usually the manager is also the owner

Capital is supplied and ownership is held by an individual or a small group

The area of operations is mainly local

Workers and owners tend to be in one home community, although the markets need not be so restricted

The business is small compared with the biggest units in its field.

Keep in mind that the number of people employed by a particular firm is directly proportional to the magnitude of its financial and human resources. If you are thinking of employment in a small business, it is safe to say that it is likely you won't be transferred. It is more than likely that the owner will be keenly aware of the individual employee's contribution on a day-to-day basis because there are relatively few employees and the owner tends to be the manager. Because it is small compared to bigger business units in its field, it may have to continually reach out for new business. It has to compete directly with larger firms having more resources, including sales and marketing resources, or else it has to be in a subcontractor or other subservient relationship with a larger business.

A small business is not just a scaled-down version of a big business. Almost all businesses start small and stay that way. Therefore, what are your chances of advancement? Although owners/entrepreneurs are generally experts in the product or service they engage in or produce, they usually possess neither the education nor the skills required to manage a business. Many small business owners who do not understand the intricacies of running a business end up making most of the decisions—at least all the crucial ones. Often they do not know how to delegate authority. An owner makes decisions in areas, such as inventory or finance, that are usually the responsibility of expert professionals in large firms. If you are highly trained in a business or financial specialty, will you resent taking orders from one who knows far less than you? Conversely, if you are a generalist, might you not learn a lot more about the total operation of a business by working in a small business rather than being off in an isolated department within a large corporation? Responsibility comes faster in a small business because fewer people have to make all the decisions. Many small businesses are family-run or, at least, employ members of the family. Would you feel that members of the family are being favored? Would you like to work for years, productively and successfully, only to see the boss's son fresh from high school be promoted to manager of the business? Will there be time for training? Funds to attend seminars and workshops?

Many small businesses are established as a means of self-employment, and as long as the owner receives a satisfactory income he or she may not wish to make the effort to expand. Where does that leave the employee who wants to advance in rank and in salary? The fewer people under you, the lower the salary. If you choose a career in big business you might advance with the tide. As the business expands, so do the employees within the department. Senior employees tend to rise to positions of management, and the more people they have working under them, the higher their salaries. So, you might work as hard or harder in a small business and yet receive a significantly lower salary. Also, because a small business often operates with very limited capital, what about adaptations you might require to accommodate yourself in the job or to advance to the next position? Can the small business afford to spend the money?

Then, there is the additional question of benefits. If you need to rely on an employer for all or a substantial part of your health care costs and coverage, a small company may not have the wherewithal to offer a comprehensive coverage package and certainly not dental and vision plans.

Ask small business owners for a list of woes and the lack of skilled workers is guaranteed to be near the top. But an increasing number of companies such as $4.5-million Jet Products have started to work with schools to address the problem.

During the past 8 years, Phoenix-based Jet, an aerospace machine company has apprenticed 38 students, mostly high school juniors and seniors who were recruited through the local school district's cooperative education program. The students worked from 4 P.M. to 9 P.M. 4 days a week. Vice-president Jim Perlow observes that the apprenticeship program helps the company by giving it the opportunity to screen and train future workers. It provides students with a real-world context for what they are studying in school.

Which financial matters are most troubling to entrepreneurs? A 1995 survey by Comprehensive Business Services, a national accounting and financial-services franchise located in Carlsbad, California, found that the managers of small businesses (those with revenues of from $100,000 to $1 million) put insurance and taxes way ahead of other financial concerns. For 73 percent of those polled, insurance was a major concern. Workers compensation received fifth place, recorded as a concern of 53 percent of those surveyed. What does this mean for those with physical disabilities? Are small business owners not leary of hiring someone who might impact upon their insurance and compensation? If applying for small business employment, be sure to have your arguments to counter this concern ready.

Many of the small firms that know of the ADA's existence consider the disabilities act to be very laudable, but they are having problems understanding the law. According to Jitendra Mishra, author of "The ADA Helps—But Not Much," published in *Public Personnel Management*, Winter 1995, "reasonable accommodation" is another term causing confusion. It would, therefore, seem like a splendid idea for you to come up with what you would consider a fitting accommodation with an estimate of cost. Or offer to pay toward the accommodation, if this will help you show determination that you want the job. Mishra points out that an additional problem with the ADA is that some costs may create a serious problem in terms of having to comply with reasonable access sections of the Act. The purchase of special equipment, such as electronic door openers and certain devices to aid the hearing-impaired, is often quite expensive and puts a strain on many small businesses. A survey by Bradford McLee, published in *Nation's Business,* April 1993, indicated that 30 percent of small business owners could not afford to make the changes that the ADA requires. McLee's article was titled "The Disabilities Labyrinth."

For small businesses, according to Mishra's article, the most controversial benefit is that of health insurance because the ADA allows insurance companies to charge businesses extra if they hire persons with disabilities due to their "experience rating." Section 36212 allows insurance companies to determine the risk taken and then charge the business accordingly. This contradiction in the law has many businesses confused. The law forces them to hire the disabled and, as a reward, their insurance skyrockets.

Another thing to keep in mind when approaching small businesses is that they generally do not have a lawyer on staff. Yet businesses are often concerned about liability and lawsuits related to their hiring of those with disabilities. Pat Gibson of Preferred Staffing says that part of his mission in placing persons with physical disabilities is to assure businessmen that fears of legal entanglements are vastly overrated when it comes to the hiring of those with physical disabilities.

Who works for small businesses? Data from the *State of Small Business,* a government report, suggests that small business is an excellent source for a first job. Two out of three Americans find their first job in a small business. The cost of training new workers is partly offset by lower wages paid to entry-level workers, who probably will move on to higher-paying jobs at bigger businesses. High school dropouts generally get their further education on-the-job at small companies. But be warned—only about three-quarters of jobholders in small business, those with fewer than 100 employees, work full-time as opposed to 90 percent in big companies. This is especially true for employees of small retail companies and certain service firms that engage in seasonal work.

An employee of a small business has a greater opportunity to come up with new solutions to production, distribution, and other problems. Big business is cumbersome, and newness flies in the face of the entrenched order. In big organizations, people are often beaten down by trying to penetrate the many layers of managers and red tape. Sometimes, when big business kills a new idea, those with the new ideas leave to form their own companies. A great many succeed.

In the last several years, an important trend has emerged. Rather than acquiring full control of a number of small companies, large corporations are buying non-controlling interest in many promising firms, thus leaving the entrepreneur-manager in charge. There has also been a trend of big businesses to create entrepreneurial units within the larger company. Here, the employees are largely left to their own devices and may even end up competing against their larger half. This was done because big business has begun to see signs of stagnation in idea output. Alliances and collaborations have often been formed to accomplish specific goals that were too demanding for either party to achieve singly.

Because 90 percent of all new jobs will be created by small businesses employing fewer than 500 individuals, according to Ronald L. Krannick, author of *Change Your Job, Change Your Life,* published by Impact Publishing, 1994, you cannot afford to overlook small business as a source of employment.

A survey conducted during the month of January 1996 sampled more than 7,000 small business owner/members of the NFIB Education Foundation. Twenty percent expected the economy to strengthen during the following 6 months while 14 percent expected the economy to weaken. Twenty-eight percent of small business owners believe that taxes are the most important problem facing small business today. Nineteen percent selected regulation and red tape. Labor quality received 11 percent. This indicates a fine opportunity for a well-qualified person with a physical disability to enter this market. Small business owners obviously believe the help they have is not of high quality and/or they have difficulty attracting quality people. Additional good news is that hiring plans improved a point from December 1995, rising to a net 16 percent of all firms on a seasonally adjusted basis. Unadjusted, 23 percent planned to expand employment, up six points from December 1995. Only 6 percent planned work force reductions. This is in sharp contrast to the plans of big business to continue cutting costs to the bone, principally by keeping down payroll costs. The frequency of hard-to-fill openings averaged 21 percent in 1994. In 1995, the average was 24 percent, indicating a much tighter labor market and increased difficulty filling open positions. Job creation in 1995 totaled 1.7 million. The frequency of reported increases in average labor compensation unexpectedly rose seven points in January 1996 to 29 percent of all firms. Plans to raise compensation also rose seven points to 13 percent of all firms, a reminder that labor markets are still tight.

Steven Solomon, author of *Small Business, USA*, published by Crown, 1986, states that in the last decade it has become evident that American small business is an important regulating force of the labor market, creating a vast number of jobs when big business and government can't. "It enhances labor market flexibility, it serves a complementary function in skills training, and it is playing both direct and indirect roles in producing the conditions for viable, future U.S.–based manufacturing." Solomon cites small business as a major factor in the great adaptability of the labor market to the strains of economic change.

In the United States, the labor market has been lubricated by the unprecedented creation of almost 20 million new jobs in the 1970s and 8 million more in the first half of the 1980s. A disproportionately large share of the new jobs were created by small business. The smallest companies created most of the jobs, even though they represent only one-fifth of total private-sector employment. Small firms with less than 500 employees created more than three-fifths of all new jobs, although these firms employ only one-half the private labor force in this country.

How good were these new jobs? Nearly one-half were professional, technical, and managerial. Many of the rest, however, paid comparatively low wages, according to William Serrin, "Jobs Increase in Number, but Trends Said to Be Leaving Many Behind," *New York Times*, October 15, 1984. This may be one of the factors causing the workplace to be increasingly divisive in terms of the haves and have-nots. The growth of small business jobs in the last decade tended to increase the proportion of low-wage and part-time employees. This is because small business, on average, pays 20 percent lower wages than big business and employs a higher percentage of people who work part-time.

Many of the jobs were created in no-tech businesses that support or utilize high-tech products. The personal computer industry has rippled across small business in terms of producers of simple accessories for computers, generating in-business-for-themselves repair people and writers and publishers of small newsletters and magazines concerned with computers. Many of these jobs are not high-paying, but they are building distribution and service infrastructure and creating the level of product demand necessary to encourage the growth of manufacturing.

The contribution of big business to employment growth is far greater in regions that are fast-growing. The contribution of small business to employment growth is conversely far greater in slower-growth areas. "In the last decade there has been a celebrated body of research which suggests that small businesses, young ones in particular, may have a greater innate propensity for job creation than big business." This is how Solomon sums up the contribution of small business to job creation.

Nonprofit Organizations

Nonprofit organizations can be very special places to work. Often the employees of nonprofits are especially dedicated. Despite the fact that many could be working for more money in other types of organizations, they stick with the nonprofit because of humanitarian motives. There has been dramatic growth in the number and size of nonprofit organizations in the last 10 years or so. Not only is the increase in numbers of employees significant, but so, too, is the increase in causes and range of causes. The needs and problems catered to by nonprofits covers cultural, social, health, environmental and a host of other realms. Yet, despite the almost Don Quixote missionary zeal, inadequate funding is the lot of many or most of these organizations. "These two considerations—the importance of the problems addressed by nonprofit organizations and the frequent paucity of available resources to address them—place a burden of heavy responsibility on those who manage nonprofit organizations to do so effectively and efficiently," says Gerald Zaltmas, editor of *Management Principles for Nonprofit Agencies and Organizations*, published by AMACOM, 1979. This burden is passed on to the lesser-status employees of the organization.

William H. Newman and Harvey W. Wallender, III, in "Managing Not-for-Profit Enterprises," published in the *Academy of Management Review*, January 1978, list a breakdown of nonprofit enterprises grouped according to services rendered:

Health—hospitals, nursing homes, and clinics

Education—universities, schools, and trade institutions

Social—welfare, child care, and family counseling agencies

Arts and culture—orchestras, libraries, and museums

A nonprofit organization is one whose major goal is not the maximization of monetary gains. Operationally, whether an organization is classified as nonprofit depends on decisions of the U.S. Internal Revenue Service (IRS). The IRS lists approximately 300 categories or classifications of nonprofit enterprises. The differences between for-profit and nonprofit are diminishing as managers increasingly apply the same or similar tools to the administration functions of both types of institutions.

What are the distinguishing features of the nonprofit sector? Terry W. McAdam lists eight in *Careers in the Nonprofit Sector*, published by The Taft Group, 1986:

1. The organizations that operate in the nonprofit sector do not generally attempt to make a profit and to retain it. In fact, the law forbids people or institutions from profiting through investments or contributions to nonprofits.

2. Primacy of cause is foremost to the majority of these nonprofits. These causes run fully across the political spectrum and address thousands of issues of interest to some segment of the population.

3. This sector has deep and healthy roots in our country's history, including our rich and varied religious heritage.

4. The health of the nonprofit sector is viewed by many as tied closely to the overall health of the entire society.

5. The heart of the sector is voluntary in nature.

6. There is greater diversity and variety in the sector. The heterogeneity of purpose for the organizations in this sector is very substantial. The purposes can often contradict each other or be totally unrelated.

7. Although direct service provision is the meat and potatoes of the sector, advocacy and activism are among the very important functions which NPOs have in our society.

8. The sector is labor-intensive. In general, it is people and their services, rather than manufactured goods, which are the output of the sector.

This view of nonprofits would suggest that only those need apply who are committed to the particular cause of the organization and who are geared toward altruism and helping others. Certainly, many will be called on to interface with the volunteers who make up the bulk of the organization and so people skills are very important. The fact of diversity implies you must be comfortable in working with people of all backgrounds. These organizations will be interested in employing people of skills with or without disabilities. Of course the fact that the industry is labor-intensive means that there just might be a job out there for you in the midst of the thousands of jobs generated by this sector.

According to Peter Drucker, author of *Managing the Nonprofit Organization*, published by HarperCollins, 1990, the nonprofit organization exists to bring about a change in individuals and in society. He points out that one of the most basic differences between nonprofit organizations and businesses is that the typical nonprofit has so many more relationships that are vitally important. In all but the very biggest businesses, the key relationships are few—employees, customers, and owners, and that's it. But Drucker maintains that every nonprofit organization has a multitude of constituencies and has to work out the relationship with each segment.

"Although successful business executives have learned that workers are not entirely motivated by paychecks or promotions—they need more— the need is even greater in nonprofit institutions. Paid staff in these nonprofits need achievement, the satisfaction of service, or they become alienated and even hostile. Drucker asks, "After all, what's the point of working in a nonprofit institution if one doesn't make a clear contribution?"

Thomas Wolf, former executive director of the New England Foundation for the Arts, writes in *The Non Profit Organization: An Operating Manual*, published by Prentice-Hall, 1984, that while nonprofits attract creative people, they also attract those who are suspicious of authority and of hierarchically arranged organizations. Individuals who come from a management background tend to be more familiar and comfortable with organizational hierarchies. "Another misconception about nonprofit organizations is that administrative jobs within them tend to be more interesting than comparable jobs in the profit sector. By and large, this is not the case," Wolf says. Finally, Wolf declares that it is not true that a nonprofit organization is a haven from the real workaday world dominated by profit-motivated corporations and big government. "It is remarkable how rapidly nonprofit organizations have become integrated into the world they are supposed to be unlike."

Federal Job Opportunities

As federal jobs continue to shrink, where are the new opportunities? *Federal Jobs* of March 8, 1996, surveys the federal job market and comes up with a few winners. Procurement clerk and technician jobs are being filled. The federal government is continuing to hire candidates to fill Procurement Clerical and Technician jobs, GS-1006, in significant numbers. Currently, more than 8,000 Procurement Clerks and Technicians are employed in federal service. There is always a high turnover of such jobs.

The major hiring agencies for these job classifications are Department of Defense agencies. However, a number of other federal agencies also have openings for these types of positions. Agencies that employ at least 100 Procurement Clerks and Technicians are the Defense Logistics Agency, almost 2,000; Navy, 1,586; Army, 1,418; Air Force, 1,261; and in appreciably lower amounts, Agriculture, the General Services Administration, Interior, Veterans Affairs, and Transportation.

More than 1,060 Procurement Clerks and Technicians received promotions in fiscal 1994, the last year for which promotion statistics are available. Most were promoted to the GS-6 level. This trend is expected to continue. Procurement Clerks and Technicians perform work that involves clerical and technical support for purchasing, procurement, contract negotiation, contract administration, and contract termination. Typical duties include: preparing, controlling, verifying, or abstracting procurement documents, reports or industry publications or other clerical support work and technical work in support of procurement tasks, such as assembling product and price data; reporting on performance of how contractors meet terms of contracts; and similar support functions. These positions require a practical knowledge of procurement operations, procedures, and programs and the ability to apply procurement policies, regulations, and procedures.

Redefining Work Arrangements

For the past several years corporate America has been redefining itself. In the wake of this transformation the economy has become global and the demographics of the workplace have changed. Due to these shifting tides, companies have begun to recognize that the needs of their employees have taken on new dimensions. As a result of these changes businesses have begun to examine the viability of alternative work arrangements.

What are the new work arrangements? The following definitions are taken from *Making Work Flexible: Policy to Practice*, published by *Catalyst*, 1996:

Flexible Full-Time Options are alternative work arrangement for full-time work and have no effect on salary, benefits, or time frame for professional advancement.

Flextime is a situation in which employees chose starting and ending hours, but usually must be at work during a core period when all employees are present.

Flexible Week is a variation on the standard workday and workweek. There are fewer, but longer days, or a "compressed workweek." The average week does not exceed 37.5 or 40 hours.

Flexplace or Telecommuting is work done at a location other than the work site, usually an employee's home, a satellite or branch office, or a client's office. Telecommuting specifies that an employee is connected to the office by use of electronic equipment (fax machine or computer or pager).

Flexible Reduce-Time Options are alternative work arrangements for fewer hours that would be considered as full-time. This affects salary, benefits, and professional advancement. But, the degree of effect is dependent upon the arrangement, its length, and company policy.

Part-Time is a reduced work schedule that can take various forms: reduced weekly hours, reduced annual hours, or transactional work, such as full-time on a specific project with time off between projects.

Part-Time Telecommuting is an example of a combined flexible arrangement. It refers to part-time at a location other than at the work site.

"Let's Be Flexible" argues Karol Rose, a workshop trainer for work/life issues and author of an article with that title in HRFocus, February 1996. In focus groups, surveys, and interviews, employees have said they can't do it all. What they want is to be good, productive workers and also have a life. To accomplish this, Rose says they need flexibility. Rose cites that in study after study these arrangements—including flextime, telecommunicating, and compressed workweeks—have proven to be win-win situations. The employer can attract and retain qualified employees, boost morale and productivity, and even cut overhead costs. The employee can meet his or her personal responsibilities while still being productive at work. Needless to say, those with a limited amount of energy or a need for time alone, or with other duties will benefit from such an arrangement.

When employees are asked what would most help them manage their work and personal lives, flexibility is the number 1 response. However varied the reasons for wanting flexibility, the payback to organizations that provide it has been consistent: improved morale and productivity both from the employees' perspective and that of management. Many managers still rely on "face time" to measure employees' performance. With flexible arrangements, they must learn to evaluate performance based on results. This is good news for a person with a disability. Making the workplace more objective in terms of measuring results rather than how a task is accomplished can only help toward objective evaluation of the work product of those with physical disabilities.

"Certain kinds of jobs can be done at home or on the road, and certain kinds can't, and no amount of technology is going to change that," says Diana Salesky, an analyst with Towers Perrin, an employee benefits consulting firm in Stamford, Connecticut, as quoted in *Crain's Small Business Report on Labor*, September 1995.

According to recent surveys by Link Resources in New York and Find/ SVP in Ithaca, New York, the number of corporate employees who telecommute has almost tripled since 1990 to 6.6 million and could reach 11 million by 2000. Most experts say that telecommuting works best in certain narrowly defined situations. "The jobs that work best for this are the ones that involve a lot of time spent manipulating data in front of a computer, such as word processing or financial analysis," commented John Challenger, an analyst with outplacement firm Challenger Gray and Christmas in Chicago. Other telecommuting candidates are sales and service employees, who tend to be gone much of the time.

Telecommuting can improve the morale of employees and even make it possible for them to continue to hold a full-time job when they have other responsibilities or are not conveniently located to the site of the business. It certainly saves the company the cost of having a desk for the worker and providing amenities. At Chicago's Ameritech Corporation, 1,500 employees work at home a few days per week. Management is hoping to increase that number. The company reports that it is realizing a considerable savings in office space.

Many companies favor a combination of telecommuting with a day or two spent at the office so that the company culture can be preserved and face-to-face meetings can be held for important matters. The combination seems to cement ties between in-office workers and telecommuters, but allows workers new freedom and flexibility to ply their trade at home.

Jennifer J. Laabs, writing in the *Personnel Journal*, March 1996, says that schedule flexibility follows in the footsteps of the empowerment trend. She cites Lincoln National Insurance, which allows people to map out their own individual career development processes but gives them the tools such as training and rotational assignments with which to accomplish their personal objectives. People want to be seen as capable of managing their careers and their lives.

Chicago-based Morningstar Inc., a publications company, employs 350 workers and offers relief from set office hours. While the office does have certain core hours, staff members can come and go as they please. Of course, customer service representatives must be there during office hours, but work groups can schedule their own hours within that framework. People work for as long as they need to to complete their work. Then they can take off, and they do not receive reproving glances.

Corporate America already has made huge concessions toward work and life balancing by providing myriad flex options, according to Laabs. Other options include job sharing and sabbaticals. Downshifters are demanding even more innovative solutions to modern life's dilemmas, and companies are beginning to respond with even more creative ideas. First Tennessee Bank in Memphis employs some 8,000 workers in 30 states. It has started to allow employees to rearrange work schedules and hours and even to restructure their jobs based on people's personal needs. Following a schedule employees themselves helped to establish, employees now work extended hours early in the month when the load is heaviest, and then they take off a day during the end of the month when business has slowed.

Hewitt Associates says that during the past 5 years, the number of employees offering programs and policies that help employees better balance their lives has grown substantially. The company, located in Lincolnshire, Illinois, found that 67 percent of more than 1,000 U.S. employers offer some kind of flexible scheduling. In 1990, the percentage was 54. Yet, few companies allow employees scheduling options on an individual basis. Flextime is offered by 73 percent of the companies; part-time employment by 65 percent; job sharing by 36 percent; compressed work schedules by 21 percent; work at home by 19 percent; summer hours by 15 percent, and other options, such as scheduling on an individual basis, 4 percent;

and at manager's option 3 percent. The total percentages exceed 100 percent because many employers offer more than one alternative work schedule.

Job Sharing

You don't have to wait to be asked. Take a pro-active stance. Seek out a company within comfortable distance of your home and target a suitable one or two to be sent a formal plan devised by you for job sharing. Find a partner and decide what each has to contribute. Decide how much time will be put in by each member of the flex-team. Agree on how fringe benefits will be distributed and how you can communicate effectively while on the job-share program. Even three can participate in a flex-time arrangement. Typical jobs that are shared are: career counselors, engineers, lawyers, secretaries, teachers, curators. Sometimes, the tasks are appropriated among the various team members, while at other times the effort is collaborative.

Patricia Lee, author of *The Complete Guide to Job Sharing*, published by Walter and Co., 1983, says that employers are discovering that job sharing has a positive effect on both worker and workplace. Some of the pluses cited by enthusiastic employers are:

Increased productivity

Opportunity to recruit from a broader labor pool

Greater flexibility in scheduling of work

More energy for the job

Reduction of absenteeism

Any or all of these can be included in your pitch for asking a company to consider job sharing.

If an interview is scheduled, come well prepared to answer such questions as:

What if one quits?

How will you deal with vacation time?

Who is really responsible for getting the job done?

What about attendance at meetings?

How is evaluation handled?

What about consideration for promotion?

What about salary increases?

Remember that the company will be more productive and save money per person when it hires a flex-team rather than the team as separate individuals.

Temping

Temping is a way of life for some. When you temp, you have formed a partnership with the temporary agency. The temporary agency is sending you on an assignment as a representative of the quality of employee it has to offer to its client companies. You need your temporary agency because it is a pipeline to work. Different services have different personalities, and it is up to you to screen out those you believe you couldn't work with successfully. You should work with an agency that is willing to carefully explain each assignment it asks you to consider, assist you with transportation issues revolving around how to get to work on time, and give you a briefing on the climate of the company. For example, some companies expect the temporary to fit right in the first day of work with little explanation as to how to do the job. Other companies are very helpful with training, including job orientation and training on-the-job. Does the work pace of the company meet yours? If a legal firm is 10 days behind in billing and this is one of your first assignments as a temp in billing, can you work up to the speed expected? If you take a job far beyond your level of experience, training and skills, you give yourself a chance to fail, and too many failures will discourage the agency from enlisting your services. Better to be honest with yourself and your agency and select only those jobs that you can handle. Don't worry. After you establish yourself as a willing, reliable worker, there will be enough jobs. You have to have a high degree of flexibility to fit in with temp work. You might be asked to take a job on a short notice, and you might be asked to take a series of short jobs when you really wanted a job lasting for a minimum of a week. By being flexible, you will be a more highly valued employee in the temp field.

Why not be a permanent temp? You'll never get rich, but you can make a living if you are willing to work at it. Temporary agencies are generally busier in reverse proportion to the slowdown of business in companies, firms, and factories. Staffing at many companies has been cut to the bone. This means that when seasonal work adds to overload and a company wishes to see if it has enough overwork to create a new position, it looks to a temporary service to supply a qualified worker. Employers save money on benefits when they hire temps, and benefits now account for up to 30 percent of the yearly salary of an employee. Because temporaries are hired for specific work assignments, those with physical disabilities can choose those jobs that match their specific skills and interests. Many temp jobs offer on-the-job training, as well. This means that the temp can count on continuing education and a broadening of the positions for which he or she may apply. Some agencies are now providing benefits, such as insurance or paid time off. Be sure to inquire.

You may choose to work under your own agreement with a specific company or you may make an arrangement with several. You can choose your shifts and days of work. You earn overtime for any work amounting to more than 40 hours in the framework of a single week. Of course, if you split work between temporary companies, this may not apply; the 40 hours has to be worked for one company.

To ensure permanent status, be sure to listen carefully to directions and do not hesitate to ask questions of the person or persons in charge of you. Remember they are aware that you are a temporary and will need some orientation to work up to an efficient level. Always be on time. If you absolutely cannot report to work on a certain day, try to arrange for your absence as soon as possible. Never fail to call your temporary service and/or the company itself to report. Follow directions given by your temporary agency to the letter. If you are working for a company directly, call immediately and speak to your supervisor, advising him or her as to when you expect to return.

Always ask for feedback on your performance. Accept criticism. Suggestions for improvement can make you a more desirable worker. Never gossip about the company to others or gossip about people in the company. Be cheerful and polite. You will never be an insider when you are a temp, but you should be regarded as a pleasant companion who is willing to join in with others at break times and lunchtimes.

Because many employees and perhaps even your supervisor are not knowledgeable about working with people with disabilities, do not hesitate to negotiate tasks that may come up within the workday that you are unable to perform or perform only with great difficulty. If you are asked to move a box that is too heavy for you, ask someone who is clearly capable of doing so to move it for you. Be sure to thank the person and offer to do something in return for the favor. Better to ask for help than to sit and grumble or feel sorry for yourself or, worse yet, attempt to do it and do it in a highly inefficient manner or do it with a resultant injury to yourself. Remember it is not unusual for workers to trade off parts of the job tasks because they are not well-trained in a particular segment of a job, do not like to perform a part of the job, or feel they can more efficiently spend time doing another part of the task. Trade off. The variety may be enjoyable to other members of the department.

Two trends in temp employment go in your favor:

1. Long-term assignments are easier to find than short-term for a day or two.

2. Some assignments are more like projects in that they are related to a specific series of tasks and outcome or replacement of a position such as a secretary for a specified length of time. These special projects or extra-long assignments can easily last for several months or up to a year or more.

Self-Employment

"About 1 out of 11 workers in the United States was self-employed in 1994," according to the Current Population Survey, which has been the lone source of data on self-employment for the past 55 years. John E. Breggar, recently retired as BLS assistant commissioner for current employment analysis, reported on this survey in the *Monthly Labor Review*, January/February 1996.

One important conclusion is that self-employment is not nearly as significant a part of employment in the United States at present as it once was. Even with a growing population, the total number of self-employed people in 1994 was less than in the late 1940s, when nearly one in five people was self-employed. The primary reasons for this are that agriculture in general and small farming in particular has diminished greatly, and there has been a marked trend toward incorporating businesses, both in the agriculture and nonagriculture sectors.

Other conclusions were that self-employment increases as one gets older, and that in terms of sheer numbers the largest amount of self-employment occurs among persons in mid-career or those between the ages of 35 and 44. With regard to occupations, sizable numbers of individuals in agriculture, construction, and retail trade are self-employed. Yet, occupationally, self-employment is even more diverse, with no single group standing out.

The employment of others in self-employed businesses is quite low. Of the more than 10 million self-employed people, only 2.2 million had employees other than themselves. Of these, 33 percent had only one employee. These numbers indicate that the basic nature of self-employment in the United States involves persons working on their own account. What undoubtedly occurs is that as a small business expands and brings on employees, the owner incorporates the business. Therefore, the self-employed remain essentially single entrepreneurs. As self-employment has diminished, incorporated self-employment and just plain "working for someone else" have increased.

If you are interested in starting your own small business, the following resources can provide help and information.

- Check with your state unemployment office for the number of your local SCORE or Service Corps of Retired Executives, sponsored by the Small Business Administration (SBA). SCORE will provide you with a number of pamphlets outlining the start-up and successful operation of a business. The Small Business Administration plans workshops and conferences at nominal charge. After you have a business plan, the SBA will be happy to work with you. SCORE volunteers will schedule an informal appointment to discuss a wide range of small-business issues and to answer specific questions you may have regarding a potential business or one you have already begun.

- The Small Business Network, 1341 Ancona Drive, La Verne, CA 91750, or (800) 825-8286 is a knowledge network of professionals that is designed to help people obtain the information they need to start, develop, and maintain a successful business. Each chapter has a panel of professionals available to all members.

- American Business Management Association, Box 111, West Hyannisport, MA 02672 is a business tax and financial-planning service for small and home-based businesses. Joining this association gives you access to a network of business consultants from your own community who specialize in helping people start a small business. Branches are in Los Angeles, San Diego, Boston, Phoenix, and San Francisco.

- CompuServe Information Service on-line videotext service lets you access expert help through your telephone via a personal computer modem. You can contact consultants in your own community. The Disabilities Forum is a source of support and information on resources and opportunities for individuals with various disabilities. The Working Home Forum offers business expertise and networking with professionals and successful home-based businesses from coast to coast.

CHAPTER EIGHT

PURSUING ESPECIALLY HOT PROSPECTS

"Not Everyone Is Downsizing" blared a headline in *Newsweek* magazine, March 18, 1996. Author Marc Levinson asked: "Are middle-class jobs disappearing?" No, insisted Levinson. "In fact, plenty are going begging." He observed that in the 1990s Willy Loman, the out-of-date salesman celebrated in *Death of a Salesman*, wouldn't have the background to get into sales. "And therein lies the real dilemma behind the downsizing of America." With giants from AT&T to Wells Fargo announcing massive layoffs and with the remaining workers getting only slim raises, who wouldn't be worried, agrees Levinson. But, he says that strange things are going on out there in the job market. While Americans fret about the demise of the good jobs they remember, the economy is creating millions of new ones that once we would never have imagined. The trouble is that many of the new jobs require skills that most of today's workers lack, according to Levinson.

Of the more than 8 million positions created since 1993, only approximately 300,000 are in durable-goods manufacturing. Retailers, by contrast, added a million. These figures lie behind the 1992 Labor Department study, which found one in six college graduates doing work that required only a high-school education. Levinson quoted economist Joe Poplin as stating that the occupational classifications used by the government are out of date; low-wage classifications, such as "services," hide a number of new high-tech jobs.

Levinson argued that technology is getting a bad rap for disrupting industry and throwing out human workers while letting machines do the work. However, the counterargument is that technology turns bad jobs into good ones. Here's an example: A customer-service representative was relocated in a bank to assume a newly created position of telephone banker. Now, she spends her time urging customers to do more business with the bank.

The Changing Complexion of Work

Computer skills alone are no salvation. Technology changes the complexion of work. Not everyone who mastered the old work will succeed at the new. Levinson cites the case of Air Products and Chemicals, who 2 years ago decided that paying librarians to look up facts was a drain on the payroll. Instead, the company formed teams of librarians to function as consultants, using computers to pull together analyses for scientists and market researchers. Because of this shift in job description and duties, there is now a two-tier pay system for librarians at the company. Those who are able to analyze information earn much more than those who shelve books.

The demand for certain new technology skills is so great that Jackson State Community College in Jackson, Tennessee, will teach manufacturing technology 24 hours a day, seven days a week.

Meeting the demands of high-tech careers often means getting an advanced degree. According to Anne Nissin, director of the Career Center of Gallaudet University, 30 percent of the school's graduates to directly to graduate school upon finishing their undergraduate degree. Many of those seeking advanced degrees do so in educational administration and counseling and psychology.

Almost three-quarters of the top industries across the United States are currently hiring people with disabilities, according to a December 1995 news release from the President's Committee on Employment of People with Disabilities. You have a chance to find a job in big business. Furthermore, as noted earlier, a majority of the human relations specialists and CEOs who were polled said they were looking for access to qualified applicants; they want to move forward and hire individuals with disabilities. When the representative companies were asked what would be most helpful to accomplish this, 51 percent called for access to qualified applicants. Part of your challenge is to figure out which sectors of big business are booming.

In 1991 about 118 million people were employed in the United States. More than 10 percent of the work force or 14.9 million people, according to *The American Almanac of Jobs and Salaries* by John W. Wright, published by Avon Books, 1994–95, occupied executive, managerial, and administrative positions. The largest single grouping in this category was teachers on the elementary and secondary school levels. About 3.2 million worked in health-related occupations and slightly more than 3 million were employed in engineering and science-related jobs. About 14 million were engaged in selling, while another 16 million worked in service industries. The standard manufacturing, construction, and maintenance sectors employed slightly more than 30.3 million or 26 percent of the total workforce.

Wright states that barring any sudden and dramatic action by the federal government to stimulate a return to manufacturing, these occupational trends will continue into the next century. White-collar, service-oriented work, especially in health care and business services, will be the major growth area. The competition for jobs will continue to be more intense than in previous years in part because of the sluggish economy, but also because of the enormous numbers in the work force. Even engineers and computer scientists have felt the pinch in recent years, although it must be noted that these occupations and others in the science and technology areas still have unemployment rates of less than 3 percent.

The Fastest-Growing Occupations

According to the Office of Employment Projections of the Bureau of Labor Statistics (BLS) in its 1995 report, the 10 fastest-growing occupations are:

Personal and home care aides with a percentage increase of 119 from 1994 through 2005

Home health aides with an increase of 102 percent

Systems analysts with an increase of 92 percent

Computer engineers with an increase of 90 percent.

In lesser percentages of increase, yet highly significant increases, are:

Physical and corrective therapy assistants and aides

Electronic paging systems workers

Occupational therapy assistants and aides

Physical therapists

Residential counselors

Human service workers (with an increase of 75 percent)

The list covers occupations requiring advanced degrees as well as fields requiring only a high school diploma or GED.

Where are the jobs of the future and what will the U.S. labor force look like in 2005? The BLS has released its projections of work force demographics and future job growth by industry and occupation by 2005.

Between 1994 and 2005, the BLS predicts that total employment will grow at a slower rate than during the previous 11-year period. The majority of jobs will be in service industries, such as business services, health care, and social services. The most significant growth of all in the business service category will be in computer and data processing services, and personnel supply or temporary service.

College graduates looking for work should have enjoyed a bull market in 1996, according to a survey just published by the National Association of Colleges and Employers (NACE), a job-information clearinghouse. The 259 employers who answered the survey said they plan to hire 24 percent more graduates this year than in 1995. Strong hiring is expected in software development and data-processing services, as well as in computer, business-machine, and chemical products manufacturing.

The labor department predicts a 69 percent increase in the number of manicurist jobs in the next decade. It also projects a 29 percent increase in the number of movie ushers, lobby attendants, and ticket takers. As movie houses struggle to compete with video stores, theatre owners are expected to boost the quality of their service; boosting the quality of service translates into more jobs.

Several studies suggest that some areas will have more jobs than workers. These jobs are in business and management; engineering; health professions; computer and information sciences; physical sciences; mathematics; and protective services. Conversely, many areas will have more candidates than jobs. These include social sciences; communications; psychology; life sciences; visual and performing arts; liberal or general studies; agriculture and natural resources; home economics; human ecology; public affairs; foreign languages; philosophy; parks and recreation; and ethnic studies.

The respective starting salaries indicate which professions are hot. Consider, for instance, that the starting salary for chemical engineers is $38,114; for mechanical engineers, $34,715, but it drops to $19,516 for journalists and $19,496 for those in natural resources, according to L. Patrick Scheetz in *Recruiting Trends, 1990–2002*, a publication of the Collegiate Employment Research Institute of Michigan State University.

Sales should prove rewarding to those with physical disabilities because salespeople are advanced on how well they sell. Salespeople are paid for production—not for their looks or their physical strength. Because many work solely on commission or on salary plus commission, a company is quite inclined to try someone with a disability because the person must actually invest more in his or her career than does the company.

Due to the supply-demand ratio, those with degrees in the health services, technical fields, and sciences will receive the highest average starting salary offers. On the other end of the spectrum, advertising, human ecology/home economics, and natural resources graduates will find estimated starting salaries to average $21,000 to $22,000. Education majors will average $20,500 for a 10-month year, and journalism and hotel/restaurant majors will average $19,000 to $20,000 to start.

During the last decade, the difference in starting salaries between the high-demand and the low-demand disciplines has been widening, as the estimated average starting salaries for a chemical engineering major ($38,000) and a journalism major ($19,000) show. The halo of the MBA degree is slightly tarnished in the eyes of some employers. Employers are finding that paying an extra premium for an MBA graduate doesn't always pay off—at least in the first position. In the long run, however, obtaining an MBA does have advantages and frequently opens doors for advancement that those holding only a bachelor's degree do not enjoy.

Factories and Robotics

Factory settings do not have a history of being friendly to those with physical disabilities. The new frontier of robotics and computer-aided manufacturing or CAD, may change all that. Marvin Cetron and Thomas O'Toole are among the authors who predict there will be more than 1.5 million robot technicians employed in this nation by the end of the century and even more during the next century.

An emerging occupation is an identifiable job needed nationally that has developed as a result of the creation of a new industry. Robotics as a part of computer-integrated manufacturing fits this definition.

Job growth is expected in the electronics divisions of defense manufacturers, computer companies, aerospace firms, semiconductor manufacturers, missile and weapons manufacturers, industrial robot manufacturers, and artificial intelligence research corporations. These firms hire engineers and technicians in robotics research, development of artificial intelligence, and manufacturing. Laser manufacturing processes within robotics factories will replace many of today's foundry tools. Materials utilization technicians with new materials created for advanced automated manufacturing technologies. Computer-assisted manufacturing specialists will be in big demand. These programs will be able to operate a production facility. The cost-cutting goal of computer-assisted manufacturing technicians is to allow flexible manufacturing cells so that every step of the production process is programmed sequentially. Human intervention is at a minimum.

Computerized vocational training technicians will develop materials for use in robotics and in automated manufacturing education programs at all levels. There will be many openings for such technicians. Automated factories use optical fibers for sensing light, temperature, pressure, and dimensions. More than 200,000 jobs will open for holographic inspection specialists who transmit information to optical computers and compare data with stored three-dimensional images. The robotics industry will have jobs for energy auditors who will use infrared measuring devices and computerized energy auditors to track energy used by robots in production. These technicians will interface with the product engineers and marketing staffs in industrial plants. Offshoots are:

Quality assurance inspectors

Security technicians

Laser/electro-optical technicians

Off-line robotics programmers

Support technicians

Fiber optics workers

Human factors technicians.

More hot job prospects within this field are:

Employee benefits

Accounting

Machine repair

Programming or design

Fund-raising for robotics societies

Venture capital raising for research and development

Grant proposal writing

Instructional media management

Computer law/paralegal administration

Sales and marketing

Advertising

Seminar/workshop promotion

Robotics publishing

Human factors research in industrial psychology

Engineering and technical writing

The March 25, 1996, *U.S. News & World Report* examines why the chip is still the economy's champ and declares that despite corporate downsizing and diminishing job prospects in traditional sectors of the economy, microprocessors have helped to create significant employment opportunities. Semiconductor companies employ nearly 300,000 workers. Computer and software firms now employ about 1 million workers. Cellular-phone companies have hired 60,000 workers during the last 10 years, and Internet service firms are growing at a blistering pace. Meanwhile, to satisfy global demand, 22 major chip factories are under construction in the United States.

Economist Nuala Beck said that in the long run, high-wage, technology-related job creation will outpace technology-related job destruction. Beck estimates that the new positions, which are being filled by knowledge workers, now represent one third of total U.S. employment.

A surprising short-term development was the increase in manufacturing employment. Manufacturing grew by 2,700 jobs from March of 1994 to the same month of 1995. Few people could imagine that such an increase could happen after the struggle manufacturing has gone through in recent years. Other manufacturing indicators such as payroll are showing the same trend. The percentage of increase in exports has increased during the first 7 months of 1995 and has exceeded the percentage increase of 1994. Electronic equipment is the dynamic force behind this manufacturing expansion, specifically beepers and cellular phones.

Re-careering Newsletter, Spring 1996, offers its own viewpoint, predicting that entrepreneurs and robots will rule tomorrow's workplace. According to its report, new infotech will not just deprive many workers of their jobs, it may leave them stranded in the cyber society as ever-faster, cheaper, and easier-to-use computers cut down the number of workers needed.

Hot Careers Requiring College

The seventh edition of *Business Today* by David J. Rachman and others, published in 1993, lists hot careers in business through the year 2000.

Two Years of College

The following careers are rated as very good to excellent and require a two-year college program:

Management trainee learns many assigned duties and usually participates in work assignments under close supervision in sales, finance, personnel, production, and similar departments. The starting salary was pegged at $19,000, and the outlook was rated as very good.

An interviewer in an employment agency helps job seekers find employment and helps employers find qualified staff. The requirements are a two-year associate degree or a four-year degree. It demands the ability to screen people and match them with jobs. Applicants for interviewer must know the requirements of jobs to be filled. A salary of approximately $16,000 may be on commission basis. The outlook is excellent and is described as a good entry-level position for personnel work in business or in government.

A customer service representative interacts with clients, researches problems, and may do order processing, usually on computers. The starting salary is $16,500 and the outlook is very good.

A computer-assisted manufacturing (CAM) production supervisor works in CAM operations and monitors production schedules to maintain an appropriate work pace. It pays $18,000 to start. The outlook is excellent.

Four Years of College

The following jobs are rated as having a very good to excellent outlook and require a four-year program:

A manufacturing production supervisor takes responsibility for or assists with operations within the manufacturing and assembly divisions of a company, including cost control, reporting systems, production schedules, etc. The starting salary is $18,000. The position is described as one of the best starting points for a career in manufacturing.

A human resources manager position may still be acquired by those holding a four-year degree, but the emphasis is on an MBA. This manager supervises all personnel departments and all facets of employment, handles workers compensation, employee benefits, salaries and wages, labor negotiations, training and records. The starting salary is $28,000. The job outlook is very good.

An operations manager uses scientific methods to evaluate and improve decisions about a company's alternative methods of operation. Four years of college and a master's program in operations research or management science is required. A strong quantitative background is important. The outlook is excellent. On-the-job training is considered important.

An international planning analyst takes responsibility for international management decisions. A four-year college degree and MBA are required as are excellent writing skills. It pays $45,000 to start. The outlook is excellent. Candidates must have general management skills as well as technical knowledge.

Executive Positions

"Hot" jobs are those for which the demand and, in many cases, the compensation, is high. The executive recruiting firm of Christian & Timbers, of Cleveland, Ohio, has compiled a list of hot careers based on thousands of interviews conducted during the course of a year. Their findings were reported in the March 1996 issue of USA Today. The survey covered a variety of industries such as information technology, financial services, insurance, health care, biotechnology, and the environment.

The following represents a compilation of the most-requested positions to be filled in the executive ranks:

General manager of Internet-related companies and chief executive officer (CEO) of technology-related start-ups. Companies competing for this talent are realizing it is difficult to find. The talent base is small and elusive because there is little experience on the Internet. These executives usually have a track record in software marketing or, at the least, an affinity for getting products to the market, as well as start-up experience.

The "new" chief executive officer. He or she is client-focused, works outside the office, empowers employees, creates almost impossible goals and wills the organization to meet them. This person has strong marketing skills with a real understanding of what the customer wants.

Vice President of content. With the advent of the new Internet-related companies, the big question is what to put on the screen to make it entertaining for the end user and to provide valuable information. The job of the vice president of content is just like that of the program manager at the television networks. The next phase to judge these people will be "ratings" in the form of usage of their offerings on the Internet. They need deal-making skills to acquire content and create programming to keep the users on-line.

Chief technology officer (CTO) is a new title for 1996. The job was created by Fortune 100 companies, which have found their chief information officers are overwhelmed with technology. The CTO helps to decide how best to apply new technology. Additionally, as financial institutions rapidly move to electronic banking, there will be a huge demand for talented people who can fill the role of CTO and manage an increasing electronic distribution environment.

Senior private banking executive is in high demand because he or she is the key to building relationships between financial institutions and the high-profile customers these institutions seek for credit, trust, and investment business.

Vice president of managed care and managed-care development is a person familiar with negotiating contracts and in obtaining new business from preferred provider organizations and others that deal with managed care for individual hospitals or hospital organizations.

In biotechnology, the vice president of transfer process is a position in which the person holding it is responsible for taking a recently approved biochemical compound from research and development to a manufacturing mode.

The mergers and acquisitions (M&A) executive. With all of the consolidation in the banking industry and substantial reshuffling in the technology market as well as in other fast-growth industries, M&A activity is on the rise. An executive experienced in this role has reemerged as a hot commodity.

Career Woman, Winter 1995 listed "Hot Jobs for the Future":

- Human service worker headed the list with an average salary of $18,000 to $21,000 and expected to increase 136 percent through 2005.

- Next was computer engineer with an average salary of $49,000 with an expected increase of 112 percent.

- Systems analyst was listed at $48,500 with a projected increase of 100 percent.

- A physical therapist averages $17 to $21 an hour and is expected to increase in ranks by 88 percent through 2005.

- The others expected to show a substantial increase are:

  Teacher of special education, $36,000

  Medical assistant, $15,500

  Radiology technologist, $26,000

Medical records technologist, $21,000

Operations research analyst, $35,000 to $64,000

Occupational therapist, $20 per hour

Kindergarten teacher, $18,000 to $22,000

Speech pathologist, $34,000

Insurance adjuster, $26,000 to $38,000

Respiratory therapist, $26,000 to $38,000

Psychologist, $30,000

Newly Emerging Careers

Newly emerging fields provide you with a ground-floor opportunity. They are not rigidified by rules and regulations. You can move around freely and look forward to quick recognition as you deserve it. In newly emerging fields there is a camaraderie and an exchange of information that inspires new inventions and improved methods. What are these futuristic jobs? Of course, we can only guess because many have not been created as yet. Work consultant Norman Feingold has suggested such futuristic job titles as "crytologist" or one who preserves people through the ages, planetary engineer, pollution botanist, and robot trainer.

Carol Kleinman in *100 Best Jobs for 1995*, described job fields set to explode in the future:

- Biotechnology and genetics will be hot areas within the medical field, especially as applied to cancer research and to the development of new foods and food products. Recently the bio-engineered tomato has appeared in the grocery's produce section.

- Communications and entertainment have received a new jolt in direction as compact disc players, VCRs, camcorders, and new types of television sets with three-dimensional effects vie for consumer attention.

- Fiber optics will make inroads into entertainment technology.

- Computers will create giant networks of information so that a new information infrastructure will emerge.

- Development and increased use of alternate fuels will provide jobs. New sources of fuel are liquid hydrogen, ethanol, methanol, compressed natural gas, propane, and electric power.

- Lasers will change medical care. The greatest impact of laser technology will be in surgery. Lasers will be incorporated into dentistry and will make a visit to the dentist truly painless because lasers will replace drills. Gallaudet University has a program for training dentists.

- Even such a well-established field as marketing will be greatly changed as lasers, scanners, personal magnetic cards, bar code technology, and electronic coupons make it easier for stores and marketing consultants to establish databases of what is being purchased by whom.

- Medical technology will depend upon high magnetic fields and the technology that powers nuclear resonance machines in hospitals will radically change the way diagnosis is conducted. Fiber-optics, tiny videocameras, and miniature surgical instruments will be used to perform pinpoint surgery.

- Robotics will be used to measure ingredients, milk cows, handle radioactive material, and perform many duties that had formerly been handled by humans.

- Now more than ever the best bets for federal employment will be found among the hard sciences, financial management, some engineering specialties, and health occupations. But even here candidates will have to contend with the downsizing trend. Among the fastest-growing governmental fields are specific engineering disciplines, lawyers, management-related workers or those who provide staff and support services such as program analysis procurement assistance, or personnel management. Some of the fastest-growing federal occupations are medical personnel, business such as procurement, IRS agents, social scientists, and investigators.

Network technician is an emerging career that doesn't necessarily require a college education. Diane P. Licht, staff writer for *Employment Review,* presents a glowing picture in the April 1996 issue. A network technician is a person who would work hand in hand with a network manager. He or she runs and designs the wires, wiring layout, or oversees the wires being laid out. He or she takes care of the physical cables and the connections and the communication techniques. The network technician is responsible for the hardware side as opposed to the software side.

When you have many computers that are going to be connected you have to decide first if you want slow speed or fast speed. There are different ways to connect the machine. These ways relate to their speed. There are other issues to consider as well. You have to know about loads on a network connection and understand the maximum loads for a network and how to split them up.

Telephone wiring is a prerequisite for this position. You have to study continually in this field. If you stop working on your education for more than 3 years, your skills will be obsolete. Computing engineering is helpful after you're at a top-level management position. Unless you're going to be a simple wire puller, you need some sort of formal education. You can become certified as an engineer or take an exam that will allow you to design cabling schemes and cabling strategies for moving high-speed data from point to another. To succeed, you need an intense interest in computers and networking.

New and emerging occupations according to L. Patrick Scheetz in *Recruiting Trends, 1992–93*, published by Collegiate Employment Research Institute of Michigan State University are:

Allied health professions including physical therapists and pharmacists

Aquatic ecologists

Biochemists

Biomedical technologists

Chemical safety engineers

Chemists, especially for novel drug delivery systems research

Chinese bilingual language specialists

Clinical nurse specialist

Communication systems managers

Computer software engineers, including computer network engineers, information systems specialists, specialized computer programmers

Corrosion engineers

Customer support and sales representatives

Distribution/logistics/operations management specialists

Economic development specialists

Environmental health and safety analysts, including safety engineers, environmental engineers, environmental/industrial hygienists, and environmental researchers

Financial planners, including stockbrokers, financial analysts, trading specialists, operations analysts, and fund developers

Industrial engineers

Integrated pest management specialists

International marketing representatives with second and third language skills

Mechanical engineers for technical sales

Nuclear medicine

Pattern engineers, including technical designers, fabric technicians, and production assistants

Performance management analysts

Photo/laser research and design specialists

Power quality analysts

Process engineers

Production engineers and managers

Quality assurance engineers and managers

Right-of-way agents

Sales/service and direct marketing representatives, including retail management trainees, account executives-outside sales, product champions, product managers

Security service supervisors

Technology transfer and deployment analysts, science and technology specialists for developing new high-technology systems

Toxicologists

Ultrasonographers.

Scheetz's list of new and emerging occupations make an informative contrast with his list of greatest employment opportunities for 1994 graduates:

Accountants, including auditors, staff accountants, associate accountants, sales accountants

Actuaries

Bank branch manager trainees, including retail banking trainees, mortgage banking processors, mortgage closing trainees, commercial lending trainees, community banking trainees, business credit analysts

Caseworkers, including juvenile court officers

Chemists

Computer scientists, including systems programmers, computer programmers, systems analysts, systems engineers, business systems analysts, computer applications development consultants

Criminal investigators

Engineers, especially chemical, civil, computer software, consulting, control, electrical, electronics, environmental, field, mechanical, microprocessor, packaging, process, project, pulp and paper, quality assurance research, research and development, and tool design

Environmental scientists

Financial planners, including stockbrokers, credit analysts, financial analysts

Fund-raising specialists

Geologists

Hydrologists

Insurance underwriters, including underwriting trainees and claims adjusters

Management trainees and interns, customer services trainees

Merchandise management trainees, including assistant buyers, merchandising executive trainees, store manager trainees, department manager trainees, retail branch trainees

Medical technologists

Microbiologists and researchers

Occupational therapists

Personnel specialists, including contract recruiters and training and development specialists

Pharmacists

Production/manufacturing managers, production manager trainees, operations managers, transportation management specialists, warehouse management trainees

Restaurant management trainees, food supervisor trainees, and food service managers

Sales representatives, including marketing representatives, sales trainees, sales/service representatives, technical sales representatives, territory managers, marketing representatives, field service/sales representatives, sales managers, customer sales representatives, account executives-outside sales.

Those with physical disabilities can easily see from the many lists of emerging and growing occupations that many are in the knowledge industry, in which physical disability should not be a handicap. The United States is in a period of substantial transformation. Peter Drucker notes that "knowledge is the primary resource for individuals and for the economy overall." Land, labor, and capital—the economist's traditional factors of production—do not disappear, but they become secondary. They can be obtained and obtained easily, provided there is specialized knowledge.

Job availability by geographical region is highly variable. While most of the country is not in a hiring mode, certain regions offer more opportunity than others. Certainly those with ambitions in politics and government should head for the Washington, DC area. According to Scheetz, the better areas are the southeastern and north central regions. On the lower end of the job scale are the south central and northwestern regions. Last of all is the northeastern region of the country. From a global perspective, there has been an enormous transfer of work opportunities to the Pacific Rim and to Latin America.

Statistics and Trends

The *Monthly Labor Review* of February 1995 contained an important article written by Lois M. Plunkert and Howard V. Hayghe, economists in the Office of Employment and Unemployment Statisticians. It was entitled "Strong Employment Gains Continue in 1994." According to the authors, the labor market turned in a very strong performance as virtually all sectors and geographic regions enjoyed substantial job gains. The largest employment increase in 10 years was accompanied by a steady decline in unemployment.

In the goods-producing sector, manufacturing, which had lost jobs steadily from early 1989 to mid-1993, rebounded in 1994, despite a drag on unemployment growth caused by continued defense cutbacks.

The services industry accounted for nearly half of the overall gains but, within the broad service-producing sector, substantial employment advances also occurred in retail trade and state and local governments.

The current economic expansion started its fourth year in 1994 and, by year end, had already lasted longer than most post–World War II recoveries. The 1994 payroll employment increase of almost 3.4 million was the best annual performance of the current economic expansion. To a large extent, the authors posit that it is possible to trace the origins of job growth in specific industries to changes in related macroeconomic or large picture factors, such as personal consumption, investment, exports and government spending, some of which are themselves influenced by trends in total employment.

As sales of goods and services grew so did the need to replace depleted inventories and provide more services to customers. But, sustained growth in factory employment was not seen until 1994 when the expansion was 3 years old. The primary manufacturing industries to profit from the strong consumer spending were motor vehicle makers and their suppliers such as producers of automotive stampings and flat glass.

The pickup in consumer spending extended not only to durable goods such as appliances and furniture but also to services. Some of the gains were in directly provided services, such as auto repair and others were in services to businesses that were straining to meet increased demand for their products.

The strong demand for more goods and services provided motivation for businesses to invest in themselves to improve productivity, expand capacity, and replace worn-out and outmoded equipment. The growing backlog of orders for capital equipment was partly responsible for employment gains in the fabricated metals, industrial machinery, and electronics equipment industries, which added about 50,000 workers each. So, by studying and keeping up with your overall field in general, you can predict how employment will fare in the principal industries, such as manufacturing and the businesses that serve manufacturing. Because all companies need general office staff and business and financial specialists such as accountants, those who are in these core job areas would ply their trade in those businesses and industries that are growing. Although a retail clerk can only work in a retail store, an accountant can work in a variety of industries and settings.

Improving conditions in many of the countries that are important purchasers of U.S. products helped to boost exports during the last quarter of 1993 and most of 1994. Industries sensitive to exports or those with at least 20 percent of their employment tied to exports in 1990 were durable goods manufacturing industries, such as computer equipment and oilfield machinery. The number of jobs in the large group of export-sensitive industries grew by 83,000 in 1994. Improved domestic demand also fueled employment in this area.

Defense cutbacks continued in 1994. Employment in industries relying on defense to support at least half of their jobs in 1987, the last year before major defense spending cuts, fell dramatically. In 1994, these defense-dependent manufacturing industries, such as aircraft, missiles and space vehicles, and search and navigation equipment lost 92,000 jobs.

The number-one growth industry was personal supply services, a group of business services that include temporary help, employee leasing, and employment agencies. This industry alone added 424,000 workers in 1994. The expanded use of temporary help continued a trend started during the expansion of the 1980s. Employers are increasingly relying on agencies that can provide workers in a variety of occupations, to whom the employer need make no permanent commitment. This enables companies to be more responsive to short-term fluctuations in demand and still keep production costs down. This trend toward temporary help is a movement against the hiring of permanent help, which adds the growing cost of benefits to a worker's salary.

Three other industries within business services made the top 20 list:

1. Computer and data processing services added 105,000 jobs in 1994.

2. Contrasted with this high-paying industry is services to buildings and miscellaneous business services, which added about 50,000 workers, but paid them less than the average hourly wage. The explanation for the rapid growth of these industries is similar to that for the expansion of personnel supply services: many of today's employers wish to minimize costs through the use of flexible work arrangements. However, firms in computer services, services to buildings, and miscellaneous services do work for clients under contract, while personnel supply agencies provide workers to clients.

3. Eating and drinking establishments added far more workers, 272,000, than any other industry, except personnel supply services. This large, labor-intensive industry continues on a strong growth trend year after year to meet the demand for convenience food and restaurant meals. The average hourly earnings in eating and drinking places are the lowest among the 288 industries. However, tips are not included in the payroll reports.

Three other types of retail stores were in the top 20:

1. After several years of buyouts, bankruptcies, reorganizations and layoffs, department stores made a comeback in 1994, adding 88,000 workers.

2. Auto dealers.

3. Furniture stores also had substantial job gains—another testament to the importance of healthy consumer demand and low interest rates, according to Plunkert and Hayghe.

Three industries from the goods-producing sector made the top 20 list: Two were in construction—electrical work and masonry, stonework and plastering—while only one—motor vehicles—was in manufacturing.

Local government, except education, was among the top job gainers, a development made possible by increased tax revenues. Most of this gain was in general administration. A comparison of average weekly earnings for 1993 shows that local government, except education, pays slightly above the average for all private industries.

Two of the remaining three economically driven industries on the top 20 list were in the above-average wage category. Trucking added 64,000 workers as the strong economy required the transportation of growing factory shipments as well as swelling imports. Motion picture production and services also had large employment gains as consumers put out more money for entertainment as well as other purchases. Finally, automotive repair shops, with earnings that are just short of the average for all private industries, continued a steady growth trend.

Five of the top twenty industries are little influenced by business cycles, but respond more to demographics and other noneconomic influences. Social services and health services each account for two of these industries and the other is public education. Among social services, child day care and residential care such as orphanages and other facilities for persons who require personal assistance but not nursing care grew primarily in response to the increase in the number of small children and the elderly. Taken together, these two social service industries added 113,000 workers, and their average pay was substantially below the private-sector average.

The small home health care industry added more jobs than any other area of health services: 67,000. The continued expansion of employment in this industry is the result of increased coverage of home care under health insurance plans, efforts to minimize the length of hospital stays, and improved technology that enables patients to be treated and cared for at home. Because of the large number of health aides employed, the average hourly earnings in home health care is below the average for all private industries. On the other hand, the other health industry to make the top 20 list, offices and clinics of medical doctors, pays above the average rate.

Kiplinger's Picks

Kiplinger's picks for the best high-knowledge fields of employment in 1996 were:

Home health care

Movie production

Support for medical professionals

Community-based social services

Child day care

Computer-software design

Veterinary services

Management consulting and public relations

Cable and pay TV

Elementary and secondary education.

For the ten fastest growing fields up to the year 2005, the magazine picks:

Home health aides

Social service workers

Household workers

Computer engineers and scientists

Systems analysts

Physical therapy assistants

Physical therapists

Paralegals

Special-education teachers

Medical assistants.

The aging trend in the U.S. population makes anything related to gerontology or geriatrics a very hot career. Demand for college graduates with paralegal training is soaring. The U.S. Bureau of Labor predicts that the number of employed paralegals will rise by 75 percent by the year 2000. According to *Changing Times* magazine, salaries at mid-sized law firms will hover around $34,000 within the next few years. The U.S. Bureau of Labor Statistics predicts that the demand for medical records technicians will rise by 60 percent in the next decade. This profession requires only a two-year degree. The Bureau of Labor Statistics notes that the travel and leisure specialties will grow 54 percent in the next ten years.

Other sources, although agreeing with the above picks, also mention the following occupations as enjoying a large growth from the late 90s to 2005:

Salespersons, retail

Waiters and waitresses

Registered nurses

General managers and top executives

Systems analysts

Guards and orderlies.

Jobs for librarians are actually much stronger than one might expect because of continued cutbacks for public library funding. But the cutbacks had the effect of discouraging young people to pursue a career in library science with the result that the number of librarians has remained constant since the 1960s. As many of the librarians retire, there are openings in many areas of the country for well-trained librarians, especially for children's librarians and academic librarians. Many large corporations are also hiring librarians to help organize their information and to tell them what outside sources of information the companies should utilize.

Jobs with Uncle Sam

Although it is true that the federal government is downsizing, it remains the Washington area's single biggest employer with some 330,000 civilian and 54,000 military employees in the metropolitan area, according to the Office of Personnel Management. The federal government accounts for about one third of the area's economic activity. Federal job turnover accounts for some 32,000 new government hires each year. Most of them are at the entry level, which is denoted as GS-4 through GS-7.

The Food and Drug Administration (FDA) is filling new jobs in drug approval testing. Congress has passed legislation that could lead to substantial hiring by the FDA, *Federal Jobs Digest* has learned. According to a senior personnel official at FDA, the FDA is committed to reviewing drugs in a timely manner and is recruiting additional personnel to accomplish this goal. The FDA anticipated that substantial hiring will be made agency-wide in the late 1990s. These new hires will be made primarily at FDA Headquarters in Rockville, Maryland. Most of these positions were in scientific fields such as consumer safety officer, pharmacist, biologist, and toxicologist, but administrative and clerical employees also were needed.

Electronics technician is among the top-20 white-collar federal jobs. Close to 19,000 electronics technicians are currently employed by the federal government. More than 3,401 individuals in this position received promotions in fiscal 1994. The average grade of electronics technicians is GS-11, and the average salary is more than $42,790. Special salary rates are available, however, in some areas of Maine and New Hampshire with the Department of Navy and the Department of Agriculture. Special salary rates are offered in areas where there are few qualified applicants. The top employing agencies are Transportation, Navy, Air Force, Army; and in lesser amounts, Commerce, Justice, NASA, Interior, Agriculture, and Veterans Affairs.

Electronics technicians perform maintenance, troubleshooting, testing, operation or development work in connection with all kinds of electronic equipment. The types of electronic equipment range from medical and laboratory equipment to radar, sonar, radio systems, and computers. Candidates must have knowledge of basic electrical and electronic theory, mathematics, or physics as well as the ability to use their hands and appropriate tools.

The "Green" Industry

Alternative technology is an umbrella term that covers a variety of ecology-related fields. It means solar instead of nuclear power, wood heat instead of imported oil, natural foods instead of overprocessed food, and recycling. To choose a career in alternative technology requires commitment and a sense of mission because not everyone's favorite color is green.

Solar is a fertile field for the small-scale entrepreneur. Nora Goldstein, writing in *In Business* cites the example of Malcolm Lillywhite, who used his college studies in physics and related sciences to develop a training and consulting firm called the Domestic Technology Institute, which deals with solar and other alternative sources of energy. One of his recent projects was a solar greenhouse in Cheyenne, Wyoming.

Goldstein reports that to meet the blossoming demand for alternative energy products, small retailers all over the country are selling an assortment of space age devices and updated versions of age-old designs. Many of these new alternatives are low-technology fields that allow people to start out by manufacturing and selling products out of their homes: a process economic observers have dubbed as "business steading," a hot new trend. Ken and Patty Spatcher own and operate New England Insect Trans, a small business in Colrain, Massachusetts, that makes and sells two types of flypaper-type devices. Ken Spatcher, a graduate of the Stockbridge School of Agriculture, did a five-month internship in the experimental orchards of a regional research center and applied some of this newfound knowledge in developing his devices and business.

Reportedly, many graduates can get their initial training and background for the green industry through volunteer work with environmental groups. Important skills to have are speaking, writing, and speed reading in order to keep up with the huge volume of literature in the new technologies.

Waste-recycling technologies open up career opportunities for graduates with degrees in marketing, sanitary engineering, and even sociology or psychology. According to engineer Bruce Anderson who works with Total Environmental Action, which publishes *Solar Age* magazine, "Most intermediate technologies require some form of mechanical engineering knowledge, whether it's heat transfer or motion." A second major skill is knowing how to deal with people. A third is the ability and willingness to work with your hands.

For further career information, *Environmental Opportunities* lists environmental jobs throughout the United States, which are generally in nonprofit organizations. Write to *Environmental Opportunities*, P.O. Box 547158, Surfside, FL 33154, or call (305) 866-0084, fax (305) 866-0091. The magazine is sponsored by Environmental Studies Department, Antioch New England Graduate School, Keene, NH 03431.

Finally, *Environmental Career Opportunities* contains a biweekly listing of more than 400 entry- to senior-level jobs across the United States. Write to *Environmental Career Opportunities*, P.O. Box 560, Standardsville, VA 22973, or call (202) 861-0592.

How Important is Foresight?

Today's job market favors "low foresight" personalities, according to career guru Richard Bolles in the *ReCareering Bulletin* (655 Rockland Rd., Suite 7, Lake Bluff, Illinois 60044). "Forget everything you were taught about planning ahead, about building for the future, about developing and following a career track." Bolles advises instead to learn to listen to your senses, to live and operate in the moment. The author of *What Color Is Your Parachute?* says that today's job market no longer favors the planners, the "high foresight" people who have an inborn ability to look into the future and see where something is leading, the ones who excelled, because of this aptitude, in the corridors of Big Business, climbing a well-thoughtout career ladder. "The job market ten to 15 years ago favored high-foresight people," he said. "It was stable, you could count on it, you could develop a career track. High-foresight people were in seventh heaven in that sort of environment."

Today's just-in-time job market, however, is geared toward a temporary and contingent work force, says Bolles. This work force is more suited to low-foresight personalities or those that career counselors used to wring their hands over because they did not neatly fit into career holes. Low-foresight people immerse themselves in the present, entranced with whatever is before them at the moment; they don't or can't plan for the future.

High-foresight people are in extreme pain in today's job market because the old ways don't work anymore, according to Bolles. But why is the high-foresight view still being trumpeted if it is no longer valid? Because all the predictions about the job market are being made by high-foresight people—these are the ones giving the speeches and the ones training the people. But, predicts Bolles, high-foresight people will have to try to switch gears to operate in more of a low-foresight mode. "Go with the flow, learn to listen to your senses. Be aware of which of your senses you like to use most—taste, smell, sight, touch, hearing, or the sixth sense of intuition."

CHAPTER NINE

BENEFITING FROM ASSISTIVE DEVICES AND TECHNOLOGY

On March 9, 1994, President Clinton signed into law the Technology-Related Assistance for Individuals with Disabilities Act Amendments of 1994 or Public Law (PL) 103-218. This reauthorization extends Congressional support of the original legislation, or PL 100-407, through March of 1999 and continues to support state efforts to implement consumer-responsive, comprehensive, statewide programs of technology-related assistance for individuals with disabilities of all ages.

Title I of the new act provides for continuation of competitive grants and technical assistance for states and establishes information and technical assistance to individuals with disabilities and other persons. Title II authorizes funds for programs of national significance, including training and demonstration projects related to assistive technology and the establishment of a national classification system for assistive technology. Title II authorizes funds to states to establish and expand alternative financing mechanisms for individuals to purchase assistive technology.

For a copy of the complete article or a list of Tech Act Projects in each state, contact RESNA, 1700 N. Moore St., Suite 1540, Arlington, VA 22209, or call (703) 524-6686 (V) or (703) 524-6639 (TT) or fax (703) 524-6630.

There are new directions in the vocational curriculum in the public school system. Decreasing deviance is an intervention aimed at decreasing differences between nondisabled and persons with disabilities. Deviations in behavior are first identified and then the training of the individual is channeled toward reducing or even eliminating these differences. As deviance is decreased, programmatic goals increase competence. A more positive view is taken as to the potential for achievement. Providing individuals with disabilities the chance to expand their opportunities for training will encourage such individuals to choose whether or not to become paid workers. It gives people with profound disabilities a chance to decide if they wish to compete and shows them how they can plan to compete.

Rehabilitation engineers are very helpful in analyzing a job in terms of redesigning workstations to suit the person with a disability, from reorganizing materials needed to perform a job, to adjusting seating arrangements. For detailed suggestions as to modifications for facilitating independence in an integrated community work setting for persons with physical disabilities, consult W. Pietruski's *Vocational Training and Curriculum for Multihandicapped Youth with Cerebral Palsy*, published by Virginia Commonwealth University, 1985.

Tom Thomson, director of the Learning Disabilities Program at Harper College in Palatine, Illinois, says adaptive equipment may be worth the money to invest in yourself in order to convince the prospective employer that you can do the job. Computer careers are the most promising. Up until 5 years ago, not that many people had computers. By the end of 1996–97, virtually everyone will have a computer. The computer will be used in a variety of activities, from budgeting to communications. Americans will be heavily dependent on the use of a computer. It will be easier for those with physical disabilities to communicate through use of e-mail.

Thomson points to a trend in the use of the computer and Internet as electronic means of setting up electronics systems enabling participants to communicate face-to-face. Use of the videocamera with a computer enables an interview to take place. By combining e-mail and Internet people can attach résumés as part of the cover letter. The résumés can be printed by the potential employer's printer and so will be received and in print instantly. This is good news, especially for people who are communication-impaired. All states have two-party relay systems, but such systems are cumbersome to use and are slow.

Attitude Barriers

The toughest barriers to employment are not physical, they are attitudinal. Thomson feels the ADA and other legislation have helped some, but that the economic employment market for people with disabilities hasn't changed all that much. He believes that organizations or agencies that receive funds from the government are quite sensitized to employing those with disabilities. Large businesses are also. "Not much has trickled down to medium and small businesses, which is ironic since small business is now the hiring engine of the country." He feels employers anticipate that those with disabilities will have a chip on their shoulders and may dwell on legal rights and certain types of protection rather than on focusing on how they can handle the job and what they can do for the employer. Thomson says the laws relating to the hiring of those with disabilities are enacted as civil rights legislation rather than affirmative action. The employment laws covering those with disabilities are directed toward leveling the playing field so that the person with a disability receives the same consideration as any job candidate. The laws covering disabilities do not establish quotas for hiring as do those laws associated with affirmative action. Many agree that the hiring of those with disabilities has not gone nearly far enough. But you can make the difference by being hired on your abilities, making a successful career, and becoming a role model for others.

Computer Adaptive Technology

For computer users with a disability, entering multiple keystrokes simultaneously is a problem. A sticky-key utility allows you to press "shift" and then a character key sequentially, one-after-the-other, in order to capitalize that letter. The sticky-key feature is such a popular function that it is often bundled with other assistive functions.

If you find data entry difficult, you might use software that will attempt to predict and finish writing the word you began to enter based on two or three keystrokes. Microsystems Software packages its HandiWORD Deluxe word prediction software with a handy sticky-key feature.

Computer software that enables you to operate a PC compatible, desktop, laptop, or notebook simply by your voice is available at affordable prices. The Dragon System's voice recognition software family includes packages allowing you to enter data and text into word processing, spreadsheet, database and other applications verbally instead of using the keyboard.

Computers have transformed Braille output production. Duxbury Software products translate print documents. Eye-tracking systems developed by ISCAN enable individuals with severe physical disabilities to operate word processing and communications software by following the eye movement of the operator. The Optelec and Microsystems market computer screen magnification software. Both packages magnify data or text entries. The packages also magnify icons and messages as well as the cursor and scrollbars.

The SeeBEEP utility from Microsystems Software visually identifies audible beeps by choosing between a message display at the cursor location or a message flashing over the entire screen and between a two-tenths of a second flash or a full two-second message.

Until Microsystems Software introduced ADAPTA-LAN, employers needed to load assistive software into individual workstations in a network separately. This meant that individuals with disabilities were unable to access more than just a few "special" workstations. ADAPTA-LAN even supports keyboard access using alternative means, such as head mouse and trackball.

The Totally-Hands-Free Voice-Activated Speaker Phone from Temasek allows you to answer the telephone by simply saying, "hello" after the second ring and to make outgoing calls by telling the phone to call. The Temasek can be fitted with a sip-and-puff mouthpiece for alternative access.

Don Johnston Development Equipment in Wauconda, Illinois, developed a product called "Ke:nx". Johnston strove to make the Ke:nx product as easy to use as the Macintosh itself. One feature tells the computer to automatically activate Ke:nx when the computer is turned on. The Ke:nx interface box is equipped for attaching alternative keyboards and switches. Specialized input devices include large and small membrance keyboards, light-touch switches, rocker switches, sip-and-puff switches, plate switches, and others. One input method adjusts the standard keyboard for one-handed use or for use with a mouthstick or wand. Those commands that require simultaneous keystrokes can be easily executed. Input methods allow for mouse functions, speech feedback, and a variety of other options. Sheldon Harris, an occupational therapist and regional coordinator for Region V of the Special Education Technology Program of British Columbia, is fond of Ke:nx for its speed output. He has students use it as an augumentative communication device because "It is easy to program and has a high quality of speech—higher than the Ecco System speech synthesizer." Popular with his students is the story writer, which can utilize Rebus symbols on alternate keyboards.

Selecting What You Need

Tommy K. Mayer challenged readers of *Careers and the disABLED* to "Unlock the Doors of Technology to Open Your Career into the Mainstream." Whereas a few years ago only a handful of companies attempted to develop and market products specifically designed for people with disabilities, now hundred of companies are doing so. Mayer suggests that one of the best ways to wade through the options available is to determine what it is you need. He says the ADA vests in you the responsibility for defining and proposing the possible reasonable accommodations you need in order to perform the essential functions of your job. Employers are not responsible to know about your specific disability or to figure out what reasonable accommodations would be necessary.

To aid you in your selection, he advises asking the following questions:

What types of assistive technology products are available to enable you to perform the essential functions of your job?

What types of assistive technology products are available to enable you to use transportation facilities of equal quality to those available to people without disabilities?

What types of assistive technology products are available to enable you to transport yourself autonomously?

What types of assistive technology products are available to enable you to effectively use telecommunications systems?

Several products are now on the market to enlarge the realm of your success as an asset to your company:

- Minimal Motion, from Equal Access Computer Technology, makes the full range of standard keyboard keys and controls accessible to an operator using as few as four keys with only tiny finger motions and neither arm nor wrist mobility.

- If you find data entry difficult, you might consider software that attempts to predict and finish writing the word you had begun entering based upon two or three keystrokes. As noted earlier, Microsystems Software packages its HandiWORD Deluxe word prediction software with a handy sticky-key feature.

- Computer software that enables you to operate a PC-compatible, desktop, laptop, or notebook simply by talking to it is available now at reasonably affordable prices. Voice for Windows from Kurzweil Applied Intelligence supports voice input for dictation, enabling you to create text, enter data, and to navigate the computer screen.

Example 1: Dan Leist

Dan Leist works in the Research Department of Met Life in Illinois. His duties are to process insurance claims and bills. He also handles discrepancies concerning claims and hospital billing. He graduated from the University of Hawaii in sociology. Those are his abilities. His disability is that he has muscular dystrophy. He can feed himself, but he can't take a shower by himself. He is in a wheelchair. The company has helped him to accommodate to the workplace. He wears a headset, and he has a well-equipped phone and a computer. The height of the desk has been adjusted so that he can comfortably use it. Because the tops of his hands point inward, he uses two pencils to type. With practice, Leist has achieved a speed of 25 to 30 words per minute.

Leist admits he was depressed for a while when he was between jobs. But his subsequent success proves "anyone can get a job." Since working, he reports that his self-esteem is much higher, and his social life has picked up dramatically. He was assisted in his job placement efforts by Chicago Private Industry Council.

As he began to adjust to his new place of business, his cheerfulness and ability to do the job drew him praise from coworkers and his supervisor. Met Life even installed a push-button door for him that operates with an electric eye. Now this device is also of use to visitors to the company who are physically disabled. A computer tray is specifically set up at the right so he can conveniently use it. This has been a tax write-off. His desk is situated right behind glass doors. Visitors to the company must walk past. Now, he feels he is an ambassador for those with disabilities because he demonstrates every day to the public that he can do the job. He is also a testament to the fact that Met Life feels those with disabilities can and should work side-by-side with those who do not have disabilities. Being a role model, he says, has helped him to come out of his shell, and now he finds himself quite at ease and competing successfully in the world of work. Being near the glass door has also picked up his social life because visitors come by to chat with him. He has been attending more company social functions and has begun to expand his social horizons.

The one thing left on Leist's wish list is a van. He is awaiting its delivery after going through miles of red tape to be granted it from the Illinois Department of Rehabilitation Service. The state grants only four custom-equipped vans per year. "It was a tough ordeal to get that van." But, he feels, it has been well worth it. His van is equipped with remote control, which is activated by a hidden button to open the doors and bring down the lift all without any effort on his part. In place of the conventional driver's seat, there is a space for his wheelchair. Just as his electric wheelchair is steered by a joystick so is his van. The van is empowering Leist to be increasingly self-sufficient. "The goal of the Department of Rehabilitation is to have those with disabilities rely on as little help as possible from others," said Leist.

Having good reliable transportation helps allay the fear of employers that those with disabilities will miss work frequently or show up late, although this has been shown to be a myth. Leist strives to have an excellent attendance record as employers tend to feel that those with disabilities will be prone to skip work for doctors' appointments or due to illness. Showing the company how responsible he is is paving the way for acceptance of the next individual with physical disabilities.

Example 2: Carol Waskiewicz

In contrast to someone with obvious physical disabilities, Carol Waskiewicz has hidden disabilities. But she is not about to cave into her serious arthritis. Rather than attempt the stairs at her office, she uses the company elevator. Even her recent brain aneurysm is proving only a temporary setback as she pursues her activities as an accountant for a large firm.

Graduating with a B.S. in mathematics from Chicago State University, she has been using her skills in computers and math in the area of accounting. After some 28 years with R.R. Donnelly Publishers, the company folded and Waskiewicz had to find new employment.

When applying for her new job, which she had located through a private employment agency, she decided not to reveal that she had had a brain aneurysm because she felt the disclosure would eliminate her from consideration for the job. After showing the firm she could do the job, she would reveal her condition.

In the meantime, she learned how to compensate for deficiencies in her short-term memory caused by the aneurysm. She says in developing a memory-aid system on her own, she has been doing her part to make the stock of "post-it" notes climb. She surrounds herself with notes both at the office and at home. Whenever she undergoes training at her place of work, she makes copious notes and reviews them each night so they will be fresh in her mind. Repetition has meant her survival. She has learned how to transfer important items and procedures from her short-term memory into her long-term memory.

She feels, after a period of depression, that she has come to grips with both her disabilities. "It's OK if I fail today, I'll start tomorrow." She displayed that high spirit when she interviewed for her accountant job. During her interview, she stressed that she was self-reliant with a sense of humor. When asked the type of coworker she would not like to work with, she answered, "One who doesn't do a good job, one who goofs off." Obviously, Waskiewicz is not in this category. She has even continued to study for her master's degree despite her operation for the aneurysm. She admits it has slowed her progress somewhat, but she is not about to give up. She will get there no matter what. She has made it her mission to encourage others with disabilities to face their conditions and to come out winners in spite of them. She herself networks with those who share her disabilities. They have gotten to laughing at themselves. "Accepting ourselves for what we are and being able to have a sense of humor are the qualities which help us to stabilize and move forward."

Example 3: Pam Holmes

When Pam Holmes was a young girl, she dreamed of one day becoming a music teacher, but the gradual loss of her hearing made it necessary to change her career plans. Becoming deaf, however, did not change her drive to succeed. She felt there was a purpose behind her having lost her hearing. That sense of purpose, according to Maureen McLaughlin, writing in *Careers & the disABLED*, Spring 1993, has led to her involvement in shaping telecommunications legislation and advocating for people with disabilities in her job at Ultratec, Inc., the world's leading manufacturer of telecommunications devices for the deaf or TDDs.

While TDDs look like small word processors, they allow the nation's 22 million people who are deaf and hearing-impaired to carry on telephone conversations by typing messages on a digital screen, sending them over a modem and receiving an immediate reply from another TDD caller.

People with Visual Disabilities

Low vision means that a person has some vision, but even with regular glasses, everyday tasks that require sight may be difficult or impossible to do. A person with low vision may have difficulty reading and writing. Some people who have low vision are "legally blind." Many people who are not legally blind have low vision and need more than regular glasses to see clearly enough to perform their jobs.

Low vision devices do not correct the cause of lost vision, but they enlarge and bring into focus objects that are blurry and difficult to see, according to the Chicago Lighthouse Low Vision Service. Many devices are lightweight magnifying lenses. These can spectacle-mounted, hand-held, attached to regular glasses, or used on a stand. Hand-held and spectacle-mounted telescopes bring distant objects, like bus signs, faces, and blackboards into focus.

Closed-circuit televisions can be helpful for reading lengthy materials. Equipped with a zoom lens, this device can project printed materials onto a screen. The user selects the desired enlargement—up to 60 times the original size with enhanced contrast. Large-print dials, special lights, and other resources can help to compensate for limited vision.

The Chicago Lighthouse provides instruction and training in all prescribed devices. Follow-up services, if needed, include additional instruction in use of low vision devices. There are follow-up evaluations at periodic intervals.

Not every low vision patient can be helped, but more than 85 percent report improvement in ability to see with the use of low vision devices, according to the Chicago Lighthouse.

People with corrective lenses can use low vision devices. Magnifying lenses do not improve overall vision but enable the user to focus more efficiently on specific tasks. The degree of vision that lends itself to successful use of these aids varies with eye conditions. If a person has some remaining useful vision, low vision devices may be appropriate.

During a low vision examination, the examiner, patient, and coordinator discuss how current vision is being utilized and the additional tasks the patient would like to be able to do. The optometrist then gears the examination to determine how these goals can be met.

The Low Vision Clinics use a variety of adaptive devices and equipment for in-depth testing. The extensive examination takes 1 or 2 hours. The clinic staff strives to prescribe devices that will provide the maximum benefit at the minimum cost.

Some standard visual devices are stocked in the clinic. If such a device is recommended, the patient can purchase it immediately. Patients can also borrow devices for a week or two to help determine their effectiveness at home or on the job. Prescription lenses, however, must be ordered specifically for the individual patient.

Low vision devices magnify print, but they also restrict the field of vision. Thus, the user must learn to move head or eye to read an entire line or to see a total screen. The clinic coordinator is available to assist patients by phone or in person. Each patient is contacted at regular intervals to determine whether the devices are working satisfactorily.

The Illinois Department of Rehabilitation Services often assists with the cost of examinations and adaptive devices, if they are used for vocational purposes. Fees are adjusted according to income. No one is denied services because of inability to pay at the Chicago Lighthouse, 1850 W. Roosevelt Rd., Chicago, IL 60608.

Nolan Crabb reviewed the digital voice recorder in *The Braille Forum*, March 1996. The Univex Business Memo SPU3A, a European-manufactured digital recorder, is distributed in the United States by E.W. Bridge ILC of Redwood City, California. The unit has a suggested retail price of $119.95. Weighing in at a mere two and one-half ounces, the Univex Business Memo is thin and small. Even when inserted into its leather case, the recorder fits easily in a shirt pocket. The memo can hold up to 400 messages and, when set to long play, can record for up to 12.1 minutes. "The Business Memo does a truly outstanding job of recording and replaying messages when you record at the lower compression rate." Crabb says that if you can't afford something like a Braille 'N Speak or a more expensive digital recorder alternative for taking notes, the Univex SPU3A Business Memo may be the machine for you. The unit can be purchased from Ann Morris Enterprises, 890 Fams Ct., East Meadow, NY 11554, or call (800) 454-3175.

Wheelchairs

The "W-word" is an article by Don and Vicki Nelson in *Exceptional Parent*, March 1996. "Although it was two and a half years ago, we vividly remember the day Andy's physical therapist first mentioned the 'W-word'—wheelchair. Our hearts sank, but we had to admit that our son's motor difficulties were becoming more apparent with each passing day." Andy, their son who had been born with cerebral palsy, was not independently ambulatory for long distances. Reporting on the newfound independence his wheelchair provides him, his parents praise the benefits of power mobility, which far outweigh their initial fears. "We now view power mobility as an alternative our son not only needs, but, more importantly, something he deserves." Andy delights in his new independence, and his parents have observed his increased self-esteem.

Mark Wright, 23, was paralyzed by a gunshot wound. He refuses to bow to his disability. He glides everywhere. He walks his dog. He visits friends regularly. He attends McHenry Community College and is planning a career in computer design. Wright owes his lifestyle to his bright outlook on life and to his $1,800 wheelchair—a mid-range price for the newest models.

Back in 1933, mechanical engineer Harry Jennings created the steel-tube design that dominates the industry today. That design remained relatively unchallenged until the 70s when wheelchair users began to protest the lack of innovation in wheelchair design. That, coupled with technological advances, led to the device of today.

The new model borrows from breakthroughs in the bicycle industry. Employing titanium alloys and aircraft-grade aluminum and plastics, the wheelchair can weigh as little as 19 pounds. It sports a flat, cushioned seat and back and adjustable features, with wheels that pop off and casters bolted on rather than welded. Younger users find the sci-fi look especially appealing.

According to the *Chicago Tribune*, February 18, 1996, Beth McCarty, an occupational therapist at Schwab, says the new models generally make a therapist's job easier. "What we're encouraging is that these individuals who are getting injured don't stay at home. Get out." That is exactly what Schwab patient Andre Moses is doing. He is in the process of applying for a high-tech model similar to Wright's. It is also possible to obtain a wheelchair through Public Aid. After the rehabilitation doctors submit a lengthy medical evaluation to a wheelchair vendor, the vendor makes a request to the state. Public Aid officials in Illinois do not approve a specific model for a patient, according to Illinois Department of Public Aid spokesperson Dean Schott. Instead, if convinced of the need, the state approves funds for mid-range quality items to meet the medical needs of the client. The vendor then selects an appropriate model.

People with Cancer

Some physical disabilities such as cancer require little accommodation on the part of the employer. Due largely to advances in medical technology and rehabilitation services, cancer patients are living longer and are more likely to return to productive work than ever before. In fact, the return to work is an important stage in recovery. Employers have a responsibility to provide cancer patients and employees with a history of cancer with a workplace free of discrimination. The following organizations can provide free information about employment of people with cancer. If you have specific questions about an employment matter, you are encouraged to use these sources:

- American Cancer Society for information on treatment and rehabilitation. The American Cancer Society provides up-to-date, consistent, medically sound answers to questions about cancer. Call (800) ACS-2345.

- Job Accommodation Network for information on accommodating employees with disabilities, including cancer patients. Call (800) JAN-PCEJ.

- Illinois Department of Human Rights for information on legal responsibilities of employers and legal responsibilities of employees, and suggestions on possible accommodations for employees with cancer.

- Equal Employment Opportunity Commission, for information on legal responsibilities of employers and legal responsibilities of employees regarding the federal Americans with Disabilities Act. Chicago District Office, (312) 353-2713; (312) 353-2421 (TDD/TT); St. Louis District Office: (314) 425-6585; (314) 425-6547 (TDD/TT).

ABLEDATA

ABLEDATA is a single comprehensive resource that can be used to locate and to compare assistive technology products. According to Alynne Landers, M.I.M., a program specialist writing in *Exceptional Parent*, March

1994, the number of choices available may surprise even the most well-informed. ABLEDATA has information on more than 19,000 products.

ABLEDATA provides an internationally renowned database of information on assistive technology and rehabilitation equipment for all disabilities and for all age groups. The project maintains and adds new records on products currently manufactured and distributed in the United States from approximately 2,500 domestic and foreign companies. In addition to commercially available products, the database also includes nearly 1,000 "do-it-yourself" designs and prototype descriptions. Covering high-tech, low-tech, and "no-tech" products designed for persons with disabilities, the scope of the database ranges from enlarged-handle utensils to the most sophisticated optical-character recognition devices or computer-screen readers. Entries in the ABLEDATA database include manufacturer and distributor information for each product, product features and specifications, and pricing data in a format that permits easy comparison among products.

ABLEDATA Product areas include:

Architectural elements

Communication

Computers

Controls

Prosthetics

Seating

Sensory disabilities

Therapeutic aids

Transportation

Vocational management

Walking and wheeled mobility

With a modem and applications software package, computer users can access electronic bulletin board service 24 hours a day. Computer dial (301) 589-3563 (1200 to 9600 bauds). There are no subscription fees. The cost is based on call from user's station to ABLEDATA office.

IBM CD-ROM ABLEDATA is available for use on IBM personal computers and Windows and DOS formats. Electronic images of many products can be put on the screen using the "Picture" option.

For noncomputer users, services are also available through voice and text telephone. For patrons living in or visiting the Washington area, a personal guided tour of the center can be arranged upon request. Contact ABLEDATA, 8445 Coles, Suite 935, Silver Spring, MD 20910, or call (800) 227-0210 or fax (301) 587-1967.

Response to the ADA

Provisions of the Americans with Disabilities Act (ADA) and the Family and Medical Leave Act (FMLA) have created the unintended consequence that injured workers may choose to take paid vacation or sick time rather than unpaid leaves. The FMLA mandates that employers cannot order employees with temporary disabilities to take light-duty jobs and a recent advisory letter from the Labor Department held that workers can take leave, if they are entitled to it under FMLA.

Title I of the ADA ensures that qualified individuals with disabilities are given equal employment opportunities. Despite the passage of this law, many companies still hesitate to hire additional disabled workers because of economic concerns and the natural fear that it will not work out. Employers are bound to get over their initial fear after they see the business sense of hiring competent disabled individuals, and may also find that the price of accommodation is not as high as they had at first thought. In fact, the Job Accommodation Network reports that 25 percent of all accommodations surveyed did not cost a cent; 57 percent cost between $1 and $500, and only 7 percent cost more than $2,000.

- HITEC Group International, Inc. has developed an IBM-compatible portable keyboard automating teletypewriter (TTY) call handling and facilitating device. The ADA requires all service providers to offer equal telephone access for TTY users, who require TTY terminals at both ends of their conversations. The new device, Keyplus, costs $799.

- According to the ADA, lighting fixtures on public area walls must not protrude beyond 4 inches.

- Microcomputer technology is increasingly used to augment the tasks of court stenographers and also is accommodating stipulations in the ADA. This profession requires intuitive transcription of colloquialism, slang terms, and often transcription of several people speaking at one time. Microcomputers can, however, efficiently translate cryptic stenographer codes into legible English. Therefore, it is not the stenographers themselves but their assistants who are likely to be made obsolete. Cheetah Systems offers a $10,000 turn-key translation system for court reporting that can convert the equivalent of 200 pages of stenotype code to English in only 14 seconds. The company is rising fast in the legal transcription industry, largely because of thorough technical support and the ability of its system to run on a standard microcomputer. The firm is currently preparing a $15,000 television captioning system.

Corporations can learn from 3M's comprehensive response to the ADA. Administrators, architects, facility managers, and employees at 3M have worked together to develop a plan to evaluate work site accessibility. The first step involved arranging a meeting between architects and facility managers to assess ADA requirements and plant needs. The second step was to conduct a survey of the plan, measuring the common areas, handicapped parking spaces, and bathroom stalls to ensure ADA compliance. Restroom upgrades required special attention to comply with building code requirements. The pressure needed to open doors was also checked. As a final step, survey results were presented in a report to management with later follow-up costs for the ADA upgrade.

The HEATH Resource Center has completed its work on the three-year, 1990–1993, federally funded study, "Postsecondary Education Program: Evaluation and Dissemination of Successful Practices." The study examines model postsecondary education and disability programs funded since 1980 by the U.S. Department of Education's Office of Special Education and Rehabilitative Services. Nineteen products were identified by the study as exemplary. HEATH disseminates 13 of these products and provides ordering information for the remaining 6. The products include guidebooks, curricula, manuals, and videos. Some are targeted toward students, while others are intended for professionals. For further descriptions of the products and for ordering information, contact HEATH and request a copy of the exemplary products order form: HEATH Resource Center, One Dupont Circle, Suite 800, Washington, DC 20036.

The law offers an opportunity for companies to lessen their property tax assessments after they have determined the modifications they have to make so that their properties would become more accessible to individuals with disabilities. The Internal Revenue Services (IRS) also provides two tax incentives designed to help companies improve accessibility. One of these comes in the form of a tax credit intended to help small businesses defray ADA-related "eligible access expenditures." The other is a tax deduction of as much as $15,000 annually for companies using their taxable income to finance modifications to their facilities. Both tax incentives are available to any company eligible under Title 26 of Section 44 and Title 26 of Section 190 of the Internal Revenue Code.

The ADA was established to ensure that transportation services would be available for people with disabilities. However, a recent Logan, Utah, study indicates that the legislation will benefit "aging disabled" people the most. Thus, transit equipment has to be designed to facilitate transportation for this group of people. In addition, transportation services staff have to be trained to relate with such commuters.

Ten transportation authorities' statements on their organization's compliance with the ADA generally express problems dealing with availability of funds for the required retrofitting of buses, paratransit, and route scheduling. Each organization has dealt with compliance using a variety of strategies congruent with its overall marketing and development plans.

The ADA of 1990 provides employers with many opportunities to tap the disabled as a work force. However, compliance with the act will require a keen understanding of the definitions and coverage of this law as well as the effects of specific provisions on employment practices. Employers are required to make such reasonable accommodations to eliminate barriers to employees with disabilities as long as these amenities will not impose undue hardships upon the employer.

Sears, Roebuck and Co.

Sears, Roebuck and Co. employs an estimated 20,000 persons with physical or mental disabilities among its 300,000 person work force. In 1947, the company was a founding member of the President's Committee on Employment of People with Disabilities. In 1954, it established the Program for the Employment of the Physically Handicapped. In 1968, it established a division of equal opportunity within its national personnel department. From 1972 to the present, its Selective Placement Program has matched the talents and skills of people with disabilities with the requirements of jobs within Sears. It has established the ABLE Program—Architectural Barrier Lessening and Elimination—to remove barriers facing employees and customers with disabilities at all Sears facilities. From 1991 to 1993, it empowered the Corporate Council on Disability Issues to identify affected employment areas and implement policy to ensure fair treatment of people with disabilities under ADA Title I. Its Corporate Council on Disability Issues was then replaced with a rotating Diversity Council, which includes employees with disabilities and direct managers of employees with disabilities. It joined the other companies to form Project Access, an organization designed to aid in ADA compliance and in the employment of people with disabilities.

"Sears continues to encounter hundreds of workplace accommodations since the adoption of the ADA, most of which are not recorded formally," says Executive Vice President Tony Rucci. Orthopedic impairments account for more than one third or 36 percent of reported disabilities, followed by cardiovascular impairments at 19 percent, internal impairments at 8 percent, sensory impairments at 7 percent, and respiratory impairments at 7 percent. Rucci comments that "In light of the trends identified in the preparation of this report, 'Communicating the Americans with Disabilities Act' by Peter David Blanck, Annenberg Senior Fellow, it is likely that fewer than 10 percent of Sears employees will self-identify as disabled and require workplace accommodations."

The report comments that these trends suggest the need for future study to guide work force planning and ADA transcendence at Sears and at other organizations. Such studies should include:

- Analysis of the extent to which particular back and spine injuries on the job account for a large proportion of disability identifications

- The relation of workers' compensation programs, "back to work" programs, and workplace strategies for maintaining a qualified, healthy, and safe work force

- The reasons why large numbers of qualified employees and potential job applicants with "hidden" disabilities are unable or unwilling to self-identify in the workplace.

Many believe that the ADA has reflected a dramatic shift in American public policy toward the equal employment of persons with disabilities. Yet studies differ in their conclusion as to whether the ADA has played or will play a significant role in enhancing labor force participation of qualified persons with disabilities and in reducing dependence on government entitlement programs. At a minimum, the resulting dialogue has been illustrative to small and large corporate entities as they attempt proactive compliance strategies.

The Blanck Report

According to the Blanck report, "Communicating the Americans with Disabilities Act," several core facts are emerging. Contrary to popular misconceptions, it is widely understood that the ADA does not require employers to hire individuals with disabilities who are not qualified or to hire qualified individuals with disabilities over equally qualified individuals without disabilities. Some argue that Title I distorts the market value of American labor, requiring employers to take "affirmative" and unduly costly measures to accommodate persons with disabilities. These conclusions are not validated by the findings in the present report. The costs of accommodating qualified workers at Sears is low and the relative economic, productivity, and safety-related benefits are high. There is no evidence that ADA implementation and transcendence have distorted the value of labor in the Sears work force. Virtually all Title I disputes studied at Sears have been resolved at a low cost without extensive trial litigation, keeping qualified employees at work.

Future research must identify the variables to be studied to achieve an understanding of the nature of an individual's disability and its relation to employment opportunity and career advancement. The report suggests that the following questions be studied:

How may substantial limitations change over time for individuals with different disabilities and for qualified men and women, younger and older workers, and workers from different ethnic groups with varying disabilities?

What objective measures, in addition to employment rates and accommodation costs, are valid indicators of effective Title I implementation?

How do individual and workplace strategies enhance ADA transcendence?

What are the emerging employment opportunities facing persons with severe disabilities?

How does ADA transcendence enhance employers' economic competitiveness?

How will structural labor market forces and an increasingly global economy affect ADA transcendence strategies?

Working assumptions are emerging that will help guide future study so that employers, policymakers, courts, and others may more effectively evaluate ADA implementation, including the study of disability policy requiring interdisciplinary analysis grounded in medicine, psychology, economics, law, ergonomics, and other fields; disability's function as a limiter of skills or capabilities; how with appropriate supports, the abilities of qualified persons with disabilities improves, and the acknowledgement that disability is a natural part of the human experience.

Companies must continue to establish systems that objectively measure the costs and benefits of accommodating people with disabilities into their work forces. Large corporations, such as Sears, or smaller companies through cooperatives or associations, increasingly require data collection systems that identify positive and challenging trends in ADA implementation to assist in business planning, dispute avoidance, and educational efforts.

Supported Employment

While supported employment has not reached its potential as an initiative, it remains full of promise. But it takes commitment from those who are involved. Despite a need for further achievements, there is encouraging data regarding the success and progress of supported employment. Up from only a few thousand involved in supported employment in 1985, there are now more than 100,000 currently so involved. As more people were absorbed into supported employment, it was clear that wages, benefits, and integration for such individuals are clearly superior to that received by individuals in day activity centers, day treatment centers, and sheltered workshops. But, there is a long road to travel. Fewer than one in eight or nine interested individuals with significant disabilities are currently able to choose a job in the community with long-term support, according to the above-mentioned article.

One of the problems noted in this article is that the vast majority of the money that buys some kind of employment or day service for people with severe disabilities supports segregation and not integration. Sheltered work is still counted as a successful vocational closure by most state vocational rehabilitation agencies.

At present, the area of vocational training for adults with disabilities is undergoing revision. Instead of being a dead end, it is increasingly regarded as an intermediate step or bridge along a continuum whose end point is employment in the outside world. The arena of the sheltered workshop is being invaded by work activities, work adjustment training, transitional employment services, and extended sheltered employment.

There was a time not too long ago when individuals with severe intellectual and physical disabilities were assigned to adult activity centers and day programs where they did not interact with peers who did not have disabilities. In other words, facilities for those with severe disabilities were segregated. Certainly, the idea that such individuals could ever engage in paid work was unheard of. Getting into a shelter and receiving pay for piecework was the ultimate goal. The very term "sheltered" connoted the idea of protection—individuals with severe disabilities were to be pro-tected. They were not seen as active members of the larger community.

But, in the 1980s, the concept of supported employment gave renewed hope for active roles in the community. The Office of Special Education and Rehabilitation Services was able to fund efforts in the direction of supported employment. Local funding agencies such as the state voca-tional rehabilitation agency or Job Training Partnerships Act (JTPA) established a mechanism for contract development with a company for on-the-job training. A supporting agency can use funding to enter into a subcontract with a partnership business for independent coworkers rather than exclusively employing its own personnel. The agency can also provide plans for achieving self-support as an improvement-related work expense.

In supported employment, there is internal support and employee assistance for skill development. Jobs are analyzed into small steps, and systematic instruction is provided at each step. Training is extended to daily living skills. Supported employees gain experience in a simulated work environment. Tasks assigned are usually sorting, assembling, and cleaning. A sheltered workshop is one of the sites of employment. A production time study is performed in order to rate the pay per piece in a facility that procures subcontract work. Semi-skilled work crews perform in groups of up to eight employees under close supervision. The employee is supervised by a representative of the agency supplying the workers. The employee is hired and is supervised by the human service agency. The individual is supported in transition jobs.

The National Agenda of Supported Employment supports:

Expanding the number of people participating in supported employment to 250,000 by 1998

Promoting greater consumer self-advocacy for supported employment

Converting segregated day programs into integrated employment programs

Promoting the implementation of the Americans with Disabilities Act

Expanding and improving the quality of supported employment personnel.

The Association for Persons in Supported Employment (APSE) endorses the expansion of supported employment and conversion to supported employment, which means expanding the number of people participating in supported employment to 50 percent of all people served by 1998 and converting segregated day programs into integrated employment programs. This requires a systems change instead of merely adding programs. To achieve this, states will be encouraged to provide higher levels of funding so that 50 percent of available funds will be dedicated to supported employment. Another objective is to have states create annual goals of the number of people with severe disabilities who participate in supported employment. The APSE advocates long-term employment support funding for people with a variety of disability labels who need and want supported employment. Also Title VI-C funds authorized through the Rehabilitation Act should be increased by 1,000 percent during the next 5 years and, further, that Medicaid, a waiver, education, and JTPA funds should be used to the maximum extent possible for supported employment.

The APSE is also proposing increased self-determination by promoting informed consumer choice and control of resources by people with disabilities; promoting greater self-advocacy among consumers who need or want supported employment. The APSE supports a policy of eliminating conflicting state and national policies that support and fund integrated employment while continuing to fund segregated vocational services. The APSE promotes the implementation of and investment in the ADA, the 1992 Rehabilitation Act Amendments, the Individuals with Disabilities Education Act, and other public policies that impact integrated employment and inclusion for people with disabilities. Another goal is to promote the implementation of and investment in the School-to-Work Opportunities Act, National Workforce Initiatives, and other broad public policies that promote inclusive opportunities for all people in work and society. Finally, the APSE seeks to expand to improve the quality of supported employment personnel. Write to the Association for Persons in Supported Employment for a schedule of conferences to be held around the country: 1627 Monument Ave., Richmond, VA 23220, or call (804) 278-9187.

The September 1994 issue of APSE's *The Advance* urges full employment of people with disabilities and says this will be accomplished when neighbors, family members, friends, and employers understand and advocate for employing people with disabilities. It states, "When ADA works, society realizes an immediate benefit-reduced welfare dependence, employment growth, and a richer, more diverse society."

Supported employment initiatives are ongoing at Sears, Roebuck and Co. Sears' participation demonstrates ADA transcendence. For example, a Sears store in Escondido, California, has begun a pilot job-sharing program in collaboration with the United Cerebral Palsy Association of San Diego County to employ people with cerebral palsy. The store is employing four individuals with cerebral palsy to maintain stockroom inventories in the expectation that they will cumulatively perform the same amount of work as one employee without a disability. The UCP provides transportation to and from work for the employees and furnishes a full-time trainer/manager at no cost to Sears. The only cost to Sears is an hourly wage of $5.29 to the UCP, which covers payroll administration for the employees. If successful in the Escondido store, this model program may be extended to other Sears stores, according to Harry Geller, Sears Workforce Diversity Regional Manager.

Students with disabilities will be receiving help to launch their careers thanks to a project initiated by Virginia Commonwealth University's Employment Support Institute (ESI). With a $57,000 grant awarded to ESI in January of 1994 by the Dole Foundation and the Funding Partnership, "Project WINS" (Work Incentive Network in the Schools) is providing training and hands-on tools such as computer software to public schools in Virginia. Project WINS will teach students and school staff from selected schools to identify when a student is eligible for Social Security Administration Work Incentives and how to use them to gain work experience and jobs for graduating students with disabilities. Work Incentives funds enable people with disabilities to purchase supports needed to perform the job of their choice. School staff, including teachers, counselors, and special and vocational education teachers, have been trained to work with students with disabilities, their parents, advocates, and employment specialists in the community for the project.

A primary goal is to arrange a variety of ways students can participate in the work force, such as paid positions with employment supports, job sampling or better access to vocational education programs. A benefit of Project WINS is that students will be learning ways the system can work for them and to make decisions about their career futures.

For more information, contact Mark Hill, ESI director at (804) 367-1992 or Chris Pellegrino, project manager at (804) 367-2665.

Supported Employment: A Case Study

The United Cerebral Palsy Associations, Community Services Division, presented a 1992 Workshop, "Natural Supports for Employment and Community Living" which discussed a number of issues related to supported employment. In his discussion of job site training and natural supports, Michael Callahan, Supported Employment Project Director for the United Cerebral Palsy Associations, presented the following case study of a young man in New Jersey who had attended a high school special education class. Jason was 18 years old. He was labeled as having moderate cerebral palsy and mental retardation. He was contacted by a local supported employment provider and asked if he would be interested in working half time during his last year of school. Jason expressed interest in working with computers. Soon a 20-hour-per-week job was found at a grocery store in his area. The job was negotiated. Jason was to enter incoming grocery inventory into the store's computer program. Jason had no previous experience with computers, and his teacher and parents doubted if he could successfully perform the job.

But, Laura, the employment specialist, performed a detailed job analysis of the grocery operation. She observed all the required job components. She got to know the supervisors and coworkers and got a feel of the culture of the market. From the beginning, Laura concentrated on clarifying the procedures and methods used by the employer. She carefully considered the training strategies used by the store manager and workers. As she planned the first day of Jason's employment, Laura decided which tasks the company would probably be able to teach and those tasks that would require more powerful teaching. She based her decision on her knowledge of Jason, which she gained through development of the Vocational Profile, and of her experience in the grocery market. Laura then met with the store manager to clarify responsibilities and to explain her role as a facilitator/consultant rather than as a primary provider of training for Jason. She then wrote step-by-step procedures for a couple of the most challenging job tasks. Starting with Jason's first day of work and continuing throughout the period she was offering support, Laura continuously evaluated whether she or someone in the market should teach each job skill.

By the end of the first month of employment, it was clear that Jason was having a great deal of difficulty accurately inputting data into the computer. Laura began to solve the problem by changing the instructional cues from primarily conversational/verbal, which was the most natural setting, to gestural cues with limited verbal. This strategy resulted in some improvement. Laura doublechecked with the manager for ways to look at the most difficult parts of the task and to see whether she could break them down into smaller, more teachable parts. Smaller parts did not seem to help Jason.

Finally, she considered an altogether different method or an adaptation of the natural method. She determined the number of suppliers, which turned out to be six, for the input that Jason had to master. Then she developed a plexiglass overlay for each of the six forms. The overlays each had color-coded positions that corresponded to the columns of the inventory sheets. Jason was taught to determine the correct overlay, to slide the inventory sheet into the device, and to align the first row of figures. The color-coded overlays provided Jason with quick visual feedback for his place on the sheet. Jason's consistency immediately began to improve. The supervisor was so impressed with Jason's productivity that he suggested that the other part-time data-entry clerk use the overlays.

This effort was so successful that the employer began to think of ways to make Jason's job easier. He was also much more comfortable with teaching new tasks that became necessary. Thus, the role of the employment specialist was able to smoothly evolve to facilitator/consultant because of the teaching strategies that referenced natural approaches from the beginning.

Callahan drew several conclusions from this case. One is that natural supports and outside facilitation is not an either/or decision. We still need both. Supported employees should be assisted to do the best work they can, and natural supports should be utilized to the greatest degree possible. Supported employment facilitators must carefully consider the manner in which they plan for and deliver instruction.

A good source for information on supported employment and job accommodation is the Center on Education and Training for Employment (CETE). It fulfills its mission both nationally and internationally by conducting applied research, development, evaluation, and policy analyses, and by providing leadership development, technical assistance, and information services. The areas of focus include the quality and outcomes of education and training for employment; the alignment of career and occupational preparation with the knowledge and performance requirements of the workplaces of today and tomorrow and opportunities for disadvantaged and special populations to succeed in education, training, and work environments. It serves the needs of small and large private-sector companies, both nationally and internationally, through job and task analysis, instructional system design, and development and skills updating.

CETE's information services include ERIC Clearinghouse on Adult, Career and Vocational Education; Vocational Instructional Materials Laboratory, Library Facilities Laboratory; library facilities and fee-based information search services; and CETE publications and newsletters. For additional information, write to: Program Information Office, CETE/OSU, 1900 Kenny Rd., Columbus, OH 43210-1090, or call (614) 292-4353, or fax (614) 292-1260.

Conclusion

Students with disabilities are young people facing a challenging time of life. Daniel E. Steere, author of "Remember When . . . Rediscovering the Heart of Transition," *The Advance*, September, 1994, observes that young people need a base of experience upon which to make informed choices about jobs, places to live, and other issues. Effectiveness in designing curricula is the degree to which these experiences are afforded. Families, not just students, experience transition. This impact can be positive as a proud family attends graduation or stressful as families realize their sons and daughters may have no place to go. Professionals must consider the pressures on families and provide needed supports to them. The dreams of students and their parents may not always be the same. Transition is a time of life in which young people struggle for independence and self-definition. Many young people struggle to develop a sense of themselves. Although much of our formal transition planning efforts focus on employment and independent living, a broader goal for most young people is to figure out who they are and why they are valued. In facilitating transition planning, these issues may need to be addressed and support may be required. Many students and their families prefer to conduct planning about the future away from the pressures of a traditional school-based planning meeting. Transition does not end when one leaves school. Few students attain optimal outcomes immediately upon graduation or the end of educational services. Transition is a longitudinal process, and those people who are willing to go the distance in providing support are often most important to a student.

A F T E R W O R D

Finally, a pep talk from Ines Torres Beilke, author of *Career Motivation and Self-Concept*, published by Kendall-Hunt, 1986. She believes that your motivation reflects the way you understand yourself. "Motivation is that inner force that moves you to behave in the world around you. It is the way you truly are toward life from your inside out." She cautions people against thinking that how they behave is caused by forces outside of themselves. "The reality is that everything you do, think, and feel comes from within you."

In Beilke's workshops, she tells students and other people that before they can change the way they perceive themselves, they need to change their self-concepts so they can behave accordingly. She gives exercises in which participants are to think positively about themselves—to picture themselves as beautiful, unique, worthwhile human beings. She claims that after you come to terms with yourself by accepting who you are, you are constructive. People cannot be motivated by force. In our era, according to Beilke, what constitutes an effective human being is the ability to think and to understand motivation. "However, unless we begin to understand motivation from the inside out, workers will not participate in, produce, and be constructively motivated to realize what they are capable of being in the redesigning of our corporate structures. In order to make changes in the outside world, one needs to be inside oneself. In order to create our future, we need to recognize how our values influence and shape the choices we make. Therefore, when we choose to be constructively motivated, we become more aware of our values, self-concepts, and personal identification." She proclaims that tomorrow's shortage is workers, not jobs, and that one of the greatest challenges facing America is "to train workers to fit today's exploding technology and stop promoting the attitude that life is free of work."

With the skills, knowledge, and motivation you've found in the preceding chapters, you are well on your way to anticipating and meeting the needs of tomorrow, today. You have the tools to define, search for, and land a challenging and rewarding job that will take you into next month, next year, and the next millennium.

We wish you every success in your journey!

A P P E N D I X

Information Technology Sources

Accent Voice Synthesizers
AICOM Corp.
1590 Oakland Rd., Suite B112
San Jose, CA 95131
(408) 453-8251
Fax (408) 453-8255

Alva Braille Displays
HumanWare, Inc.
6245 King Road
Loomis, CA 95650
(916) 652-7253
(800) 722-3393
Fax (916) 542-7296

IBM Screen Reader/2
IBM Special Needs Systems
PO Box 1328
Boca Raton, FL 33429-1328
(407) 443-2000
(800) 342-6672

IBM Voicetype II Voice
Recognition System
Dragon Systems
320 Nevada Street
Newton, MA 02160
(800) 825-5897

Kurzweil Readers and Scanners
Xerox Imaging Systems, Inc.
9 Centennial Drive
Peabody, MA 01960
(508) 977-2000
Fax (508) 977-2148

Multivoice Synthesizers
Institute on Applied Technology
300 Longwood Avenue
Boston, MA 02115-5737
(617) 735-6486
Fax (617) 735-6882

NEC Monitors
NEC Technologies
1414 Massachusetts Avenue
Foxborough, MA 01719
(800) 632-4636

Workplace Accommodations

The following organizations can provide information on employment and
information technology for accommodating those with physical disabilities at the place of work of their choice.

Chicago Lighthouse for the Blind
1850 W. Roosevelt Road
Chicago, IL 60608

Iowa Creative Employment Options
John A. Nietupski, Ph.D., Associate Director
257 HS
University of Iowa
Iowa City, IA 52242-1011
(319) 356-4664

Job Accommodation Network
West Virginia University
918 Chestnut Ridge Road
Suite 1, P.O. Box 6080
Morgantown, WV 26506-6080
(800) 526-7234

**President's Committee on the Employment
  of People with Disabilities**
1331 F Street, NW
Washington, DC 20004-1107
(202) 376-6200
TDD (202) 376-6205

Program Able
Audrey Walker
c/o Sears, Roebuck and Co.
3333 Beverly Road, EC-233A
Hoffman Estates, IL 60179
(847) 286-8168

Project Access
Joe Dragonette, President
205 W. Wacker Drive, Suite 2200
Chicago, IL 60606
(312) 424-5300

Recording for the Blind
20 Rozell Road
Princeton, NJ 08540
(609) 452-0606
(800) 221-4792

Wisconsin Employment Resources, Inc.
Sue Kidder, Director
1310 Mendota Street
Suite 107
Madison, WI 53714
(608) 246-3444

Agencies for Further Information

These agencies offer information on services for the physically disabled
and on the Americans with Disabilities Act.

Administration for Children, Youth, and Families
330 C Street, SW
Washington, DC 20201
(202) 205-8347

Administration on Developmental Disabilities
200 Independence Ave., SW
349 F Humphrey Building
Washington, DC 20201
(202) 690-6590

American Federation for the Blind and Gallaudet University
(202) 223-0101 (V/TDD)

Association of Handicapped Student Service Programs
  in Post Secondary School Education
(800) 247-7752 (V/TDD)

Department of Transportation
(202) 366-9305
(202) 202-7687 (TDD)

Equal Opportunity Commission
(800) USA-EEOC
(800) 800-3302
(202) 663-4494 (TDD)

National Information Center for Children
  and Youth with Disabilities
P.O. Box 1492
Washington, DC 20013-1492
(800) 999-5599
(703) 893-6061
(703) 893-8614 (TDD)

National Institute of Neurological Disorders and Stroke
9000 Rockville Pike
Building 31, Room 8A-16
Bethesda, MD 20892
(301) 496-5751

National Library Service for the Blind and Physically Handicapped
Library of Congress
1291 Taylor St., NW
Washington, DC 20542
(800) 424-8567
(202) 707-5100

Office of Special Education and Rehabilitation Services
Clearinghouse on Disability Information
U.S. Department of Education
Switzer Building
330 C Street, SW
Room 3132
Washington, DC 20202-2524
(202) 205-8723

President's Committee on Employment of People with Disabilities
1331 F Street, NW, Suite 300
Washington, DC 20004-1107
(202) 376-6200
(202) 376-6205 (TDD)

Regional Disability Business Accommodation Centers
(617) 349-2639
(617) 354-6618 (TDD)

Senate Subcommittee on Disability Policy
113 Hart Senate Office Building
Washington, DC 20510
(202) 224-6265

U.S. Architectural Transportation Barriers Compliance Board
(800) USA-ABLE

Disabled American Veterans
807 Main Avenue, SW
Washington, DC 20024
(202) 554-3501 (Voice/TT)
(202) 554-3581

National membership organization of service-oriented veterans with disabilities, their families and survivors. DAV works to lower the rate of unemployment among veterans with disabilities and to prevent discrimination against them.

National Council of Disability
1331 F Street, NW
Suite 1050
Washington, DC 20591
(202) 272-2004
(202) 272-2022 (Fax)
(202) 272-2074 (TT)

NCD is an independent federal agency appointed by the President and confirmed by the Senate. It is charged with addressing, analyzing, and making recommendations on public policy issues that affect people with disabilities. The National Council originated and developed the first draft of the Americans with Disabilities Act, which was signed into law on July 26, 1990. It distributes a free monthly publication, *The NCD Bulletin.*

National Easter Seal Society
230 W. Monroe St., Suite 1800
Chicago, IL 60601
(312) 726-6200
(312) 726-1497 (Fax)
(312) 726-4258 (TT)

NESS is a nonprofit community-based health agency dedicated to increasing the independence of people with disabilities. Easter Seal offers a wide range of high-quality rehabilitation services and programs to assist adults and children with disabilities and their families. Easter Seal centers offer employment opportunities for physical, occupational, speech, and other rehabilitation professionals. A publication catalog is available at no cost.

Testing

ACT Test Administration
Box 4028
Iowa City, IA 52243
(319) 337-1332
(319) 337-1701 (TT)
(319) 337-3020 (Fax)

American College Testing will arrange for individual administration of the ACT assessment for students with physical or perceptual disabilities. Accommodations may include use of large-type or braille editions or audiocassette tapes. For further information, call or write for a Request for Special Testing.

American Association for the Advancement of Science
Project on Science Technology and Disability
1333 H St., NW
Washington, DC 20005
(202) 326-6630 (Voice/TT)
(202) 371-9849 (Fax)

Supported Employment

Association of Persons in Supported Employment
5001 W. Broad Street
Richmond, VA 23230
(804) 282-3655

Assistive Technology

ABLEDATA
8455 Colesville Road
Silver Springs, MD 20910-3319
(800) 346-2742 or (800) 227-0216
(301) 588-9284

> Consumer referral service that maintains a database of more than 17,000 adaptive devices from 2,000 companies.

Adaptive Device Locator System
Academic Software
331 W. 2nd St.
Lexington, KY 40507
(606) 233-2332

Advanced Rehabilitation Technology Network
25825 Eshelman Avenue
Lomita, CA 90717
(310) 325-3058

Alliance for Technology Access
1128 Solano Avenue
Albany, CA 94706
(510) 528-0747

American Foundation for Technology Assistance
Route 14, Box 230
Morgantown, NC 28655
(704) 438-9697

American Occupational Therapy Association
1383 Piccard Drive
Rockville, MD 20849
(800) 843-2682

American Physical Therapy Association
1111 N. Fairfax Street
Alexandria, VA 22314
(703) 684-2782

American Speech-Language Hearing Association
10801 Rockville Pike
Rockville, MD 20852
(800) 638-8255
(301) 897-5700

Apple Computer
World Disability Solutions Group
20525 Mariana Avenue
Cupertino, CA 95014
(408) 974-7910
(408) 974-7911 (TDD)

Assistive Device Center
6000 J Street
Sacramento, CA 95819
(916) 278-6422

AT&T Special Needs Center
2001 Route 46
Parsippany, NJ 07054
(800) 233-1222 or (800) 833-3232

Bureau of Services for Visually Impaired
5535 Southwick Boulevard
Toledo, OH 43614
(419) 866-1669

Clearinghouse on Computer Accommodations
General Services Administration
18 and F Street, NW
KGDO #2022
Washington, DC 20405
(202) 501-4906

Computer Electronics Accommodations Program
U.S. Dept. of Defense
5109 Leesburg Pike
Falls Church, VA 22041
(703) 756-8811

Congress of Organizations of the Physically Disabled
16630 Beverly Drive
Tinley Park, IL 60477
(708) 532-3566

Direct Link for the Disabled
P.O. Box 1036
Solvang, CA 93464

Goodwill Industries of America
9200 Wisconsin Avenue
Bethesda, MD 20814-3896
(301) 530-6500
(301) 530-0836 (TDD)

Assistive Technology Producers

Here is a list of some manufacturers of products that can assist you in the workplace:

A-T Solutions
P.O. Box 3304
Narragansett, RI 02882
(401) 783-9661
(401) 783-9036 (Fax)

Center for Applied Special Technology (CAST)
39 Cross Street
Peabody, MA 01960
(508) 531-8555
(508) 538-3110 (TTY)
(508) 531-0192 (Fax)

Caption Center
WGBH Educational Foundation
125 Western Avenue
Boston, MA 02134
(617) 492-9225 (TDD)
(617) 562-9590 (Fax)

Conference-Mate Systems
466 Kinderkamack Road
Oradel, NJ 07649
(201) 967-5500
(201) 967-9078 (Fax)

Descriptive Video Service
125 Western Avenue
Boston, MA 02134
(800) 333-1203

Dragon Systems
320 Nevada Street
Newton, MA 01960
(800) 825-5897
(617) 527-0372 (Fax)

Duxbury Software
435 King Street
P.O. Box 1504
Littleton, MA 01460
(508) 486-9766
(508) 767-5964 (Fax)

Equal Access Computer Technology
39 Oneida Road
Acton, MA 01720
(508) 263-6437
(508) 263-6537 (Fax)

Fred Sammons
P.O. Box 32
Brookfield, IL 60513
(800) 323-5547
(708) 325-4602 (Fax)

Home Automation Technology
300 Billerica Road
Chelmsford, MA 01824
(508) 250-9080
(508) 250-1811 (Fax)

ISCAN
125 Cambridgepark Drive
P.O. Box 2076
Cambridge, MA 02238
(617) 868-5353

Kurzwell Applied Intelligence
411 Waverly Oaks Road
Waltham, MA 02154
(617) 893-5151
(617) 893-6525 (Fax)

Microsoft
One Microsoft Way
Redmond, WA 98052
(800) 426-9400
(206) 936-6735 (Fax)

Microsystems Software
600 Worcester Road
Framingham, MA 01701
(800) 828-2600
(508) 626-8515 (Fax)

NYNEX
125 High Street, Room 1356
Boston, MA 02110
(617) 743-9450
(617) 743-4108 (TTY)
(617) 757-7643 (Fax)

Optilec
6 Liberty Way
P.O. Box 729
Westford, MA 01886
(800) 828-1056
(508) 692-6073 (Fax)

Prentke Romich
1022 Heyl Road
Wooster, OH 44691
(800) 262-1984
(617) 242-2007 (Fax)

Quartet Technology
11 School Street
Chelmsford, MA 01863
(508) 692-9313
(508) 251-4951 (Fax)

Synergy—Adaptive Innovations
66 Hale Road
Walpole, MA 02032
(508) 668-7424
(508) 668-4134 (Fax)

Technology for Independence Engineering
529 Main Street
Charlestown, MA 02129
(800) 331-8255
(617) 242-2007 (Fax)

Temasek
21 Airport Boulevard, #G
San Francisco, CA 94080-6518
(415) 875-6666
(415) 875-7608 (Fax)

Zygo Industries
P.O. Box 1008
Portland, OR 97207-1008
(800) 234-6006
(503) 684-6001 (Fax)

BIBLIOGRAPHY

Barnett, Lynn (Ed.) *Directory of Disability Support Services in Community Colleges.* Washington, DC: Association of Community Colleges, 1992.

Blanck, Peter David. "Communicating the Americans with Disabilities Act, Transcending Compliance: A Case Report on Sears, Roebuck and Co." Annenberg Washington Program, Communications Policy Studies, Northwestern University, Evanston, Illinois. Washington, DC, 1996.

Transcending Compliance: 1996 Follow-up Report on Sears, Roebuck and Co.

Bolles, Richard. *Recareering Bulletin.* Lake Bluff, IL, 1996.

Dawson, Kenneth M. and Sheryl N. Dawson. *Job Search: The Total System.* New York, NY: John Wiley & Sons, 1988.

Epilepsy Foundation of America. *The Workbook: A Self-Study Guide for Job Seekers.* Landover, MD: Epilepsy Foundation, 1991.

HEATH Resource Center. *How to Choose a College: Guide for the Student with a Disability.* Washington, DC: The HEATH Resource Center, 1993.

Kennedy, Joyce Laine and Thomas J. Morrow. *Electronic Job Search Revolution.* New York, NY: John Wiley and Sons, 1995.

Kleiman, Carol. *The 100 Best Jobs for the 1990s and Beyond.* Chicago, IL: Dearborn Financial Publishers, 1992.

Krannich, Ronald L., Ph.D. *Change Your Job, Change Your Life.* Manassas Park, VA: Impact Publications, 1994.

Krannich, Ronald L., Ph.D. and Caryl Rae Krannich, Ph.D. *Discover the Best Jobs for You.* Manassas Park, VA: Impact Publications, 1991.

Martin, Phyllis. *Martin's Magic Formula for Getting the Right Job.* New York, NY: St. Martin's Press, 1987.

Riley, Margaret, Frances Roehm, and Steve Oserman. *The Guide to Internet Job Searching.* Lincolnwood, IL: VGM Career Horizons, 1996.

Rusch, F. and R. Schutz. *Vocational Assessment.* Seattle, WA: Exceptional Education, 1992.

Scheetz, L. Patrick. *Recruiting Trends, 1990–2002.* East Lansing, MI: Collegiate Employment Research Institute, Michigan State University, 1992.

Wright, John. *American Almanac of Jobs and Salaries.* New York, NY: Avon Books, 1995.

VGM CAREER BOOKS

BUSINESS PORTRAITS
Boeing
Coca-Cola
Ford
McDonald's

CAREER DIRECTORIES
Careers Encyclopedia
Dictionary of Occupational Titles
Occupational Outlook Handbook

CAREERS FOR
Animal Lovers; Bookworms; Caring
People; Computer Buffs; Crafty
People; Culture Lovers;
Environmental Types; Fashion Plates;
Film Buffs; Foreign Language
Aficionados; Good Samaritans;
Gourmets; Health Nuts; History
Buffs; Kids at Heart; Music Lovers;
Mystery Buffs; Nature Lovers; Night
Owls; Number Crunchers; Plant
Lovers; Shutterbugs; Sports Nuts;
Travel Buffs; Writers

CAREERS IN
Accounting; Advertising; Business;
Child Care; Communications;
Computers; Education; Engineering;
the Environment; Finance;
Government; Health Care; High
Tech; Horticulture & Botany;
International Business; Journalism;
Law; Marketing; Medicine; Science;
Social & Rehabilitation Services

CAREER PLANNING
Beating Job Burnout
Beginning Entrepreneur
Big Book of Jobs
Career Planning & Development for
    College Students &
    Recent Graduates
Career Change
Career Success for People with
    Physical Disabilities
Careers Checklists
College and Career Success for Students
    with Learning Disabilities
Complete Guide to Career Etiquette
Cover Letters They Don't Forget
Dr. Job's Complete Career Guide
Executive Job Search Strategies
Guide to Basic Cover Letter Writing
Guide to Basic Résumé Writing
Guide to Internet Job Searching
Guide to Temporary Employment
Job Interviewing for College Students
Joyce Lain Kennedy's Career Book

Out of Uniform
Parent's Crash Course in Career
    Planning
Slame Dunk Résumés
Up Your Grades: Proven Strategies
    for Academic Success

CAREER PORTRAITS
Animals; Cars; Computers;
Electronics; Fashion; Firefighting;
Music; Nature; Nursing; Science;
Sports; Teaching; Travel; Writing

GREAT JOBS FOR
Business Majors
Communications Majors
Engineering Majors
English Majors
Foreign Language Majors
History Majors
Psychology Majors
Sociology Majors

HOW TO
Apply to American Colleges and
    Universities
Approach an Advertising Agency and
    Walk Away with the Job You Want
Be a Super Sitter
Bounce Back Quickly After
    Losing Your Job
Change Your Career
Choose the Right Career
Cómo escribir un currículum vitae en
    inglés que tenga éxito
Find Your New Career Upon
    Retirement
Get & Keep Your First Job
Get Hired Today
Get into the Right Business School
Get into the Right Law School
Get into the Right Medical School
Get People to Do Things Your Way
Have a Winning Job Interview
Hit the Ground Running in Your
    New Job
Hold It All Together When You've
    Lost Your Job
Improve Your Study Skills
Jumpstart a Stalled Career
Land a Better Job
Launch Your Career in TV News
Make the Right Career Moves
Market Your College Degree
Move from College into a
    Secure Job
Negotiate the Raise You Deserve
Prepare Your Curriculum Vitae

Prepare for College
Run Your Own Home Business
Succeed in Advertising When all Yo●
Succeed in College
Succeed in High School
Take Charge of Your Child's Early
    Education
Write a Winning Résumé
Write Successful Cover Letters
Write Term Papers & Reports
Write Your College Application Essay●

MADE EASY
College Applications
Cover Letters
Getting a Raise
Job Hunting
Job Interviews
Résumés

ON THE JOB: REAL PEOPLE WORKING IN...
Communications
Health Care
Sales & Marketing
Service Businesses

OPPORTUNITIES IN
This extensive series provides detaile●
    information on more than 150
    individual career fields.

RÉSUMÉS FOR
Advertising Careers
Architecture and Related Careers
Banking and Financial Careers
Business Management Careers
College Students &
    Recent Graduates
Communications Careers
Computer Careers
Education Careers
Engineering Careers
Environmental Careers
Ex-Military Personnel
50+ Job Hunters
Government Careers
Health and Medical Careers
High School Graduates
High Tech Careers
Law Careers
Midcareer Job Changes
Nursing Careers
Re-Entering the Job Market
Sales and Marketing Careers
Scientific and Technical Careers
Social Service Careers
The First-Time Job Hunter

VGM Career Horizons
a division of *NTC Publishing Group*
4255 West Touhy Avenue
Lincolnwood, Illinois 60646–1975

CAREER
SUCCESS
for
PEOPLE
with
PHYSICAL
DISABILITIES

SHARON F. KISSANE, PH. D.

VGM Career Horizons
a division of *NTC Publishing Group*
Lincolnwood, Illinois USA

Library of Congress Cataloging-in-Publication Data

Kissane, Sharon F.
    Career success for people with physical disabilities / Sharon F.
Kissane.
        p.   cm.
    Includes bibliographical references
    ISBN 0-8442-4175-X (alk. paper)
    1. Vocational guidance for the handicapped—United States.
2. Physically handicapped—Vocational guidance—United States.
I. Title.
HV1568.5.K57 1997
650.14'087—dc20   96-27799
                                                             CIP

Published by VGM Career Horizons, a division of NTC Publishing Group
4255 West Touhy Avenue
Lincolnwood (Chicago), Illinois 60646-1975, U.S.A.

5 6 7 8 9 VP 9 8 7 6 5 4 3 2 1